IMAGES
of America

MUNCIE

THE MIDDLETOWN OF AMERICA

IMAGES
of America

MUNCIE

THE MIDDLETOWN OF AMERICA

E. Bruce Geelhoed

ARCADIA
PUBLISHING

ISBN 978-0-7385-0733-0

Published by Arcadia Publishing
Charleston, South Carolina

Printed in the United States of America

Library of Congress Catalog Card Number: 00-106100

For all general information contact Arcadia Publishing at:
Telephone 843-853-2070
Fax 843-853-0044
E-mail sales@arcadiapublishing.com
For customer service and orders:
Toll-Free 1-888-313-2665

Visit us on the Internet at www.arcadiapublishing.com

Contents

ACKNOWLEDGMENTS

I wish to thank a number of helpful people who have assisted me in acquiring the photography necessary to complete this book about Muncie. First, I am especially indebted to my colleagues at Ball State University. John Straw, head of the University Archives and Special Collections, and Michael Twigg, his assistant, guided me in the identification of photos from Ball State's extensive library of photography. Paramount among these collections are the recently acquired Spurgeon-Greene photographs (BSUA-SG), which are a unique treasure of materials about experiences of life in Muncie. Photographs from other collections in the Ball State University Archives (BSUA) were also valuable contributions to the book.

Second, I wish to thank Ed Self, director of Photographic Services at Ball State, and John Huffer, his assistant, for providing some contemporary photographs about life at the university and in Muncie. Likewise, I owe a special debt of gratitude to Jerry Cole, Educational Media Coordinator at the Ball State Teleplex, and James Smith, his student assistant; as well as David Marini, Instructional Designer at the Ball State Teleplex, and Barbara Krall, his assistant, for their expert work in preparing the photographs for the publisher.

Third, another group of helpful people assisted me in obtaining photographs from various community sources. Jan Jobe and Michelle Mumaw of the Minnetrista Cultural Center not only helped to identify photos from the Center's extensive collection, but also made some valuable technical contributions to the book. Other individuals helped to obtain photographs from their organizations. These included: Joyce Beck, Judith La Casse, and Susanna Hinds of Ball Associates; Judith Campbell of Ontario Corporation; Kim Campbell of Paws, Incorporated; Phillip Dunn of Ross Supermarkets, Incorporated; Michael Galliher of Boyce Forms Systems; James Garringer, who provided photographs from Westminster Presbyterian Church; Elise Hayden, Annette La Pradd, and Jon Price of Keihin Aircon North America; William Miller, who provided photographs from College Avenue United Methodist Church; Matt Pierce of Marsh Supermarkets, Incorporated; Gary Smith of Maxon Corporation; and Terry Wood of First Merchants Corporation. Deborah Geelhoed, Hurley Goodall, Donald Shondell, and Roger Pelham provided photographs from their personal collections. Thanks to all of these fine people for their support and cooperation, and to my wife, Deborah Geelhoed, for her continued love and friendship.

Finally, I wish to dedicate this book to three individuals who have helped to make America truly aware of Muncie as Middletown. These include C. Warren Vander Hill, provost and vice president for academic affairs at Ball State University; Dwight W. Hoover, professor emeritus of history and founding director of the Center for Middletown Studies at Ball State; and Wiley W. Spurgeon, retired executive editor of *The Muncie Star*. For over three decades now, through their research, writing, publishing, lecturing, and overall enthusiasm for our community, each of these men have expanded the national awareness of Muncie as America's representative community and its historic importance to the social science profession. Any errors of fact or interpretation are my own.

E. Bruce Geelhoed
Center for Middletown Studies
Ball State University
Muncie, Indiana

INTRODUCTION

THE MOST STUDIED COMMUNITY IN AMERICA

Between 1924 and 1927, a team of social science researchers led by Robert S. Lynd and his wife, Helen Merrell Lynd, came to Muncie, Indiana, to conduct a research project which dealt with everyday life in a mid-sized American community. Funded by the Institute for Social and Religious Research, an arm of the philanthropy of John D. Rockefeller Jr., the research team collected data, conducted interviews, analyzed newspaper sources and public records, and began to assemble a profile of community life as lived by the ordinary citizens of Muncie. In 1929, Robert and Helen Lynd published the results of their study in a book titled *Middletown: A Study in Modern American Culture* (New York: Harcourt, Brace). To the surprise of the Lynds and their sponsors, *Middletown* became a national bestseller, and this academically oriented, clinically written book ultimately represented a landmark in the literature of American sociology. *Middletown* also had another significant impact: it identified Muncie as the "representative" mid-sized American community. Almost overnight, Muncie became "Middletown," the barometer of social attitudes, customs, beliefs, and behavior in the American heartland.

While the Lynds conducted their research in Muncie, they experienced life in a city that was enjoying all the benefits of the 1920s-era prosperity. Fueled by the expansion of the auto and glass industries, Muncie's industrial sector boomed during this period. The Ball Teachers College, located in the northwest sector of the city, was growing and becoming a source of community pride. Local commerce thrived, and the community's outlook was positive and enthusiastic. Munsonians believed that the future promised even more progress and prosperity.

When the Great Depression struck the United States in the late 1920s and 1930s, however, Muncie did not escape the effects of this industrial nightmare. Unemployment rose, joblessness appeared to be a way of life for thousands of workers, and the positive attitudes of the 1920s gave way to chronic anxiety and despair. At the request of his publisher, Harcourt, Brace, Robert Lynd returned to Muncie in 1935 (without his wife Helen) to conduct a follow-up study to *Middletown* and to analyze the effects of economic deprivation, instead of prosperity, upon the community. In 1937, Robert and Helen Lynd published *Middletown In Transition: A Study in Cultural Conflicts* (New York: Harcourt, Brace). While the second study written by the Lynds failed to receive the critical acclaim afforded their first book, it nevertheless provided a further glimpse into the dynamics of a city that was rapidly becoming a research laboratory for social scientists.

Following the publication of *Middletown* and *Middletown in Transition*, the next 50 years witnessed a steady progression of social scientists to Muncie to study various aspects of community life. Studies that appeared subsequent to those of the Lynds sought to prove, disprove, or modify many of the central conclusions of the original Middletown books. Between 1977 and 1982, sociologists Theodore Caplow, Howard Bahr, and Bruce Chadwick conducted a replication of the Lynds' original studies on the occasion of the 50th anniversary of *Middletown*'s publication. Their study, funded by the National Science Foundation, became known as "Middletown III" and resulted in the publication of two books by Theodore Caplow: *Middletown Families* (Minneapolis: University of Minnesota Press, 1982) and *All Faithful People* (Minneapolis: University of Minnesota Press, 1983). At the same time, but independent of "Middletown III," filmmaker Peter Davis was producing his six-part documentary, entitled

Middletown. By the mid-1980s, Muncie had unquestionably become the most studied mid-sized community in America.

In 1965, the small college that Munsonians knew during the 1920s as Ball Teachers College had grown to become Ball State University. Then in 1980, Ball State capitalized on the attention generated within the academic community on "Muncie as Middletown" by establishing the Center for Middletown Studies. The purpose of the Center was to promote research and scholarship on Muncie as Middletown according to the literary tradition of Robert and Helen Lynd. Dwight W. Hoover, professor of history at Ball State and a recognized scholar in the fields of social and intellectual history, as well as urban history, was the founding director of the Center. Hoover published several Middletown-related studies during his tenure as director from 1980 to 1991, including *Magic Middletown* (Bloomington, Indiana: Indiana University Press), a photographic history of the community during the years of the Gas Boom. Following Hoover's retirement in 1991, E. Bruce Geelhoed, professor of history and a specialist in American business history, was appointed to direct the Center.

During the 1990s, the fascination with Muncie as Middletown has resulted in the publication of even more studies dealing with life in the community. In 1995, Gregory H. Williams published *Life on the Color Line* (New York: Dutton), his autobiographical account of growing up in Muncie during the 1950s when the community was sharply divided along racial lines. In 1997, Dan Rottenberg published an edition of oral histories entitled *Middletown Jews* (Bloomington, Indiana: Indiana University Press), which provided insights into the lives and struggles of the small number of Jewish families who lived in Muncie during the 20th century. In 2000, the Italian sociologist Rita Caccamo published *Back to Middletown* (Palo Alto, California: Stanford University Press), which traced the character and evolution of Middle America in the context of the Lynd studies. Finally, by decade's end, Caplow, Bahr, and Chadwick undertook still another sociological project in Muncie, titled "Middletown IV," whose results will be published later in 2000.

As the 21st century unfolds, Muncie as Middletown will continue to attract the attention of social scientists, journalists, filmmakers, and dramatists. As a social laboratory, the community continues to fascinate researchers who seek to capture a glimpse of life as it's lived in the American heartland.

One

The Muncie of the Lynds 1920s and 1930s

When Robert and Helen Lynd came to Muncie in 1924 with their team of researchers, they worked under the sponsorship of the Institute for Social and Religious Research, an organization which belonged to the philanthropic network of John D. Rockefeller Jr. In some of his previous writings, Lynd had expressed serious criticism of the Standard Oil Company, a corporation in which Rockefeller was a major stockholder. Nevertheless, Rockefeller's organization agreed to fund Lynd's research, which was initially designed to explore the ways in which religion might help to ease the strife between management and labor in a small community.

When the Lynds arrived in Muncie, they entered a growing city with a population of 38,000. The city's economy had recovered sufficiently from the post–World War I recession and was reflecting the renewed industrialization of the 1920s. Muncie's economy rested on a strong industrial base, anchored by such local mainstays as the Ball Brothers Manufacturing Company, makers of glass containers for home canning and food preservation; the Kitselman Brothers Company, manufacturers of woven wire fence products; and the Maxon Premix Burner Company, which was quickly emerging as a leader in the combustion products industry.

Other exciting new developments had also unfolded in the early 1920s. In 1921, General Motors Corporation announced that it planned to locate a transmission manufacturing plant for its Chevrolet division in Muncie. The General Motors operation was an addition to a community that already boasted the presence of the Warner Gear Company, itself a major auto parts supplier. In 1928, General Motors added to the community's industrial profile by transferring some of its Delco battery manufacturing capacity to Muncie.

Also, in 1918, the State of Indiana established the Eastern Division of the Indiana State Normal School in northwest Muncie, the first branch campus of a state college in the history of Indiana. Enrollment on the Muncie campus continued to grow until, by 1929, the school had reached sufficient size to be granted its independence from Indiana State. The new institution, named the Ball State Teachers College, enabled Muncie to become the home of a fourth public institution of higher education in Indiana.

Beginning in the 1930s, however, Muncie found itself in the grip of the Great Depression as the economic slowdown in the nation's manufacturing sector led to serious increases in unemployment locally. At the request of his publisher, Harcourt, Brace, Robert Lynd returned to Muncie in 1935 to begin work on a second community study. On this occasion, however, Lynd and his researchers (minus Helen Lynd, who remained behind in New York) stayed only for six months, rather than for two years as they had with their initial Middletown experience. Lynd expected to find that the attitude of Munsonians toward individualism and *laissez faire* capitalism would have changed due to the difficult economic times, but he discovered instead that the local population retained much of the belief system that characterized it one decade earlier.

The two studies by Robert and Helen Lynd, *Middletown* and *Middletown in Transition*, placed Muncie upon the nation's literary consciousness as the "representative" American community. Three other events during the 1930s, however, brought Muncie to national attention. The first event occurred in October 1937, when Margaret Bourke-White, the celebrated photojournalist for *Life* magazine, published her photo-essay entitled, "Muncie, Indiana Is the Great U.S. Middletown." Bourke-White's published images of Muncie opened America's eyes to "Muncie as Middletown" and its homes, schools, factories, churches, and hospital. With a circulation that numbered in the hundreds of thousands, *Life* popularized Muncie in a profound way.

The second event occurred in late October 1939, when Eleanor Roosevelt visited Muncie as the first stop on a two-week speaking tour. Mrs. Roosevelt came as the guest of the local Kiwanis Club, and she spoke on the evening of October 25th to a capacity audience at the Muncie Fieldhouse, the city's palace for high school basketball, and the largest facility of its kind in the country. The First Lady's topic was "The Future of America Rests With Its Youth." By this point in her life and career, Roosevelt had become a national media figure by virtue of her syndicated column, "My Day," her frequent radio appearances, and her lecture tours. During a press conference that she held with reporters shortly after arriving in Muncie, Roosevelt mentioned that she had read the two Middletown studies and recommended them for reading by others. Likewise, she mentioned the Middletown books in a later column of "My Day."

The third event occurred at the time of the First Lady's visit in late October 1939. During the 1930s, Muncie had become a hotbed of private aviation, and two pilots, Robert McDaniels and Kelvin Baxter, decided to attempt an endurance flight which, if successful, would enable them to break the world's record for days spent aloft. McDaniels and Baxter both came from modest working-class families and conceived of the idea of an endurance flight as a money-raising venture which would earn them enough money to pay for tuition at a flight school. McDaniels and Baxter succeeded in staying aloft for over 21 days, thereby breaking the world record and winning enough money in sponsor fees and pledges to cover their expenses for a flight school in Cincinnati. Mrs. Roosevelt, by sheer coincidence, was in Muncie on the day when McDaniels and Baxter returned to earth and she agreed to appear with them in celebration of their achievement.

By the end of the 1930s, therefore, Muncie had become the Middletown of America. Such a development was unforeseen 15 years earlier, when the Lynds first arrived in Muncie. In his monograph, *Middletown Revisited* (Muncie, Indiana: Ball State University, 1991, p. 5) historian Dwight W. Hoover observed: "The irony of the situation must strike us even today. Two young researchers [Robert and Helen Lynd] with no experience or preparation in social research enter a town that was chosen at the last minute to do a religion study financed by a man [John Rockefeller Jr.] whom the senior researcher [Robert Lynd] had attacked." Nevertheless, Muncie could not escape its past any longer; it was on the way to becoming the social laboratory of the United States.

Robert S. Lynd was the co-author of *Middletown* and *Middletown In Transition* with his wife Helen Merrell Lynd. These were the two pioneering sociological studies of Muncie, Indiana. (BSUA.)

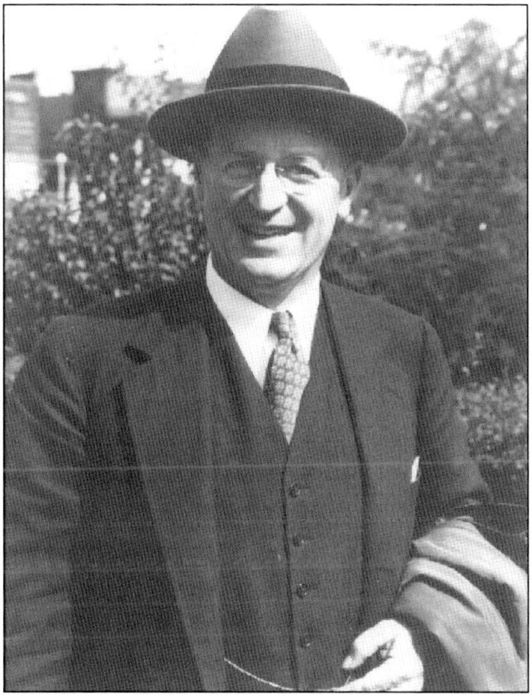

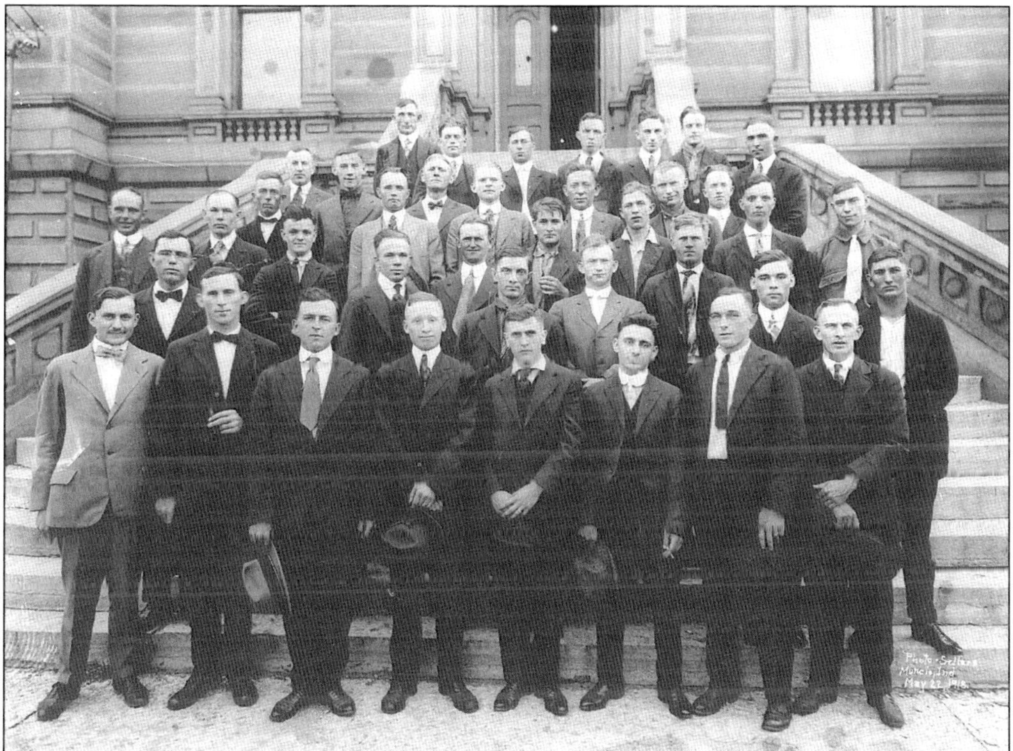

Enlistees gather for a group photograph on the steps of the Delaware County Courthouse before leaving for active military service in World War I. (BSUA.)

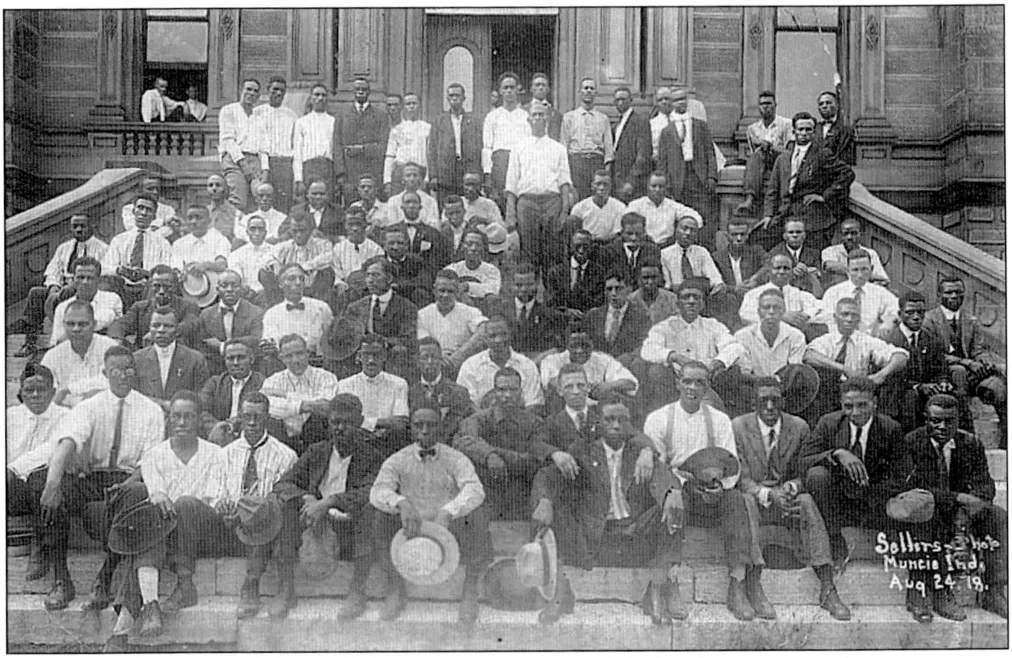

African-American enlistees gather for a group photograph before leaving for military service in World War I. (BSUA-Sellers Collection.)

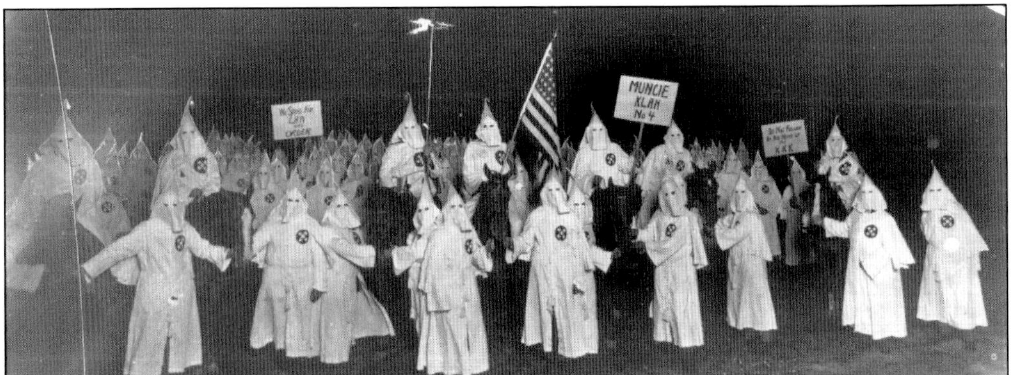

One of the less savory aspects of life in Muncie during the 1920s was the influence of the Ku Klux Klan in several prominent sectors of the city's life. (BSUA-Sellers Collection.)

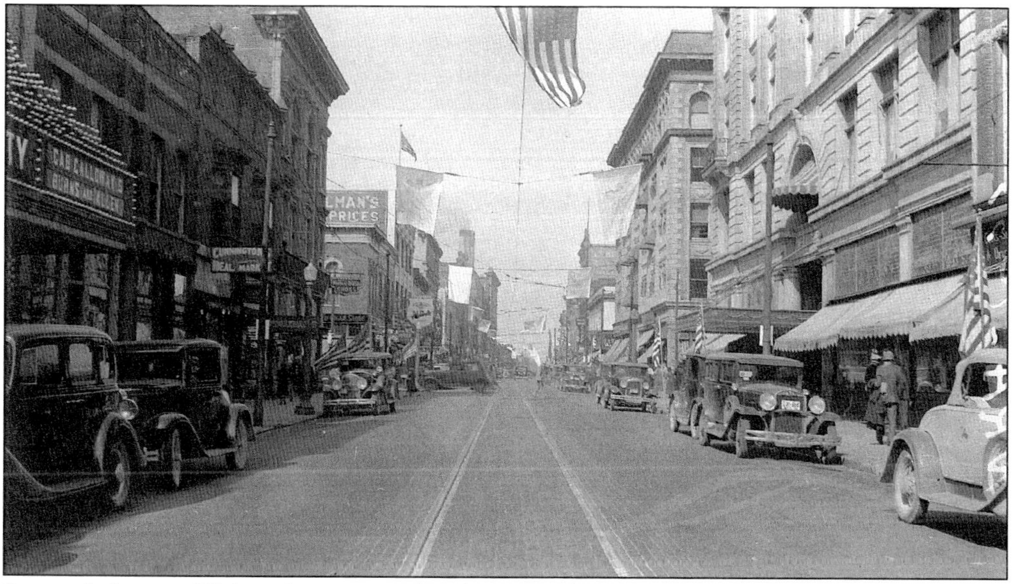

Pictured above is Walnut Street in 1933, the main shopping thoroughfare in the heart of the city. (BSUA-SG.)

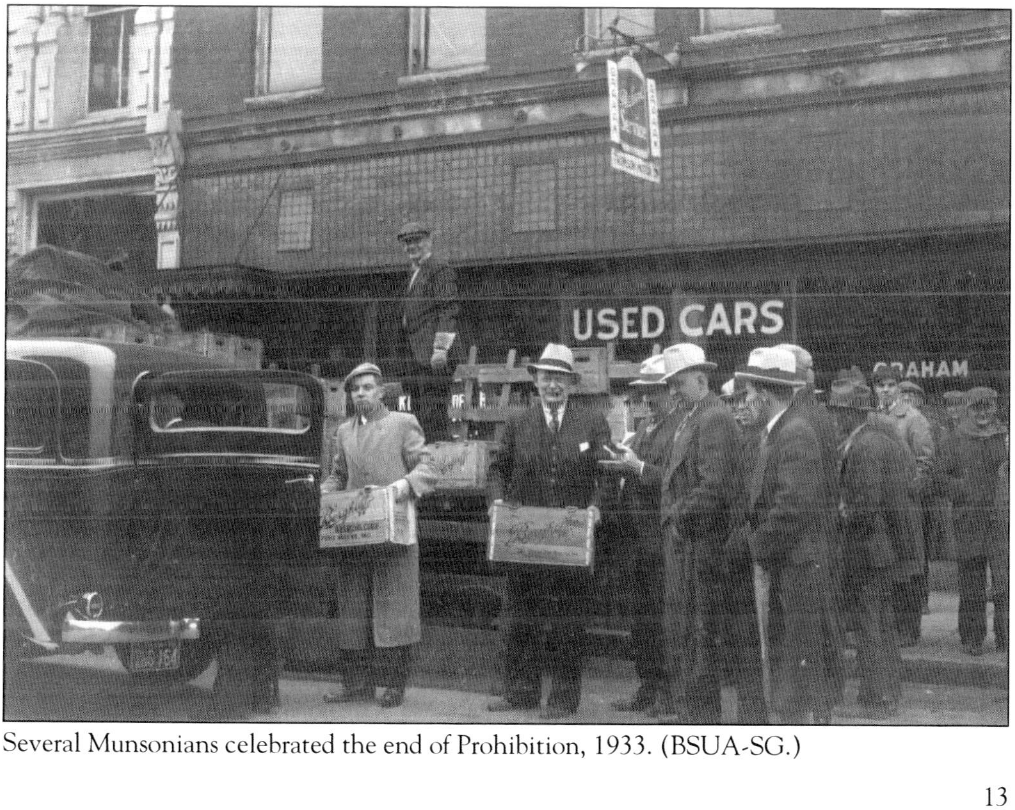

Several Munsonians celebrated the end of Prohibition, 1933. (BSUA-SG.)

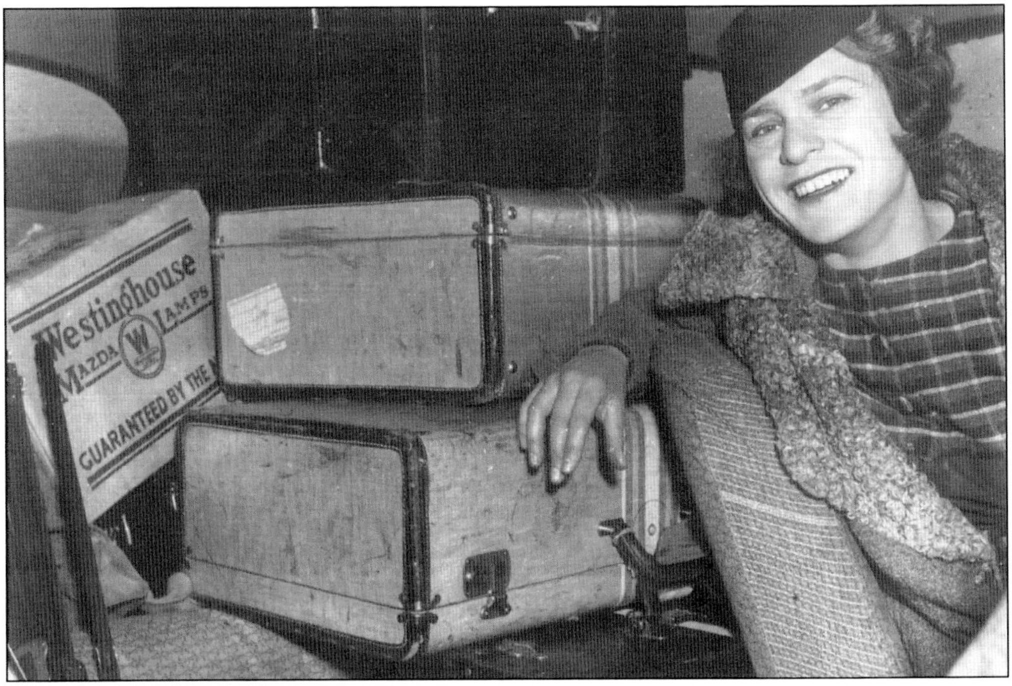

Photojournalist Margaret Bourke-White arrived in Muncie in 1937 to prepare for her photo essay to be published in *Life* magazine. Her essay, "Muncie, Indiana Is the Great U.S. Middletown," appeared in *Life*, May 10, 1937, and gave a visual picture of the community which the Lynds had described in their books. (BSUA-SG.)

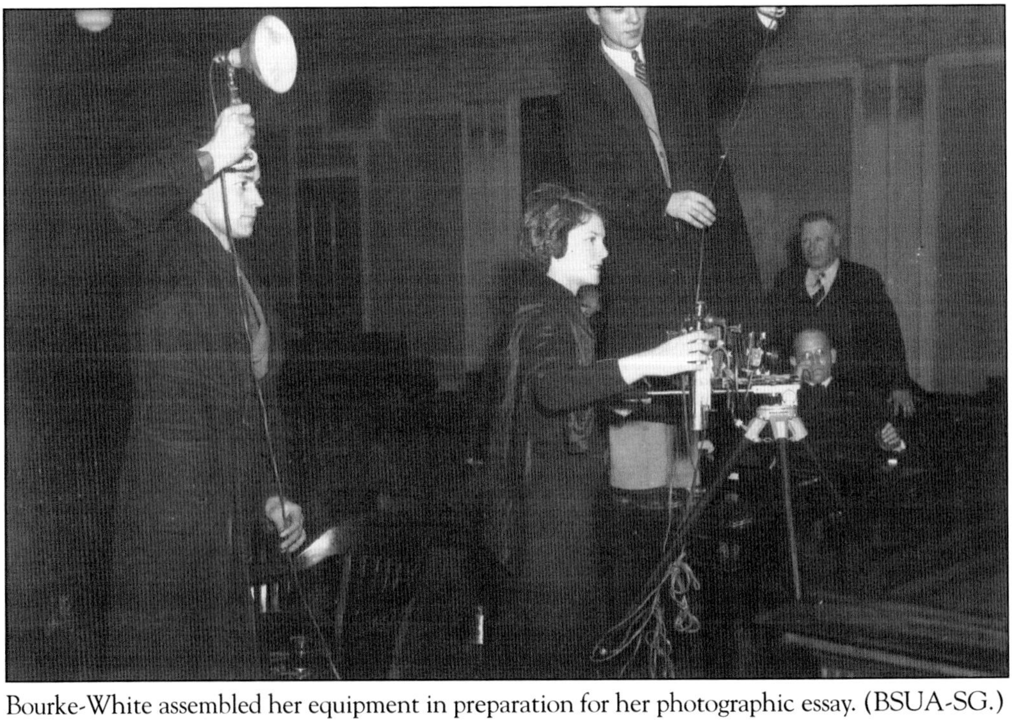

Bourke-White assembled her equipment in preparation for her photographic essay. (BSUA-SG.)

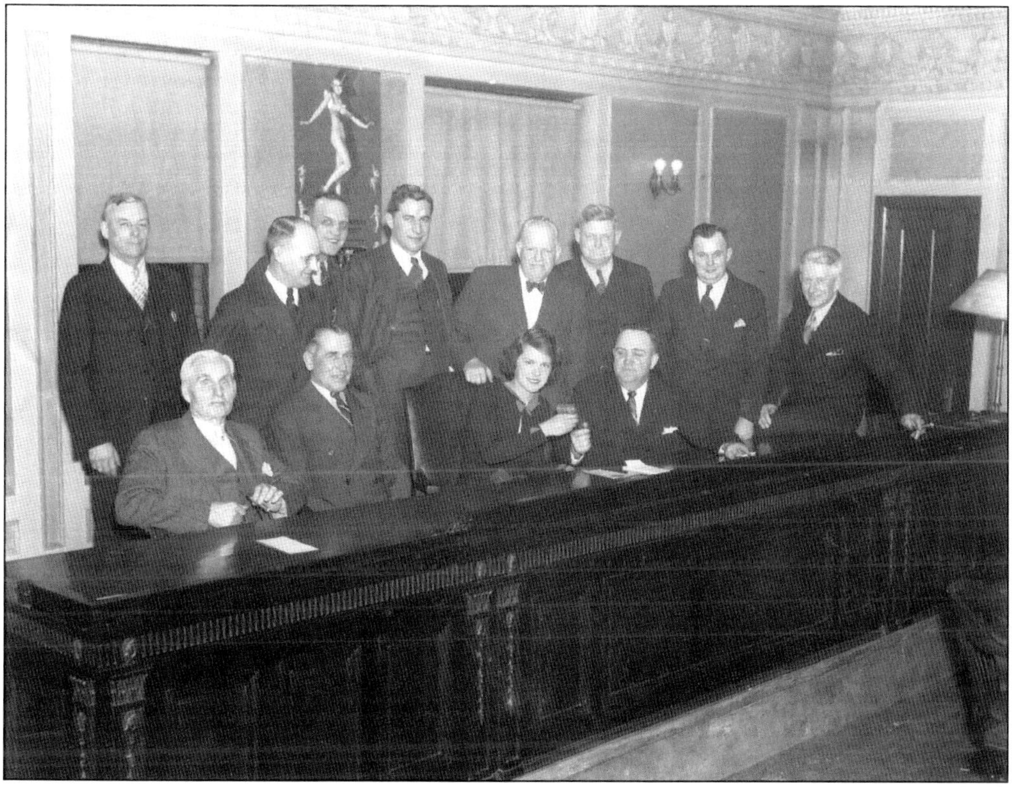

Bourke-White posed with members of the Muncie City Council. *Life* readers undoubtedly saw the pin-up of Betty Grable on the wall of the Council chambers. (BSUA-SG.)

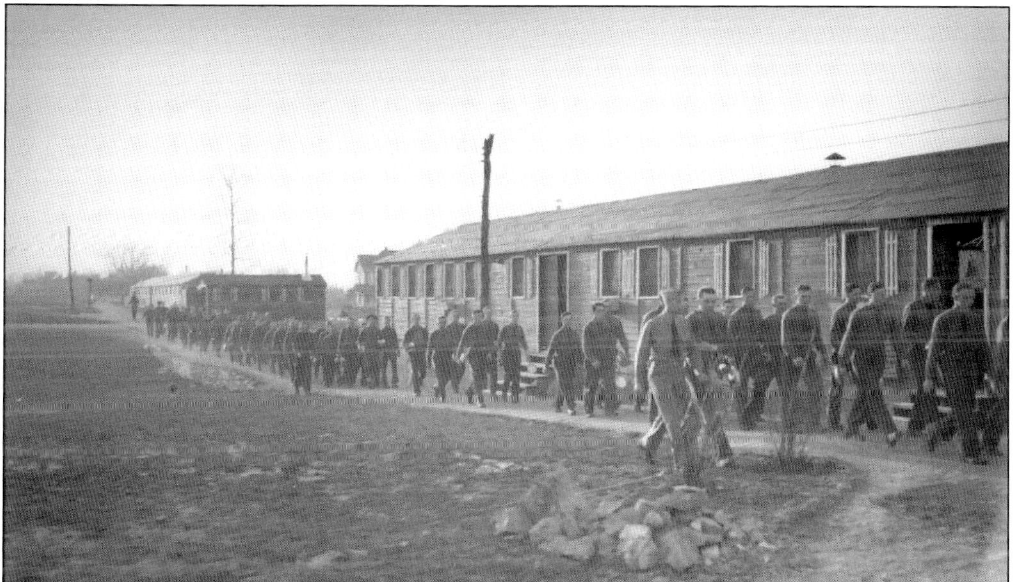

The Depression had a serious impact on Muncie's economy, leading to record levels of unemployment. In this photo, a group of young men begin their daily routine at a camp for the Civilian Conservation Corps (CCC). (BSUA-SG.)

Eleanor in Middletown: October 25, 1939

Eleanor Roosevelt's visit to Muncie in October 1939 occurred at the invitation of the Muncie Kiwanis Club. Concerned about the effects of the Depression upon the nation's youth, the First Lady spoke often about the need to keep young people involved in the economic, political, and social life of the community. Mrs. Roosevelt received a warm reception in the community, and her speech that evening was delivered to a capacity crowd.

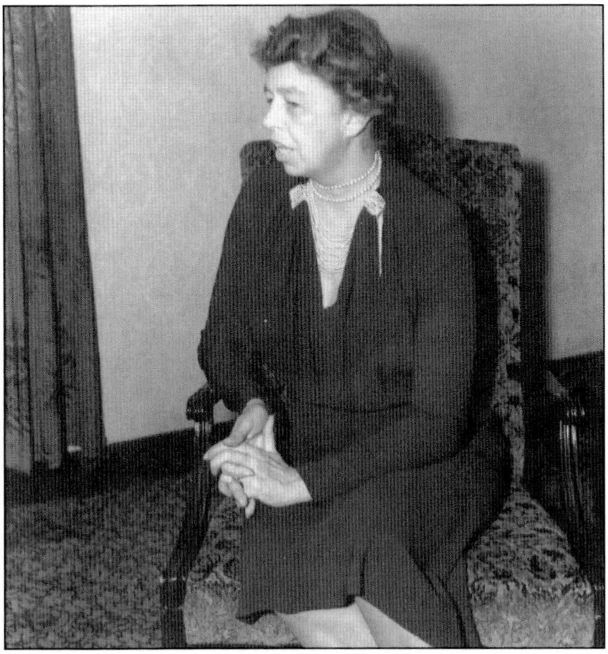

Shortly after arriving in Muncie, Mrs. Roosevelt held a brief press conference for local reporters in her room at the Hotel Roberts. (BSUA-SG.)

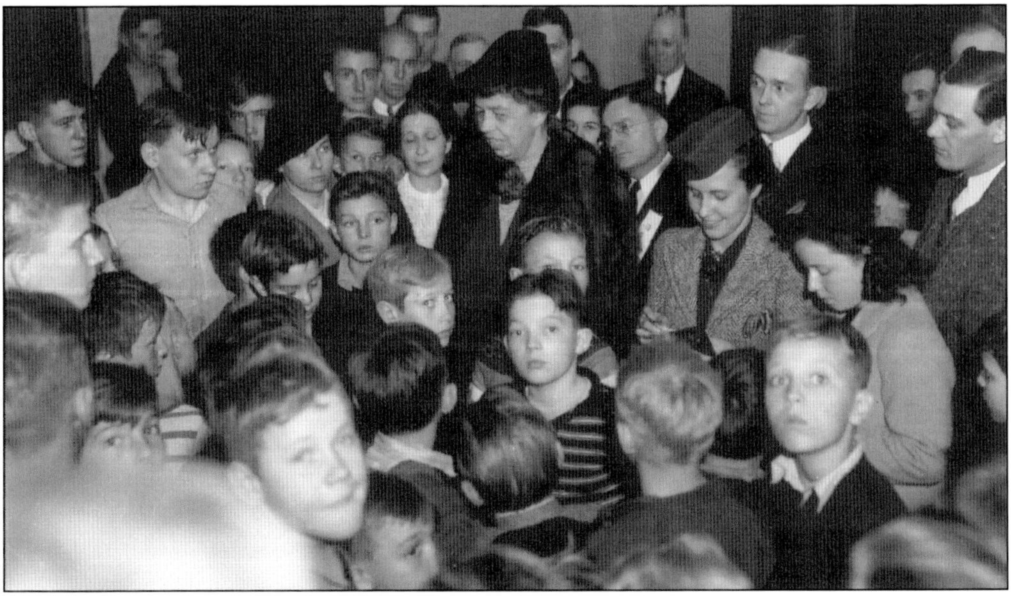

One major appointment in the First Lady's itinerary was her visit to the local Boys Club. In this photo, she is shown talking with the members of the club and their adult sponsors. (BSUA-SG.)

As this photo shows, Mrs. Roosevelt (rear) enjoyed her conversations with the members of the Boys Club. (BSUA-SG.)

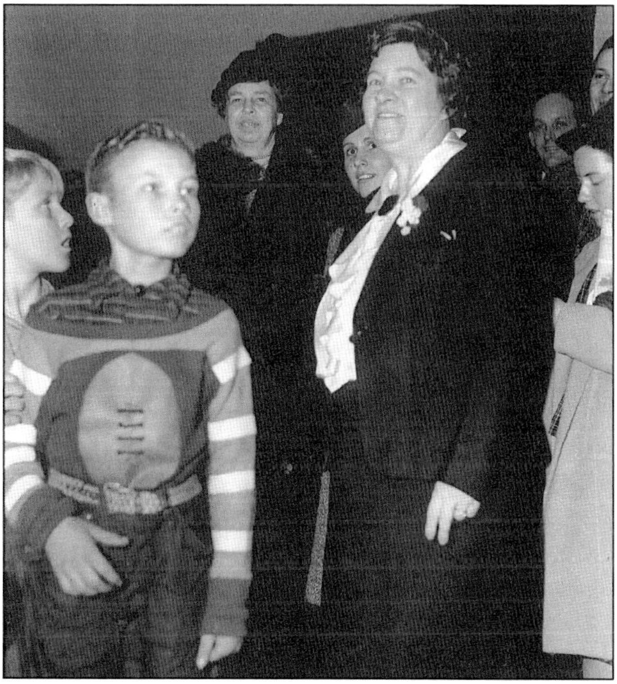

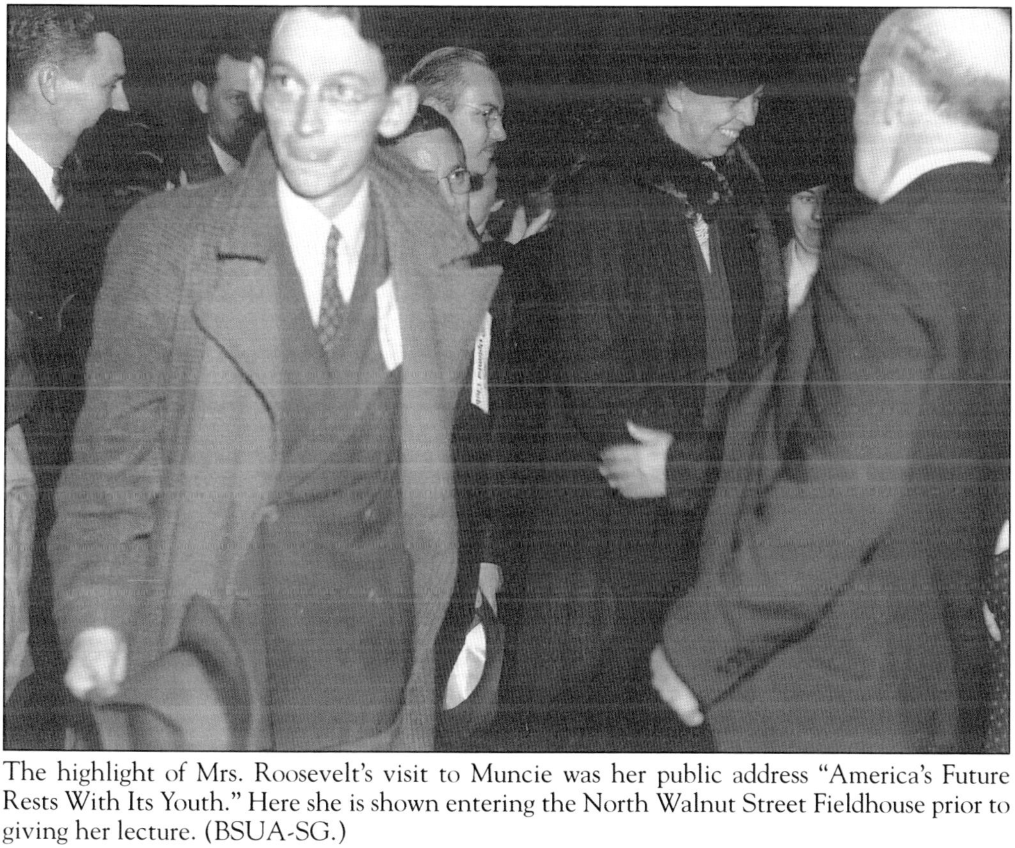

The highlight of Mrs. Roosevelt's visit to Muncie was her public address "America's Future Rests With Its Youth." Here she is shown entering the North Walnut Street Fieldhouse prior to giving her lecture. (BSUA-SG.)

The Emergence of Normal City, 1920–1940

In 1917, industrialists Frank C. Ball and Edmund B. Ball, with their wives, purchased the building and grounds of the Muncie National Institute, a defunct normal school located in the northwest part of the city. Immediately after they made their purchase, the two Ball brothers began negotiations with state government to transfer their property to the state for the purpose of locating a branch of the Indiana State Normal School. The new institution became known as the Eastern Division of the Indiana State Normal School. The Ball family gave generously to the college in the early 1920s and, in recognition of that fact, the school was renamed Ball Teachers College in 1922. In 1929, with its enrollment now surpassing one thousand students, the school was granted independence from Indiana State and became the Ball State Teachers College. Also, in 1929, Ball State opened its Burris Laboratory School, a kindergarten through grade twelve school, which served the children living in the adjacent neighborhoods.

At the same time that the Ball family was providing financial assistance to the college, it was actively supporting plans to build a comprehensive medical facility in Muncie, in close proximity to the teachers college. In 1929, Ball Memorial Hospital opened its doors, its support having come from a generous contribution from the family in memory of Edmund B. Ball, who died in 1925. Ball Memorial Hospital quickly grew into a regional medical facility, the largest of its kind between Indianapolis and Fort Wayne.

The area in Muncie where this activity took place was known as Normal City, in recognition of the numerous attempts to build a viable teachers college in the neighborhood between 1898 and 1918. By 1930, Normal City had become the educational center for east central Indiana, its medical center, and the locale of several attractive neighborhoods. The transformation of Normal City during the 1920s was one of the hallmark developments in Muncie's history.

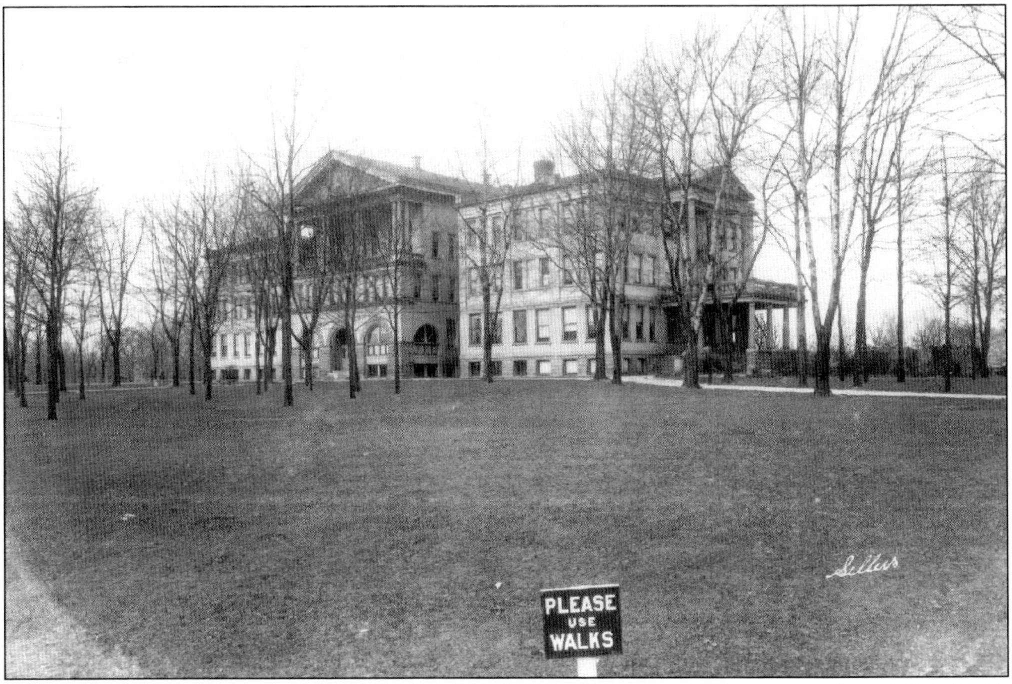

Pictured is the administration building on the Ball State campus. Constructed in 1898–1899, the building was the home of four independent normal schools—all of which failed. In 1917–1918, Frank C. Ball and Edmund B. Ball, along with their wives, purchased the college property at a bankruptcy auction and then donated their acquisition to the State of Indiana. The new school became a branch campus of the Indiana State Normal School at Terre Haute. (BSUA.)

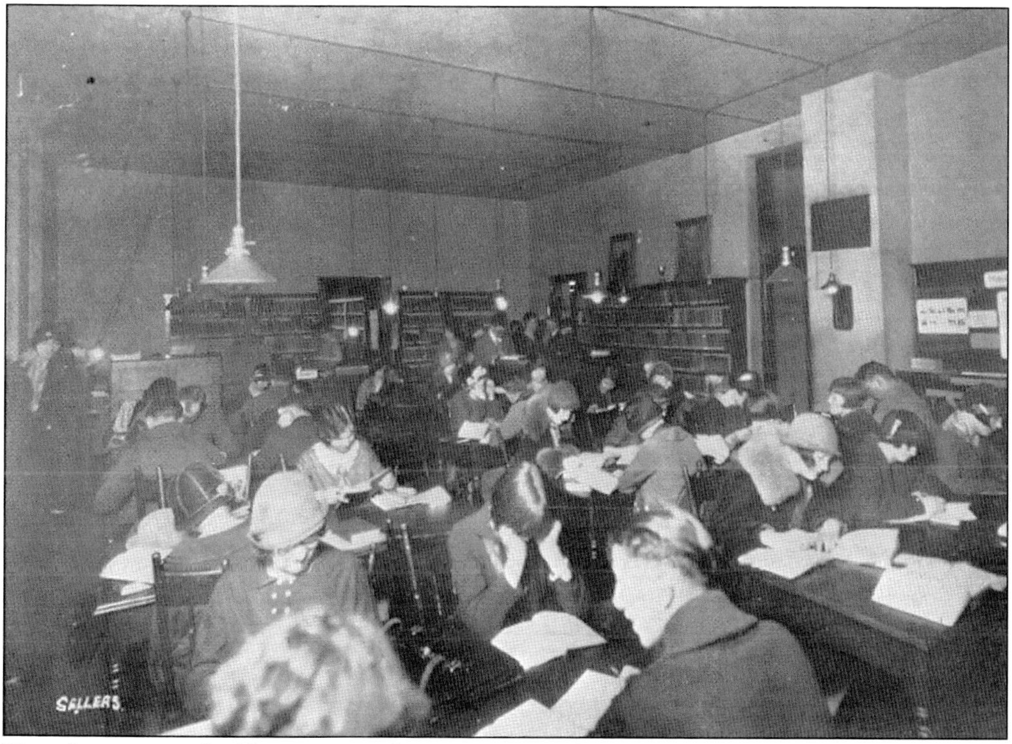

The administration building contained a separate room that served as the school's library. (BSUA.)

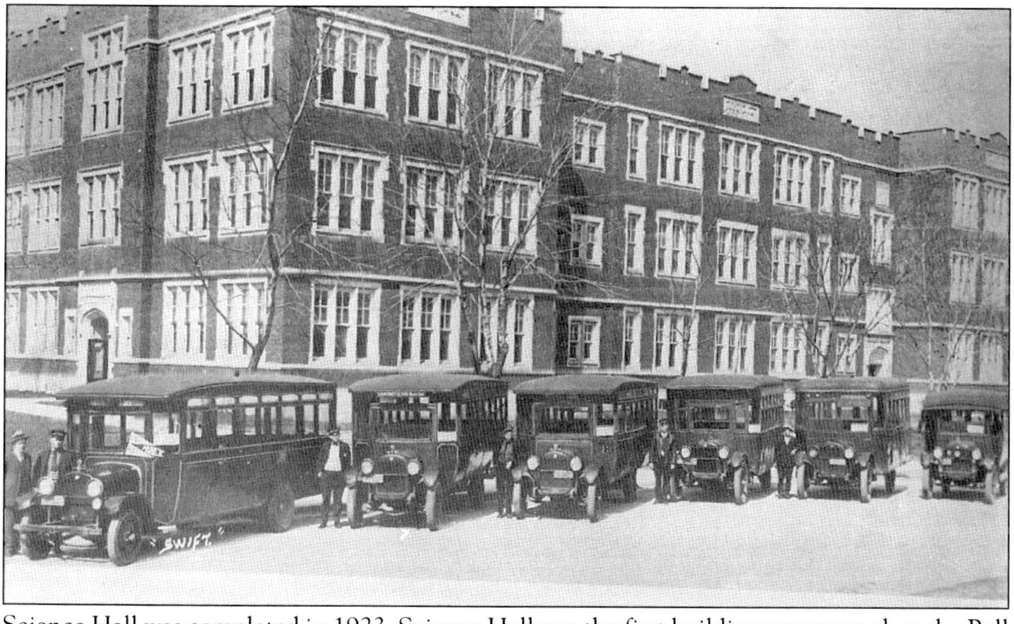

Science Hall was completed in 1923. Science Hall was the first building constructed on the Ball State campus that was built entirely by state appropriation. (BSUA.)

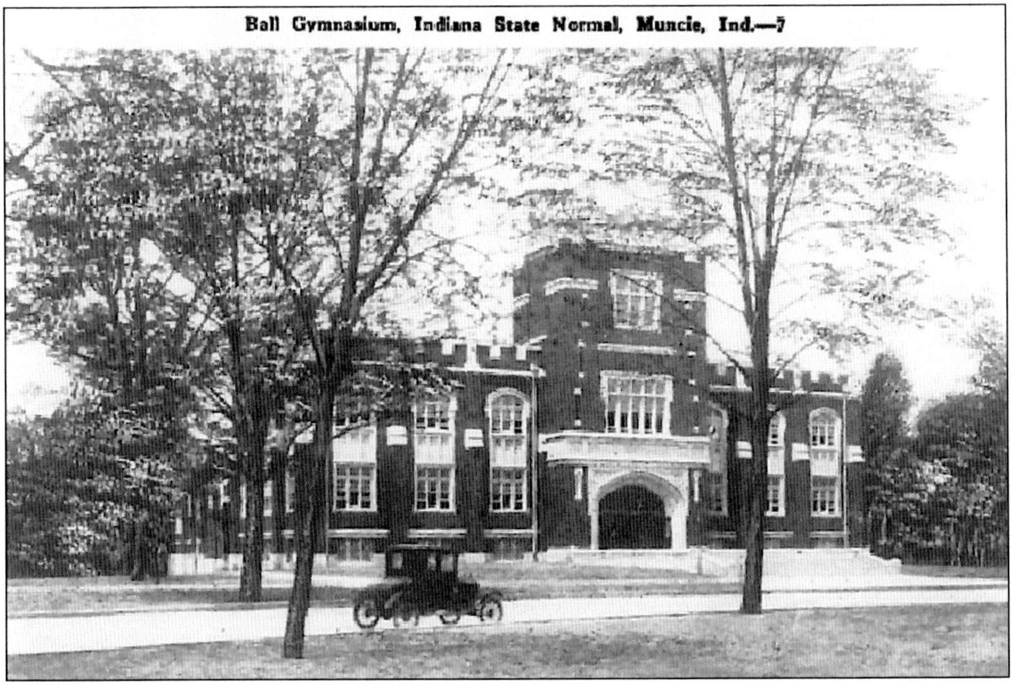

Ball Gymnasium was completed in 1924–1925. Ball State's first modern facility for physical education and athletics was built with a $250,000 gift from the Ball family. (BSUA.)

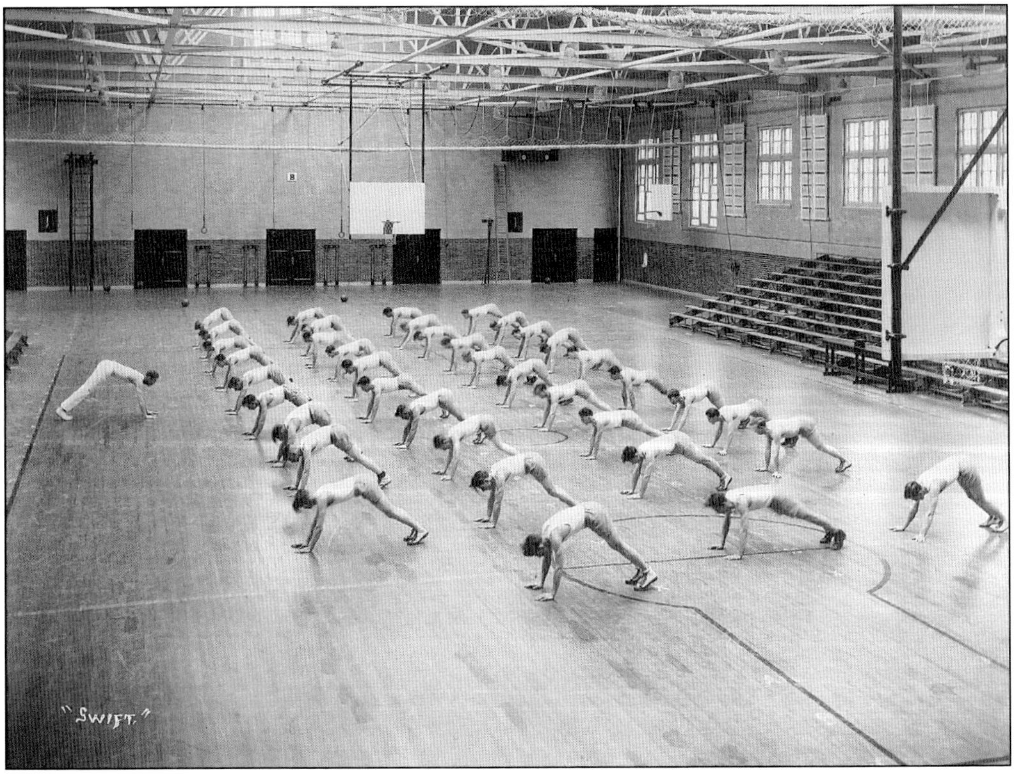

A men's physical education class meets in Ball Gym. (BSUA-Swift Collection.)

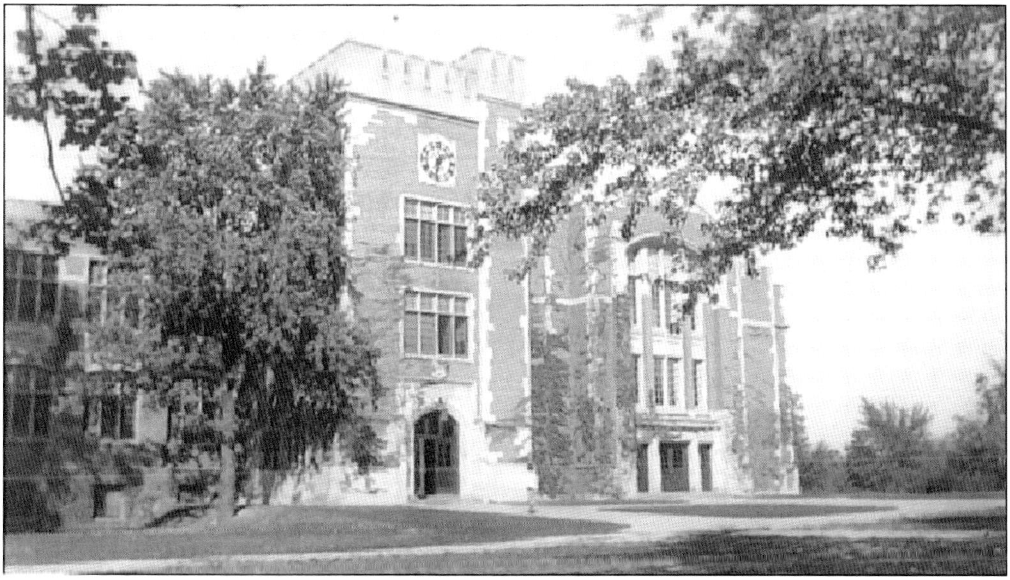

Shown here is the Library and Assembly Hall. Ball State's second state-supported instructional building was completed in 1926–1927. (BSUA.)

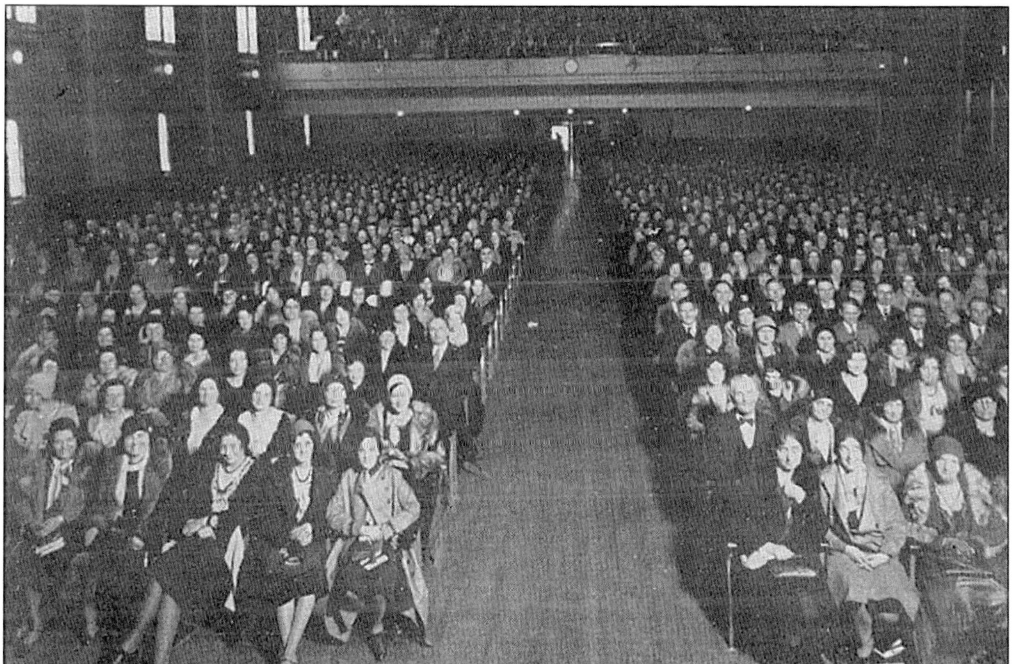

One of the first public events in Assembly Hall was a program for mothers of Ball State students on Mother's Day in 1927. (BSUA.)

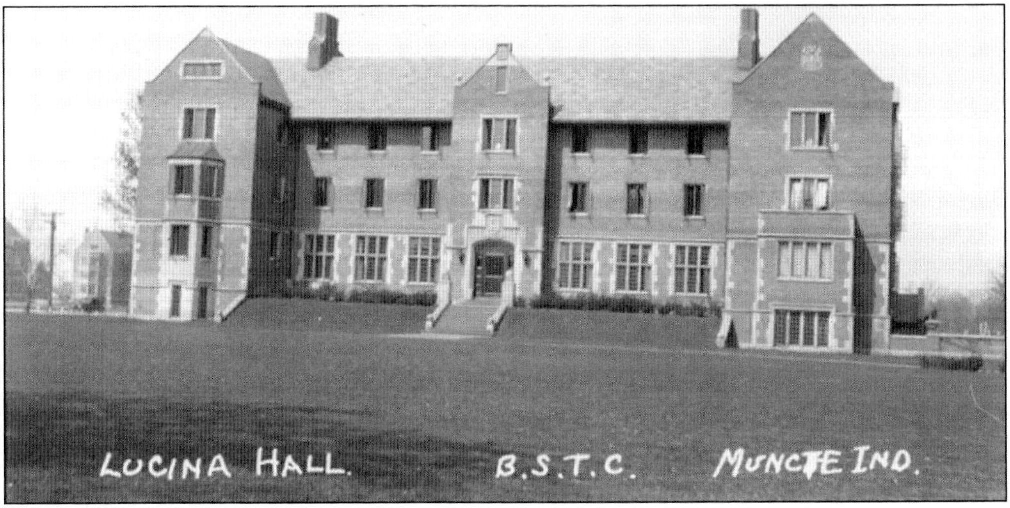

Lucina Hall, the first residence hall for women at Ball State, was completed in 1928. Lucina Hall was built with funds provided by the Ball family in honor of Lucina Amelia Ball, a sister of the five Ball brothers. (BSUA.)

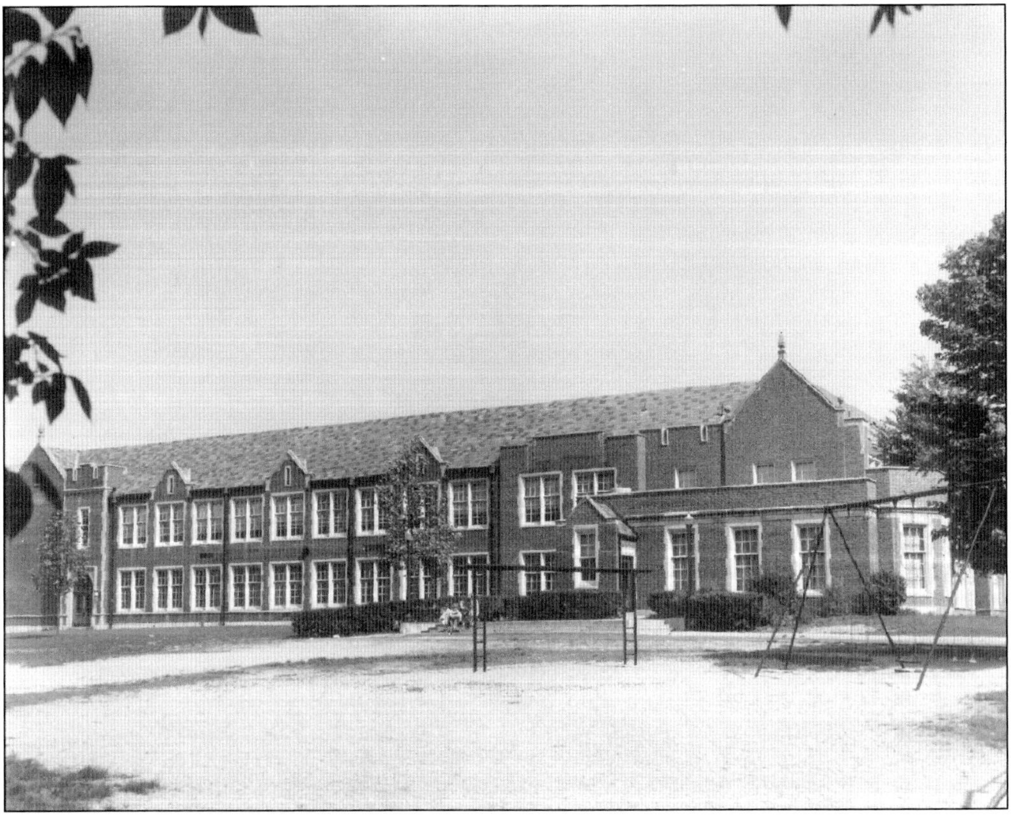

The Burris Laboratory School, a modern new structure for both elementary and secondary students, was completed in 1929. Named in honor of Ball State's first president, Benjamin Burris, the school operated as a joint effort between Ball State and the Muncie City Schools. (BSUA.)

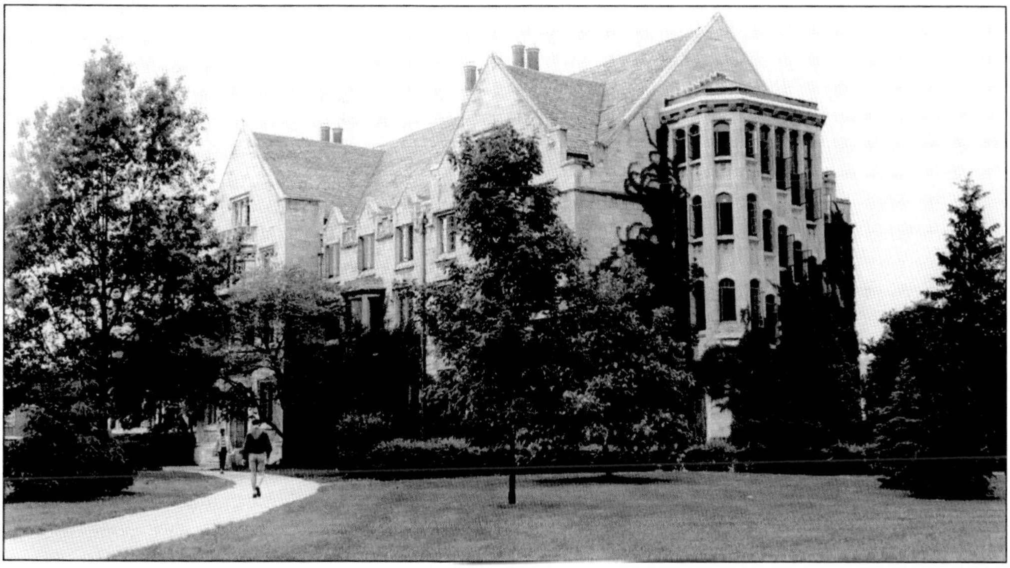

Elliot Hall, the first residence hall for men at Ball State, was completed in 1938. Elliott Hall was constructed with funds provided by Frank C. Ball in honor of his son, Frank Elliott, who died in an airplane accident in 1936. (BSUA-SG.)

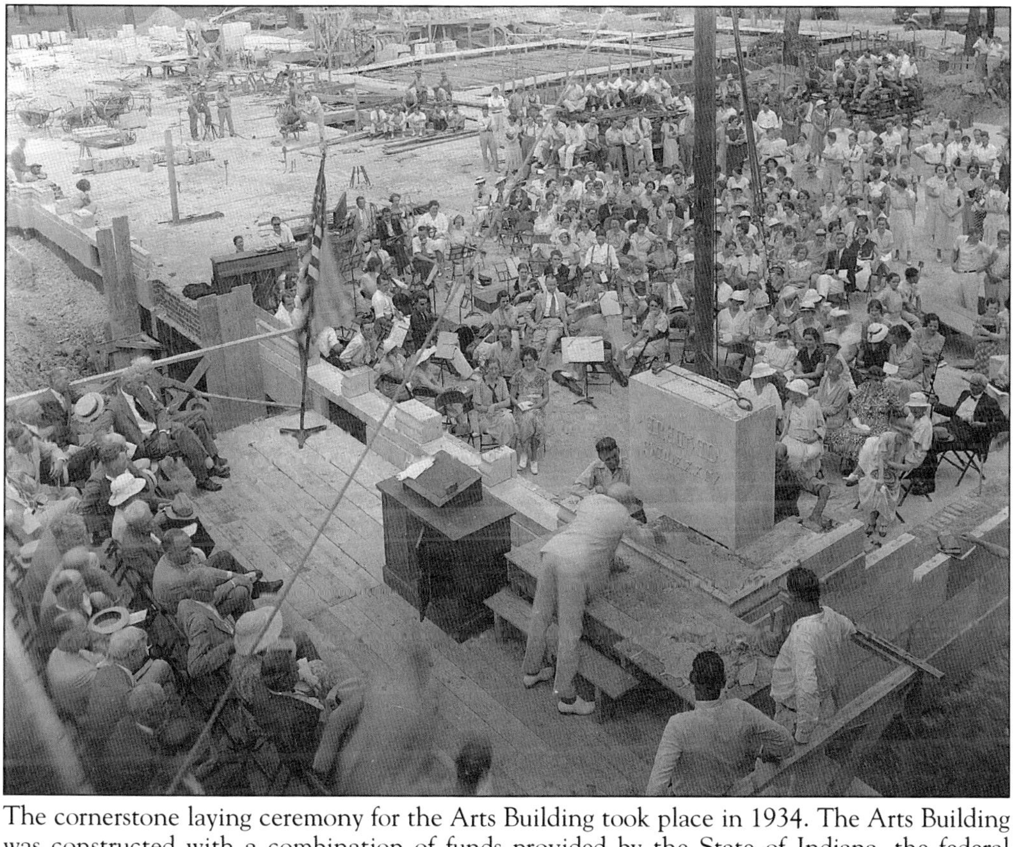

The cornerstone laying ceremony for the Arts Building took place in 1934. The Arts Building was constructed with a combination of funds provided by the State of Indiana, the federal government, and private donations. (BSUA.)

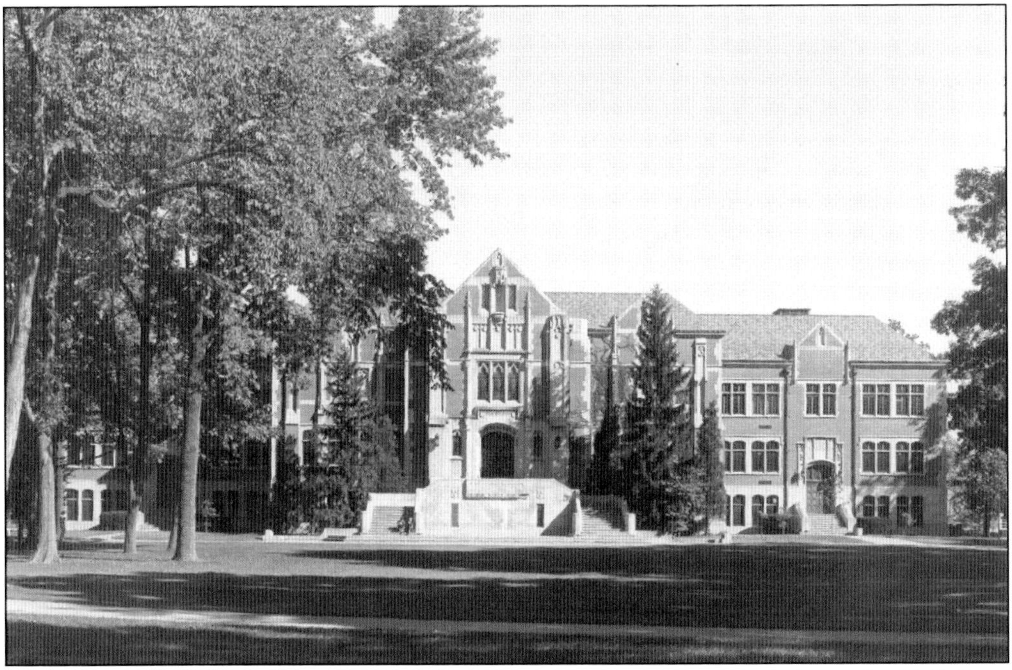

The completed Arts Building is pictured overlooking the main quadrangle on the Ball State campus. The building (with its magnificent lawn) has become the historic site of Ball State's annual commencement ceremonies. (BSUA.)

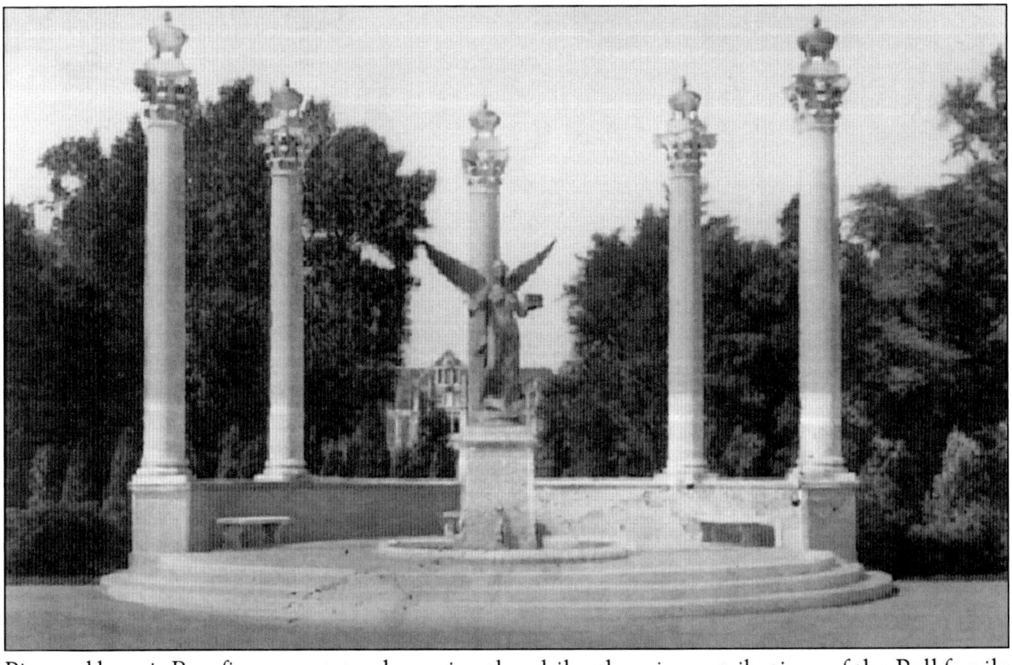

Pictured here is *Beneficence*, a statue honoring the philanthropic contributions of the Ball family to the college and community. Although not built as part of Ball State's master plan, *Beneficence* has come to symbolize Ball State's identity. The statue and surrounding landscape were the work of Daniel Chester French and Richard Henry Dana. (BSUA.)

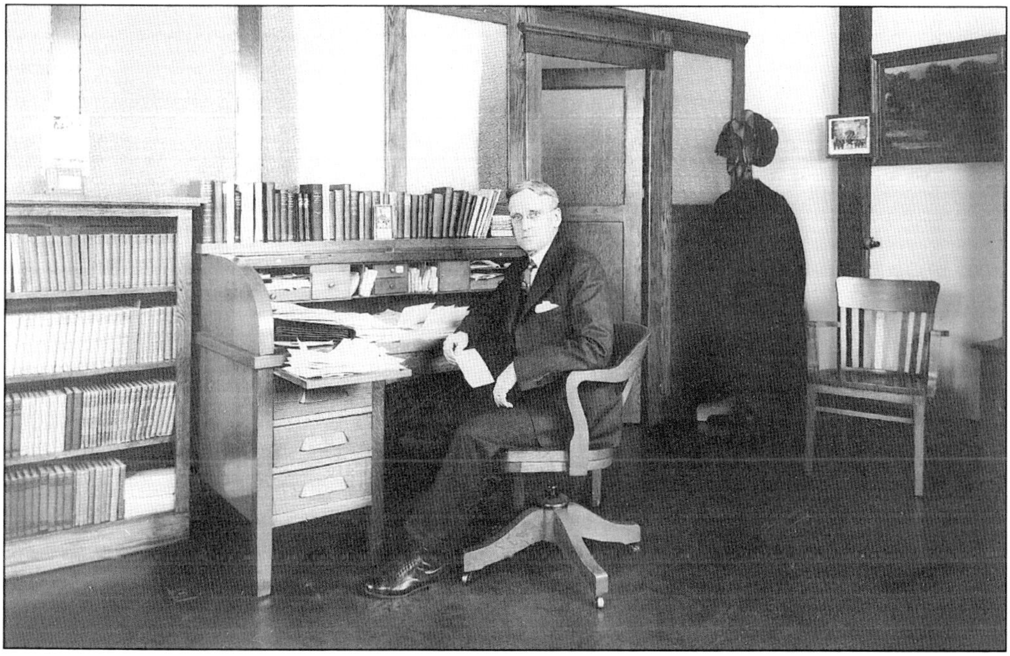

Pictured is Lemuel A. Pittenger, president of Ball State Teachers College, 1927–1942. Pittenger was the "indispensable man" in Ball State's development during its first two decades. (BSUA.)

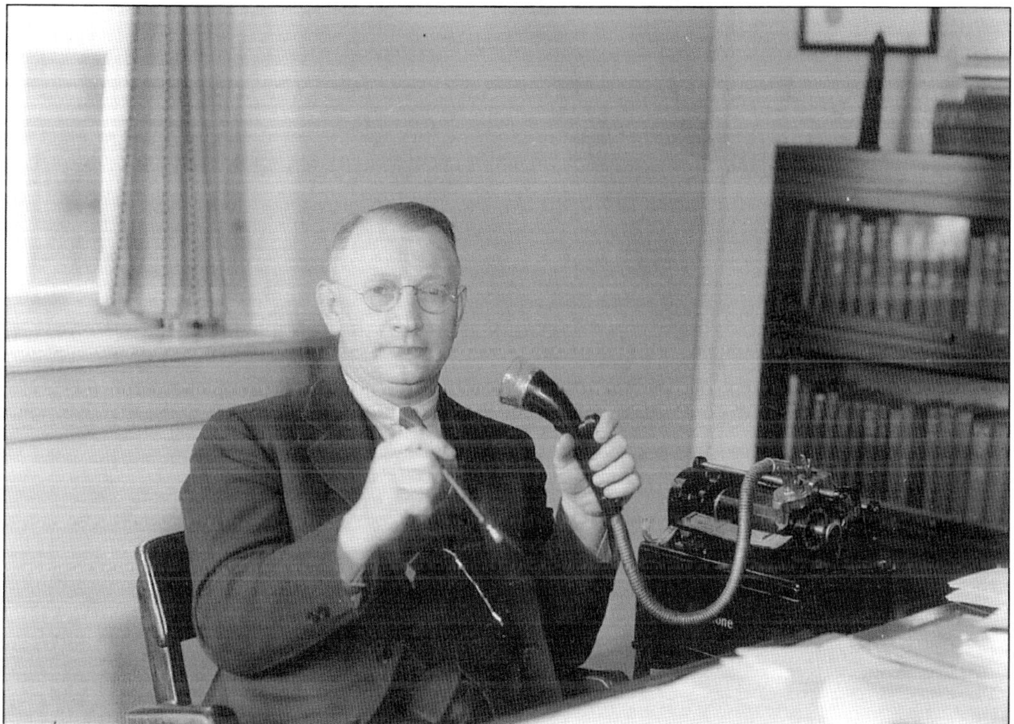

Ralph W. Noyer, dean of the college at Ball State, 1927–1952, is pictured here. A scholarly gentleman who was also known for his wit, Noyer oversaw the teaching and learning process at Ball State for a quarter-century. (BSUA.)

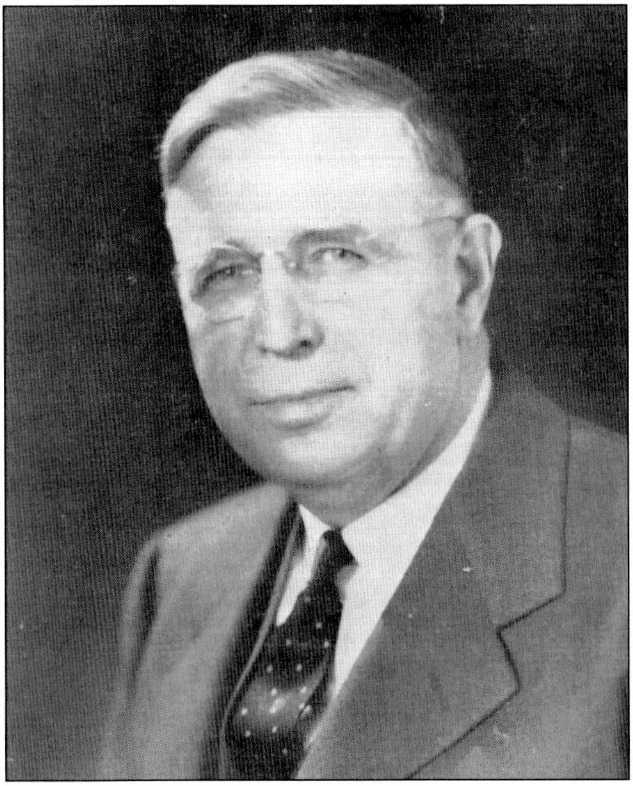

Winfred E. Wagoner, Ball State's business manager and controller, 1924–1947, is pictured at left. Wagoner managed Ball State's finances for over two decades. Then, between 1943 and 1945, he served as Ball State's acting president following the retirement of L.A. Pittenger in 1942. (BSUA.)

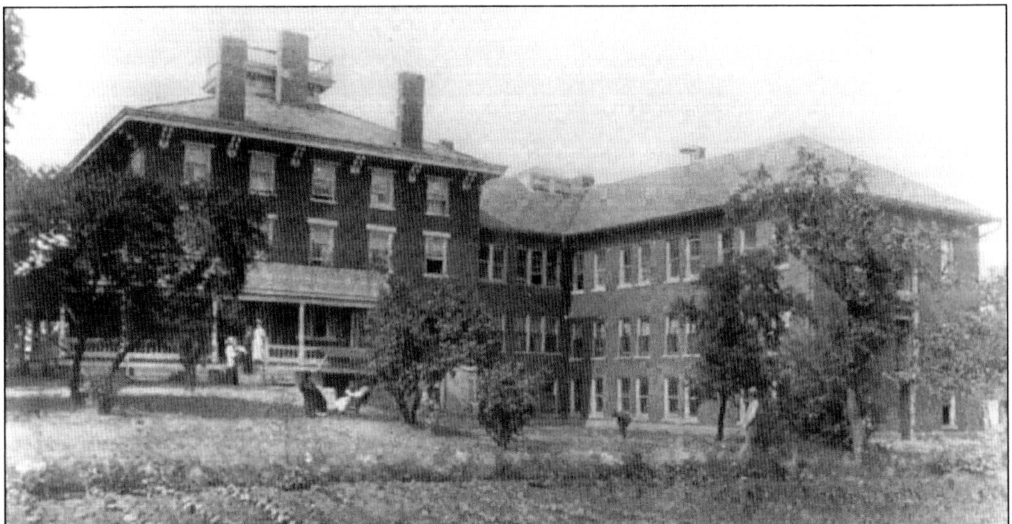

The Muncie Home Hospital was completed in 1905. The Home Hospital was Muncie's first attempt to operate a community-wide medical facility. (BSUA.)

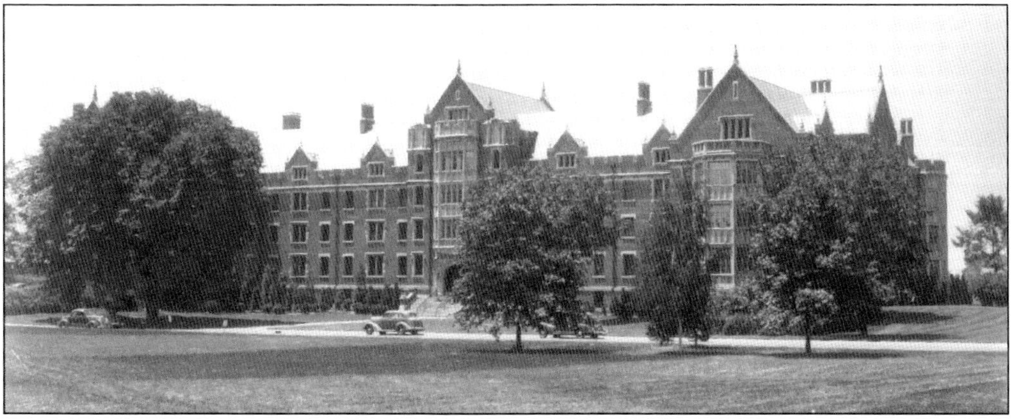

Ball Memorial Hospital was completed in 1929. Ball Hospital was built with funds provided by the Ball Brothers Foundation—the Foundation's first major philanthropic project. (BSUA.)

NON-STOP TO NOWHERE: OCTOBER 25, 1939

Muncie became a regional center for private aviation during the 1930s. Much of the impetus for this development came from Edmund F. Ball, son of Edmund B. Ball, and Frank E. Ball, son of Frank C. Ball, who became experienced pilots during this decade. The two cousins formed the Muncie Aviation Company and Muncie Airport, Incorporated, two aviation ventures that attracted the interest of many working-class young men in the community. Robert McDaniels and Kelvin Baxter had dreams of becoming pilots for one of the major national commercial airlines, and they attempted their endurance flight in 1939 as a money-raising venture toward their goal of attending flight school and obtaining their instrument ratings. The endurance flight captivated Muncie in October 1939, with as many as 20,000 people coming out to the Muncie airport to view the endurance flyers when they flew over Muncie for supplies of food and fuel.

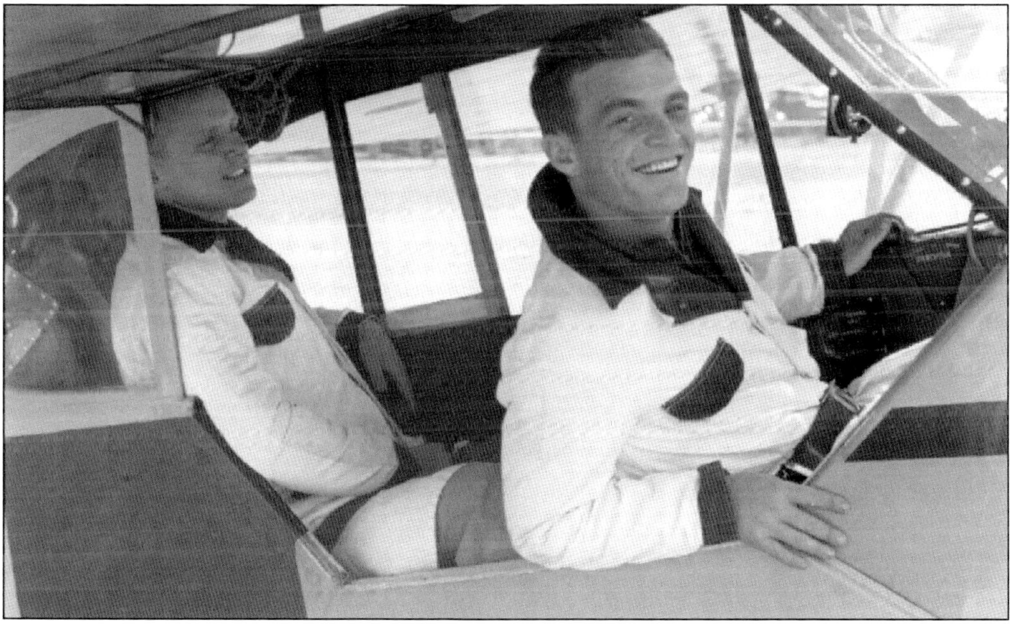

Pictured here are Robert McDaniels and Kelvin Baxter in their small aircraft before taking off on their endurance flight. (Roger Pelham.)

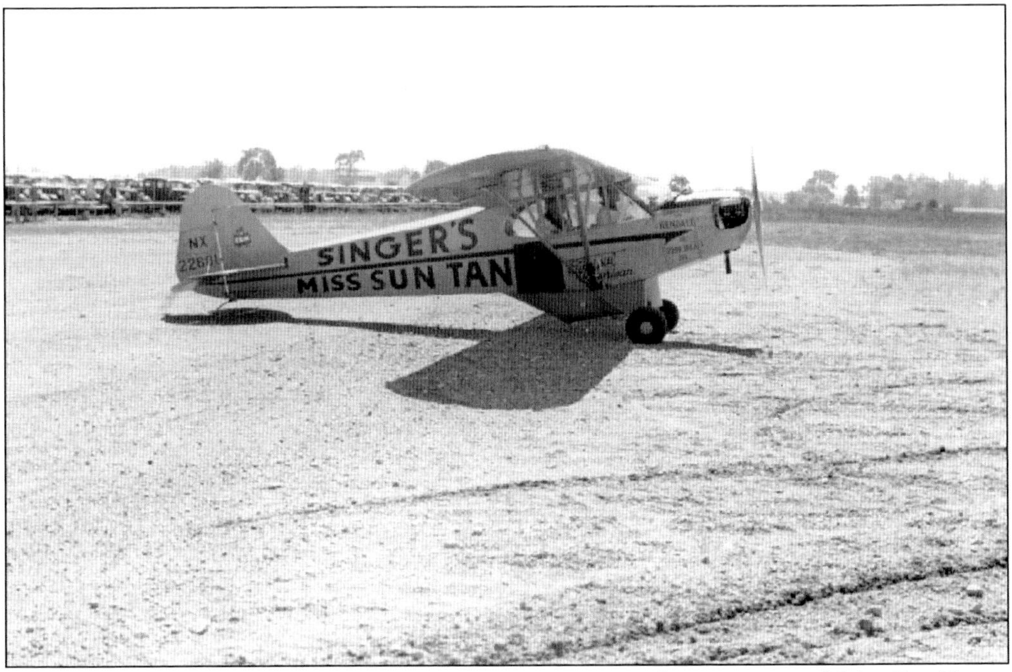

The plane flown by McDaniels and Baxter was a Piper J3 Cub. It was named *Miss Sun Tan* in recognition of a new brand of bread being introduced by the Muncie Baking Company. The Muncie Baking Company was owned by businessman Harry Singer, and he was one of the sponsors of the endurance flight. (Roger Pelham.)

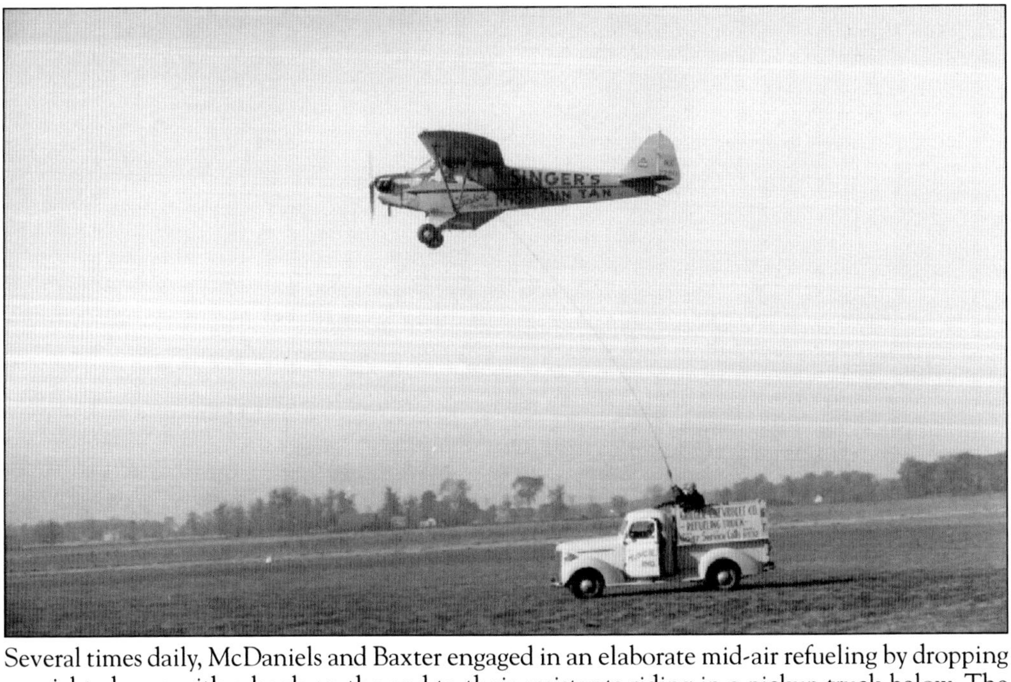

Several times daily, McDaniels and Baxter engaged in an elaborate mid-air refueling by dropping a weighted rope with a hook on the end to their assistants riding in a pickup truck below. The assistants provided fuel and food to the airmen flying above. (Roger Pelham.)

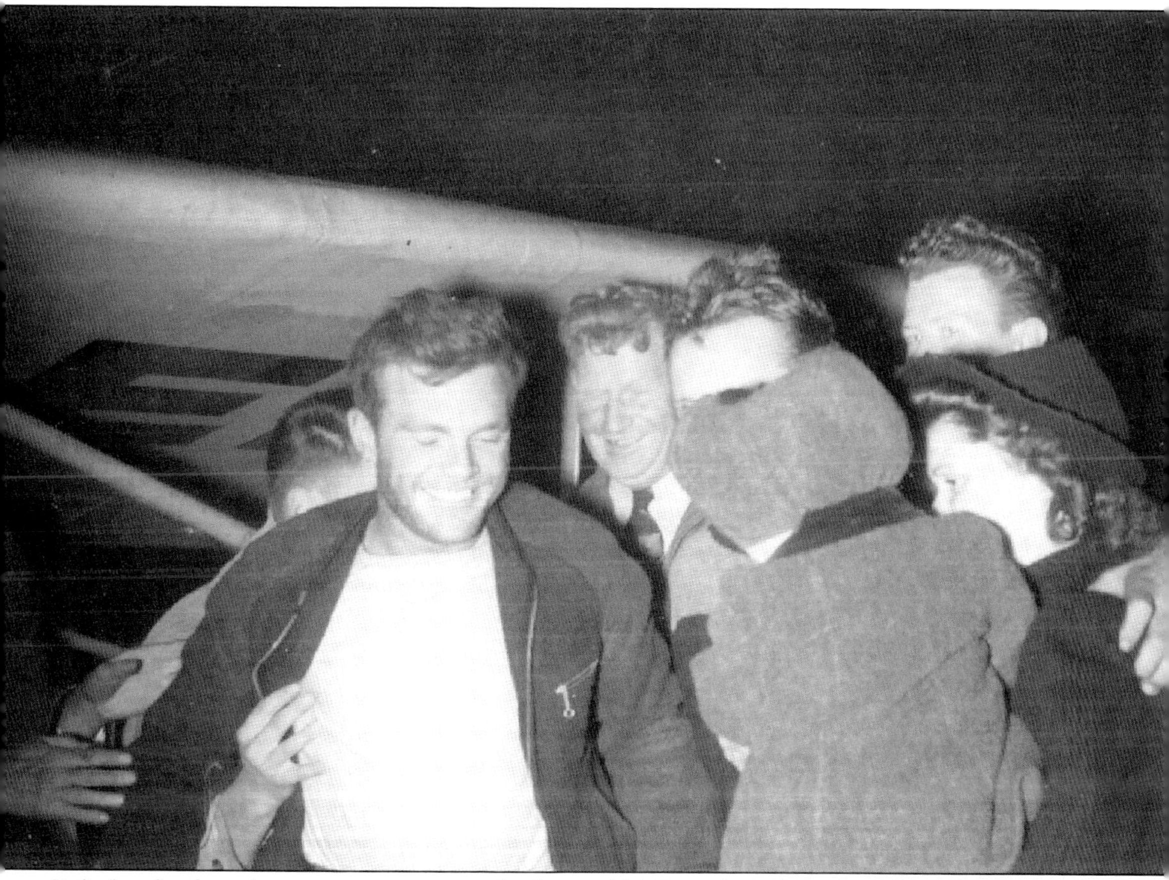

Relief and exhaustion were apparent on the faces of McDaniels and Baxter when they finally landed after setting a new endurance flight record. (Roger Pelham.)

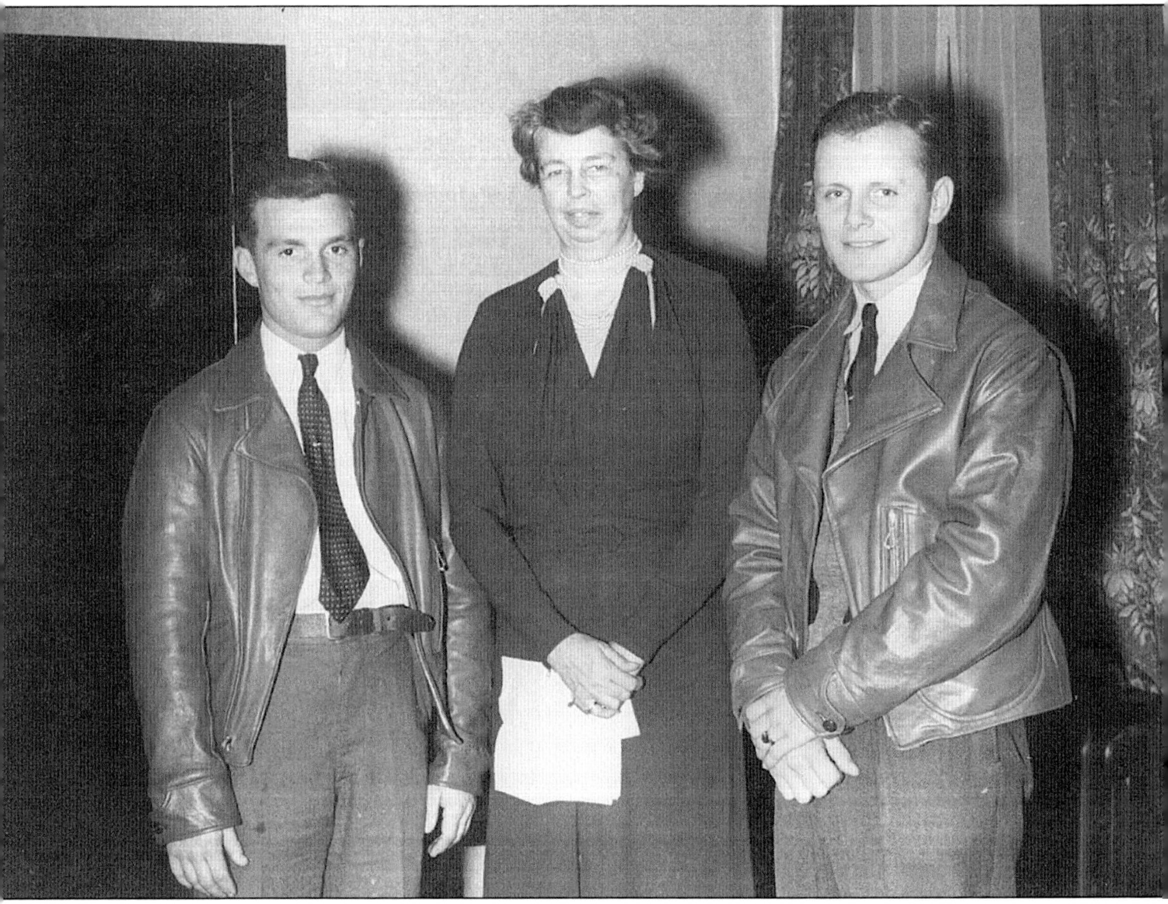

Following their record-breaking flight, McDaniels and Baxter were able to meet Eleanor Roosevelt, then in Muncie for a speaking engagement. The First Lady congratulated the two aviators on their achievement. (Roger Pelham.)

Two

Making a Living

In their Middletown studies, the Lynds and their research team focused on several characteristics of daily life in the community. These areas included economic life, family life, the training and education of young people, the practice of religion, the use of leisure, and participation in community activities. Of these six areas, the Lynds were particularly attracted to the economic life of the community, which they described under the title of "getting a living." In their analysis, the Lynds described the types of work that Munsonians performed, their attitudes toward their work, and the variety of occupations which existed in the community. Central to an understanding of the Lynds' analysis of working life in Muncie was their division of the work force into two distinct groups. "The working class" was comprised primarily of employees who worked with "things," producing the tools and products of the modern economy. "The business class" was comprised of those individuals who worked with "people," mainly those in the professions and in the managerial occupations who directed and oversaw the work of the "working class." In the Middletown of the Lynds, approximately 70 percent of Muncie's employees belonged to the "working class;" the remainder belonged to the "business class." (*Middletown*, p. 22)

On the Job

In one section of *Middletown* (pp. 53–72), the Lynds wrote about "the long arm of the job" and how occupations served to define individual behavior and attitudes, in addition to providing a means to a livelihood. These photos show a variety of Munsonians engaged in their occupations.

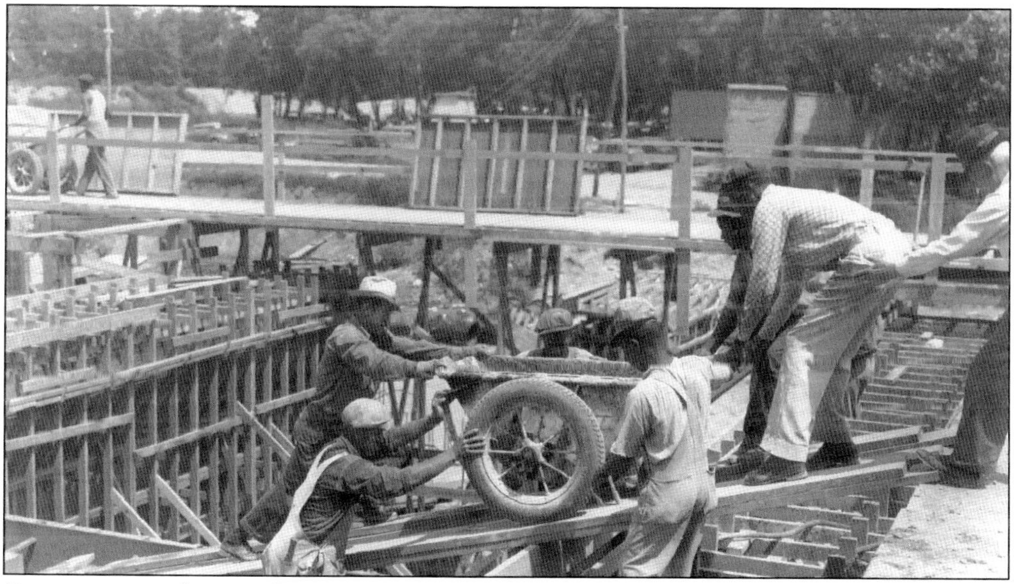

Construction of a modern wastewater treatment facility was a major Depression-era project in Muncie. Taken in 1939, this photo shows workers employed on the construction of the facility.(BSUA-SG.)

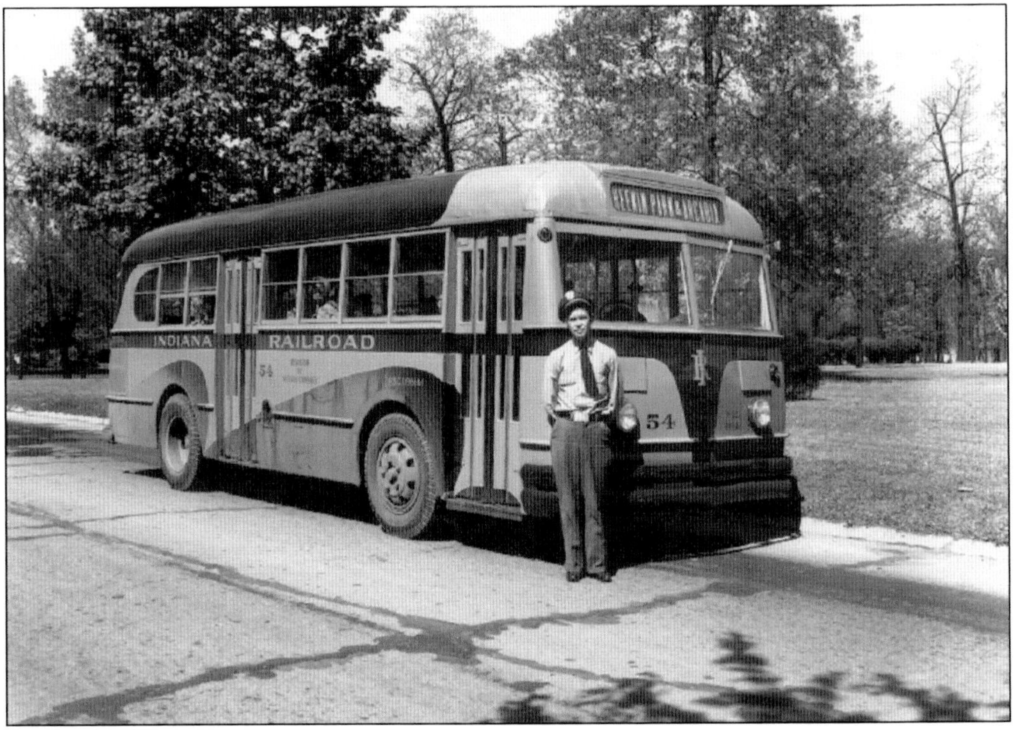

The local bus system provided inexpensive transportation for Munsonians during the 1930s and 1940s. One driver poses for a photograph outside of his bus. (BSUA-SG.)

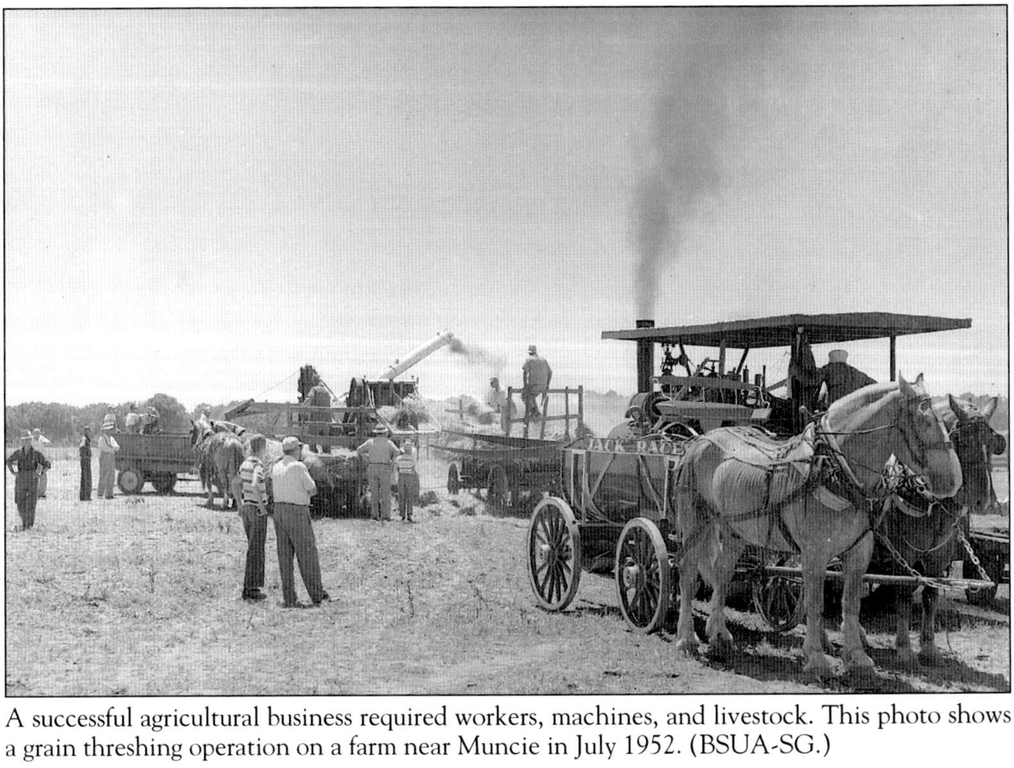

A successful agricultural business required workers, machines, and livestock. This photo shows a grain threshing operation on a farm near Muncie in July 1952. (BSUA-SG.)

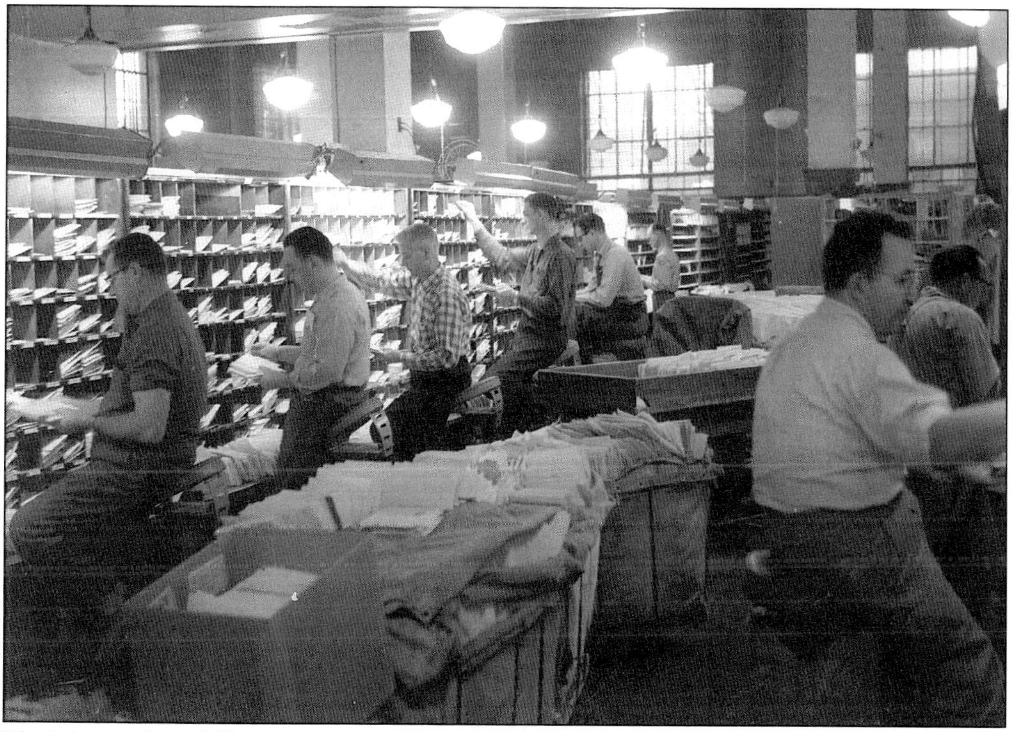

The Muncie Post Office was a hectic place during the Christmas holidays. Here postal workers sort mail during the Christmas rush in December 1957. (BSUA-SG.)

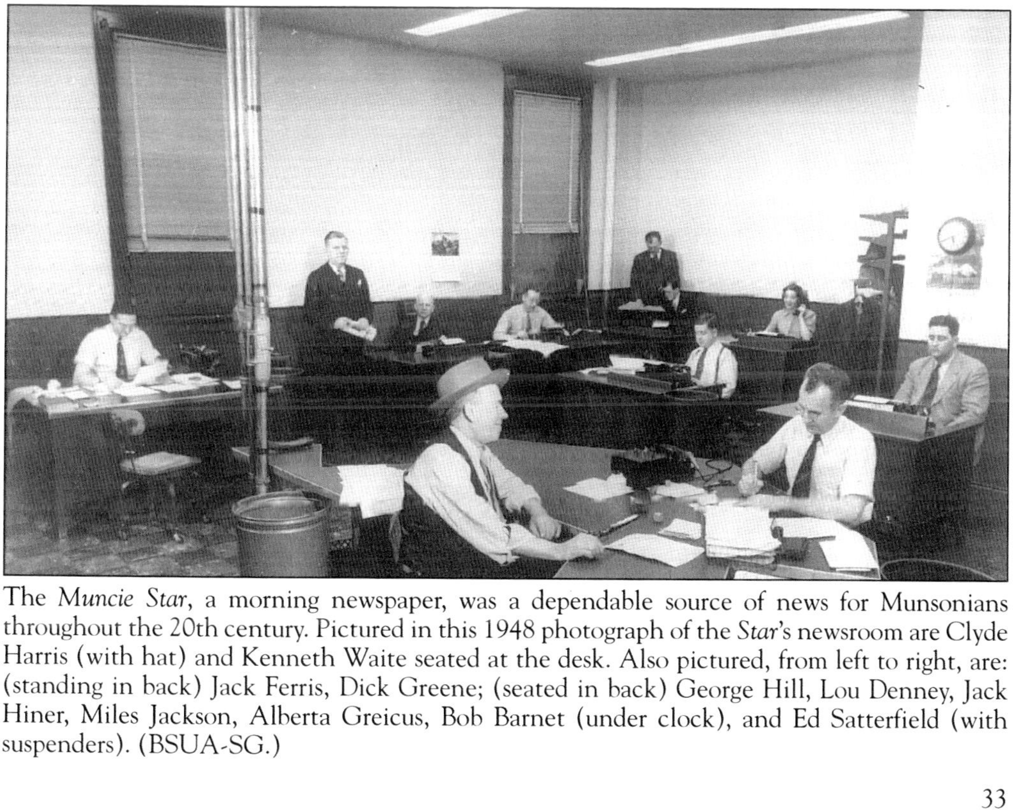

The *Muncie Star*, a morning newspaper, was a dependable source of news for Munsonians throughout the 20th century. Pictured in this 1948 photograph of the *Star*'s newsroom are Clyde Harris (with hat) and Kenneth Waite seated at the desk. Also pictured, from left to right, are: (standing in back) Jack Ferris, Dick Greene; (seated in back) George Hill, Lou Denney, Jack Hiner, Miles Jackson, Alberta Greicus, Bob Barnet (under clock), and Ed Satterfield (with suspenders). (BSUA-SG.)

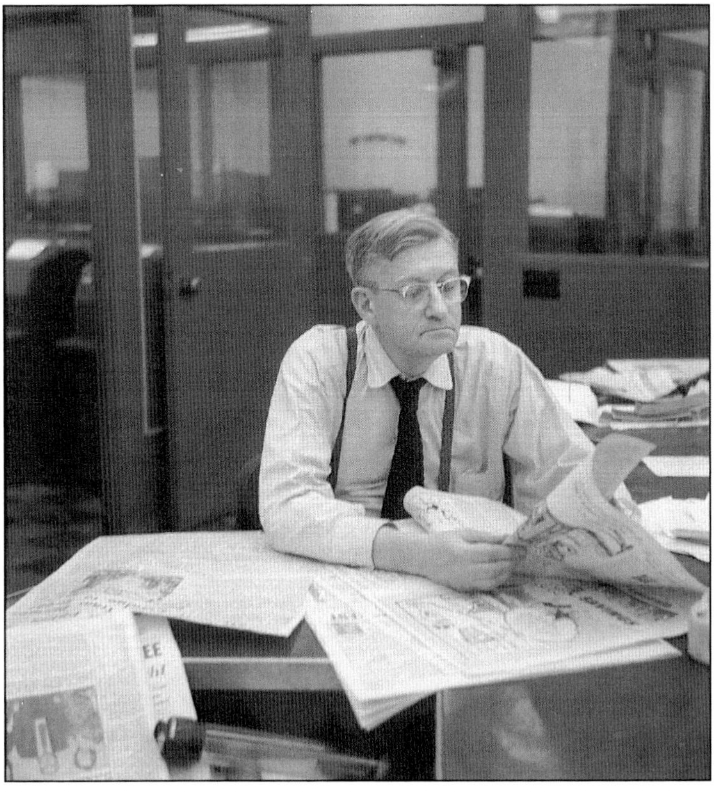

Herbert A. Silverburg, columnist for the *Evening Press*, reads the latest edition. (BSUA-SG.)

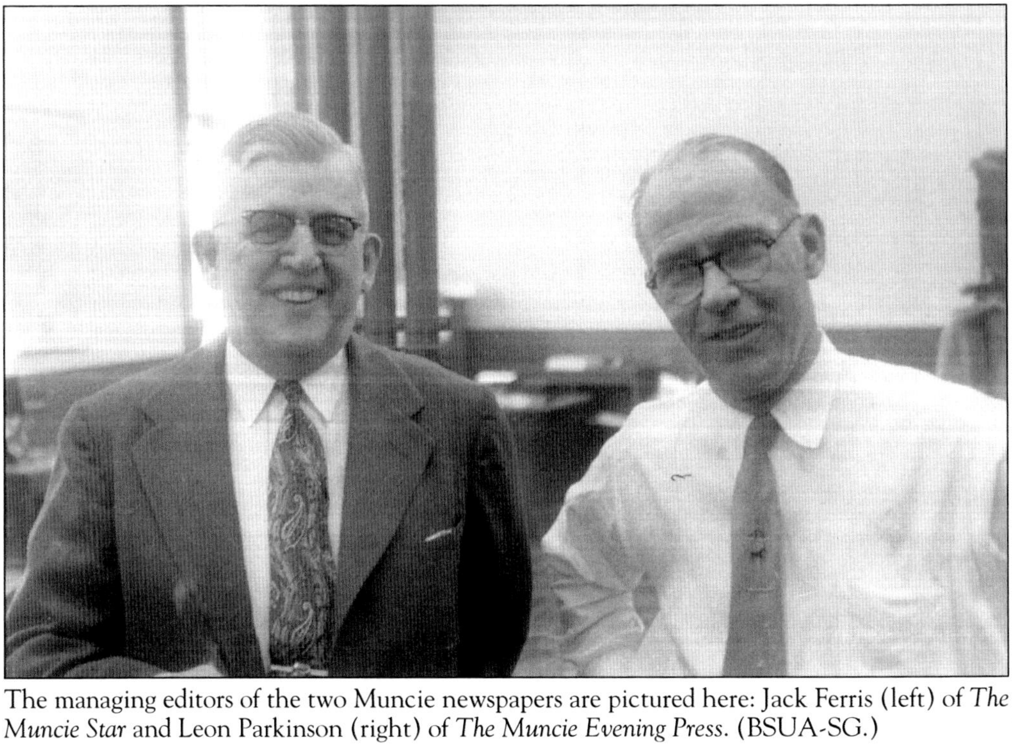

The managing editors of the two Muncie newspapers are pictured here: Jack Ferris (left) of *The Muncie Star* and Leon Parkinson (right) of *The Muncie Evening Press*. (BSUA-SG.)

John Blair was the first African American appointed to the Muncie Fire Department. Blair began his career on the fire department in April 1958. (Hurley C. Goodall.)

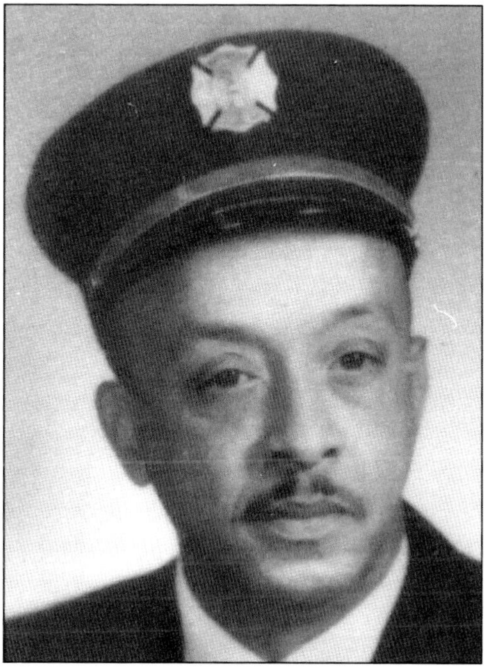

THE INDUSTRIAL EXPERIENCE

During the 1920s, Muncie developed rapidly into a center of manufacturing for central Indiana. Several national corporations operated in the city, and the community was well served by an extensive rail network. The city's development as a center of industry also helped to define the community's profile as a place "where people made things" which contributed to a better life for everyone. The city's industrial development proceeded throughout the 20th century until the recessions of the 1970s and 1980s, after which the industrial profile of the community began a decline.

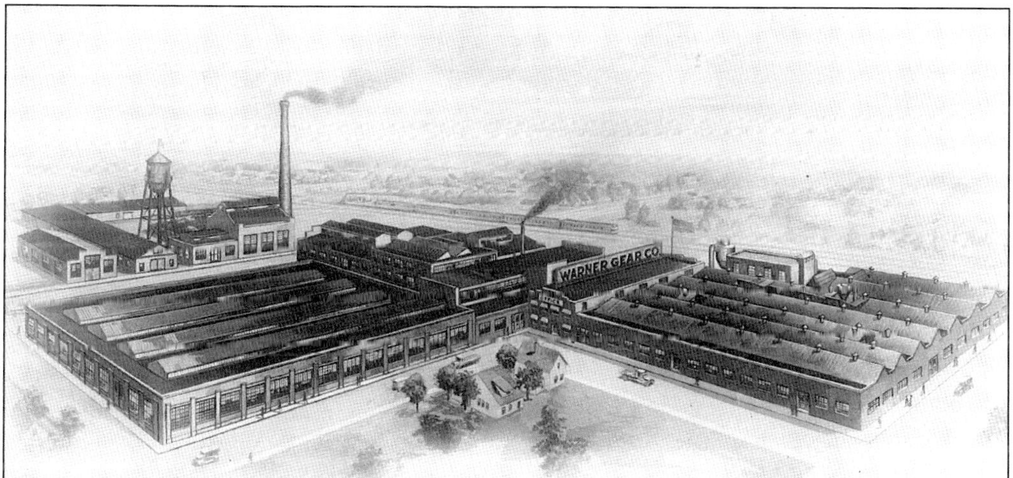

Muncie has historically been associated with manufacturing, specifically with the auto parts industry. The photo shows an artist's conception of the massive Warner Gear (now Borg Warner Automotive) complex near downtown Muncie. (BSUA-Warner Gear Collection.)

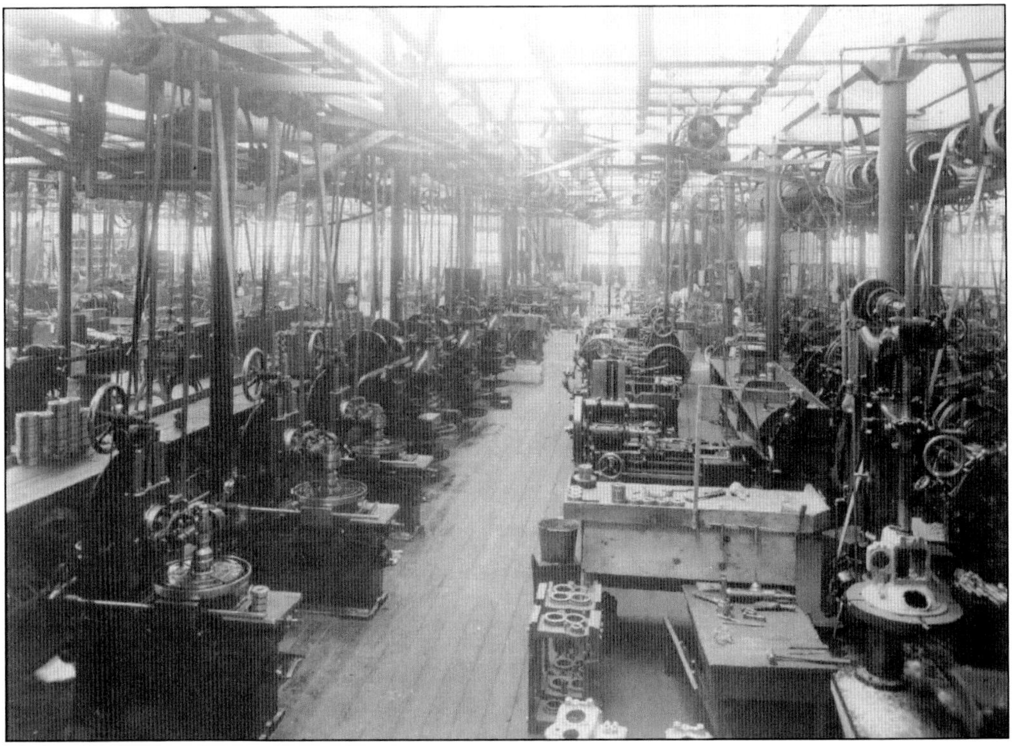

Pictured is the factory floor of Warner Gear during its heyday as a manufacturer. (BSUA-Warner Gear Collection.)

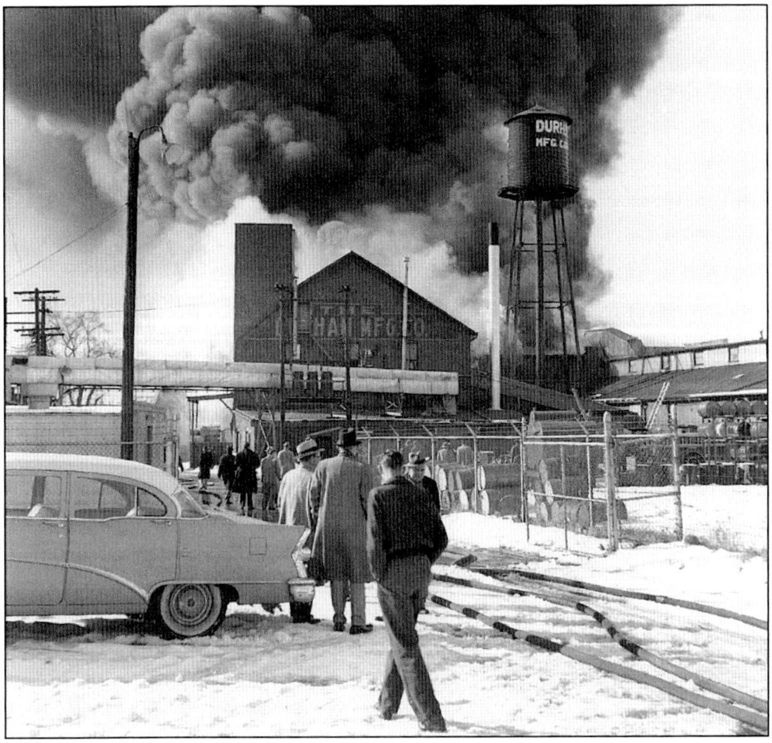

Even in the modern era, fire is the great enemy of the manufacturing industry. This photo shows a destructive fire ablaze at the Durham Manufacturing Company in February 1956. (BSUA-SG.)

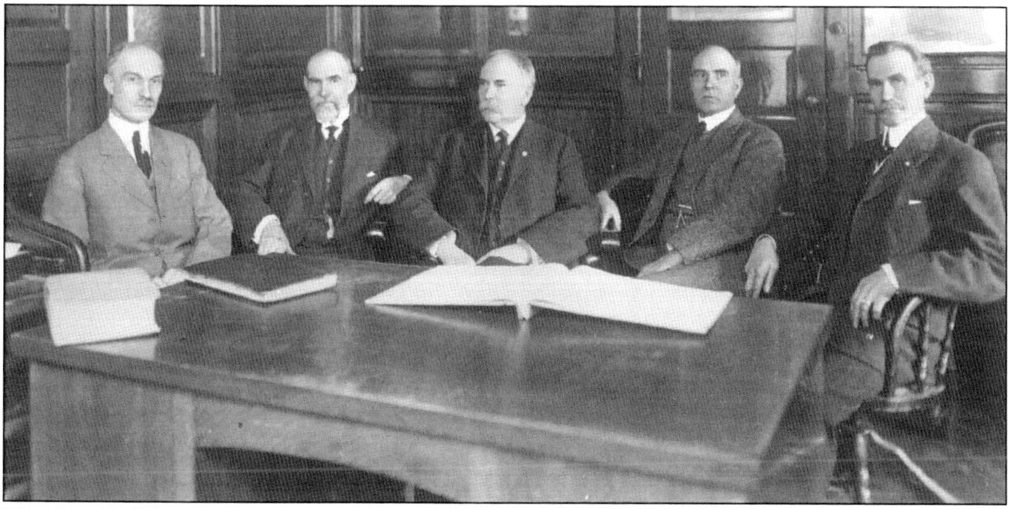

The five Ball brothers who moved to Muncie from Buffalo, New York, in 1887, and built the city's first large-scale industrial operation are pictured above. Their company, the Ball Brothers Manufacturing Company, specialized in the production of glass containers for home canning and food preservation. The five brothers were, from left to right: George Alexander Ball, Lucius Lorenzo Ball, Frank Clayton Ball, Edmund Burke Ball, and William Charles Ball. (BSUA-Richard Roller Collection.)

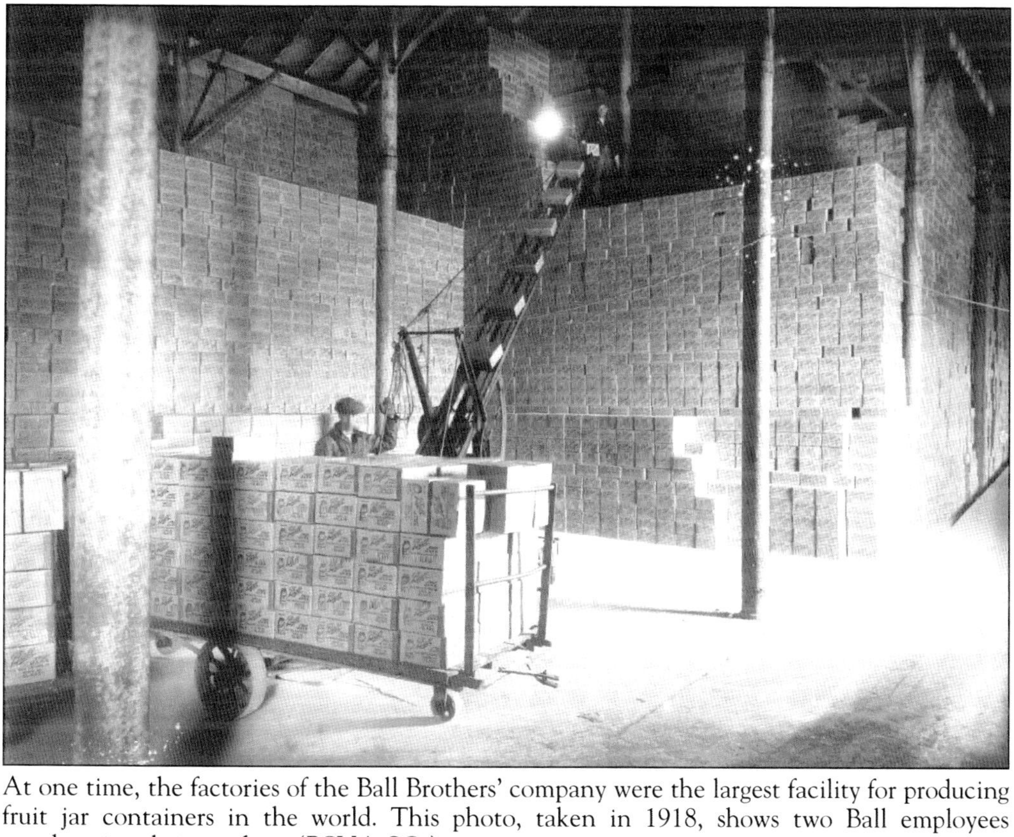

At one time, the factories of the Ball Brothers' company were the largest facility for producing fruit jar containers in the world. This photo, taken in 1918, shows two Ball employees warehousing their product. (BSUA-SG.)

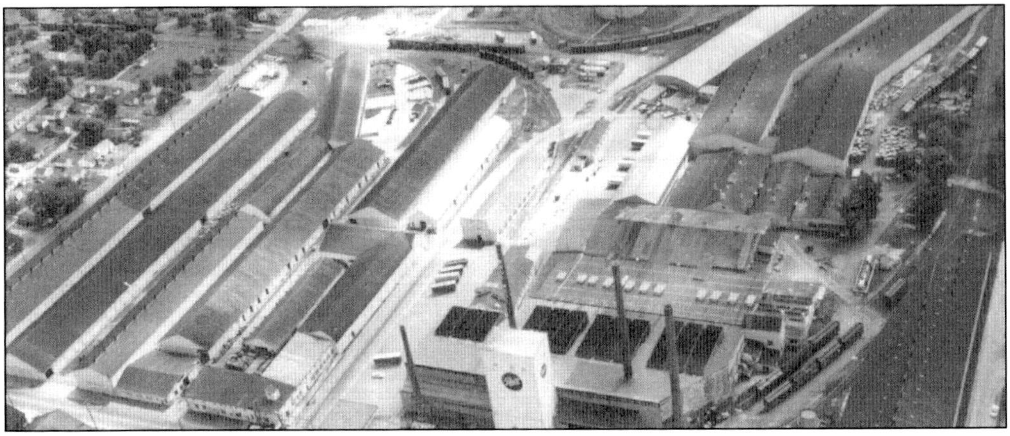

An aerial view of the massive Ball Brothers manufacturing complex on Macedonia Avenue in southeast Muncie is pictured above. (BSUA-SG)

Shopping in Muncie

Muncie's retail profile during much of the 20th century consisted of numerous neighborhood shopping centers which contained locally owned, and locally operated, stores and shops. The city's central business district was "downtown," along Walnut Street, but this circumstance changed once neighborhoods began to develop away from the city center. By the end of the 20th century, most Munsonians shopped at centers and malls well away from the central city.

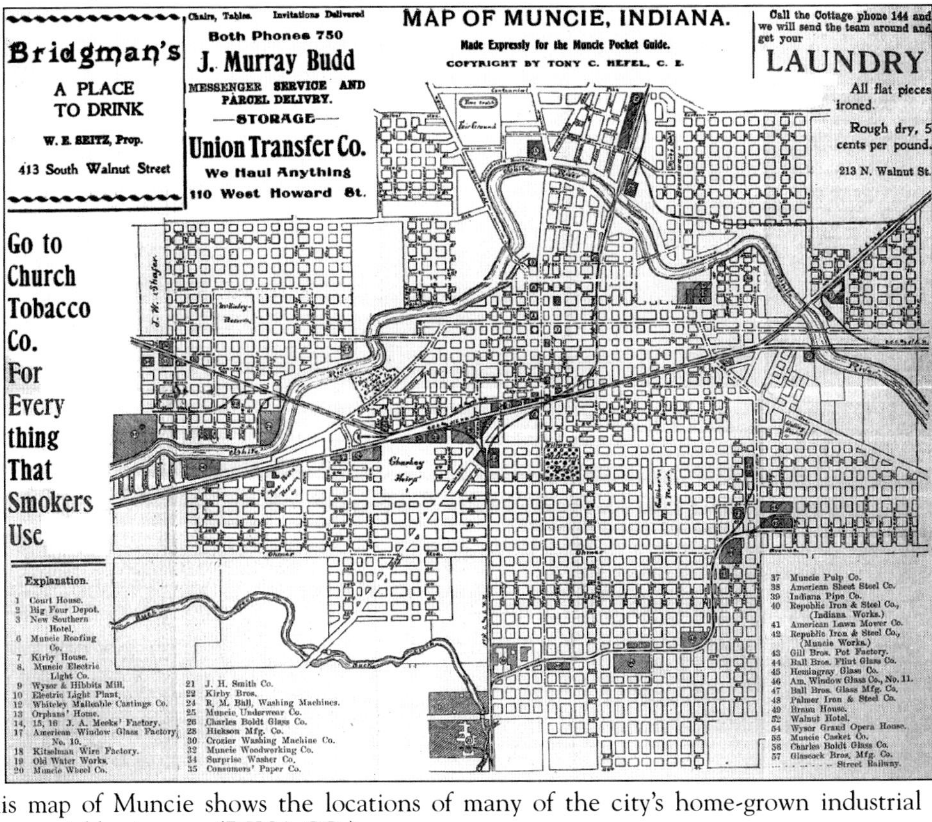

This map of Muncie shows the locations of many of the city's home-grown industrial and commercial businesses. (BSUA-SG.)

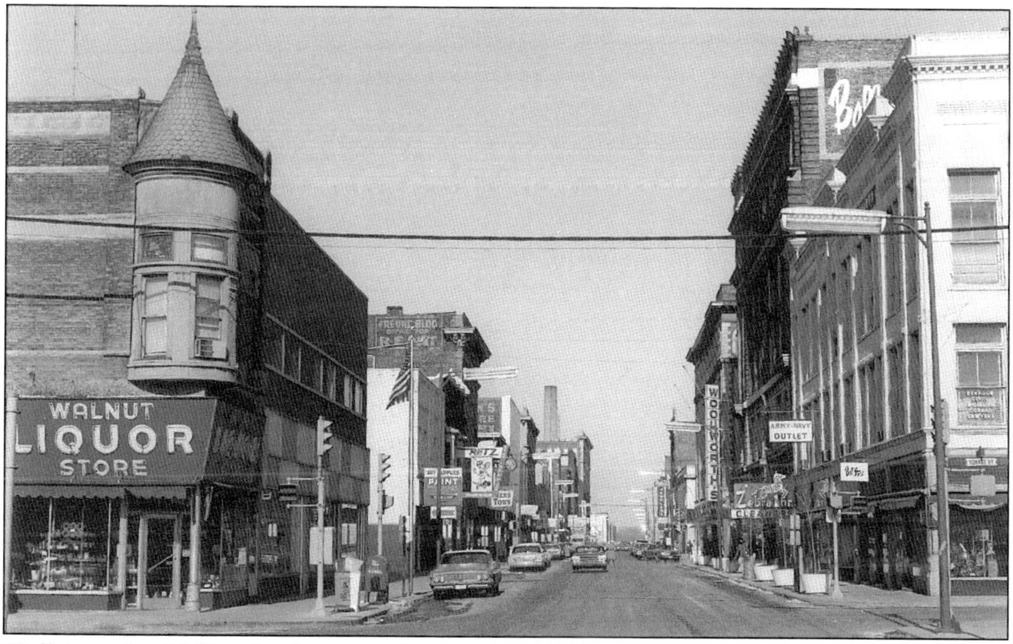

Well into the 1960s, the shopping district along Walnut Street was the home of the small businesses which attracted the attention of writers such as Robert Lynd. The names on the storefronts show the community's support for its local retailers. (BSUA-SG.)

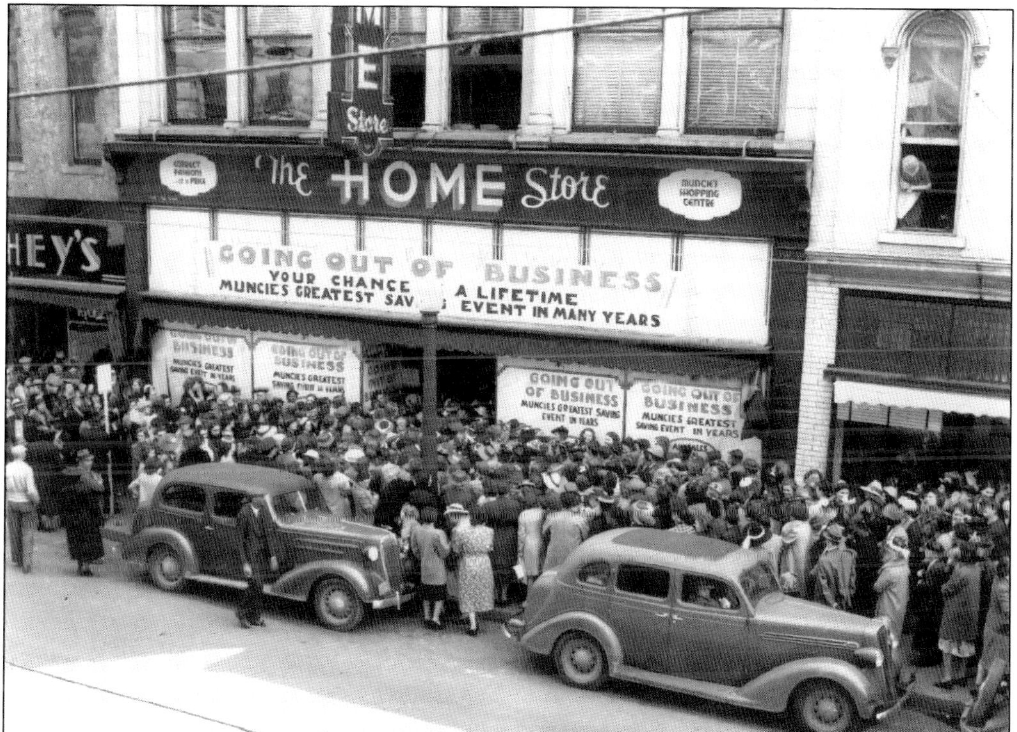

Few events attracted a crowd of shoppers like a well-publicized "Going Out Of Business Sale." (BSUA-SG.)

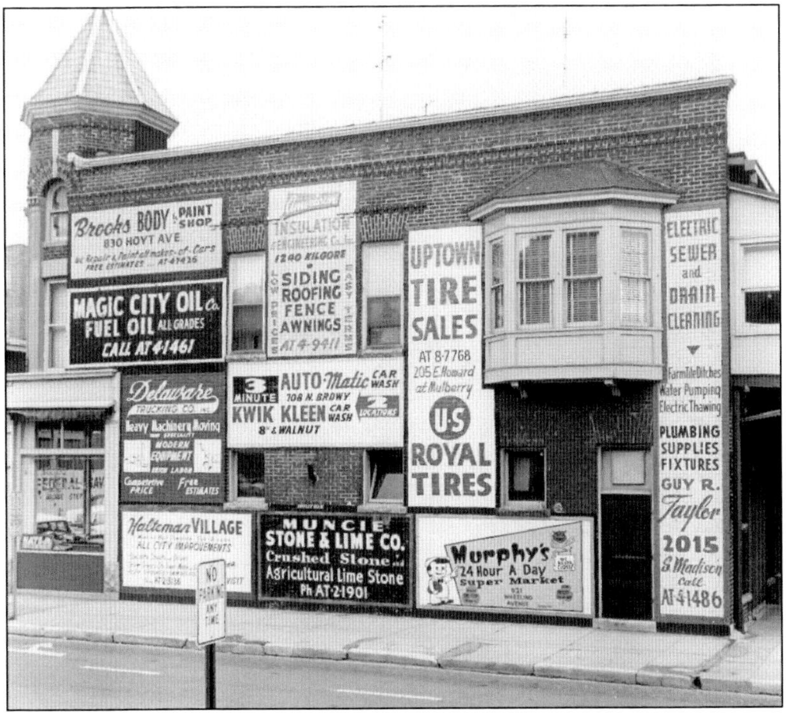

Local retailers often took advantage of their buildings to post advertising for other Muncie companies. Taken in 1960, this photo shows advertising for at least a dozen businesses on the side of the store. (BSUA-SG.)

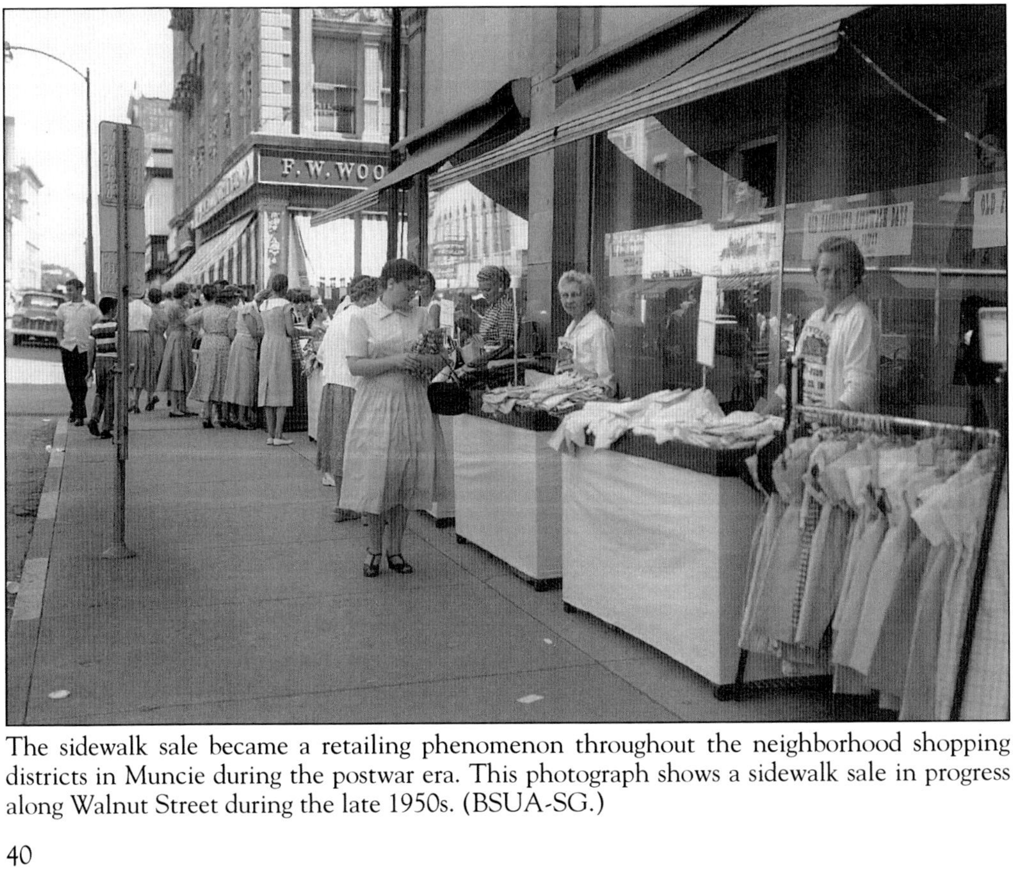

The sidewalk sale became a retailing phenomenon throughout the neighborhood shopping districts in Muncie during the postwar era. This photograph shows a sidewalk sale in progress along Walnut Street during the late 1950s. (BSUA-SG.)

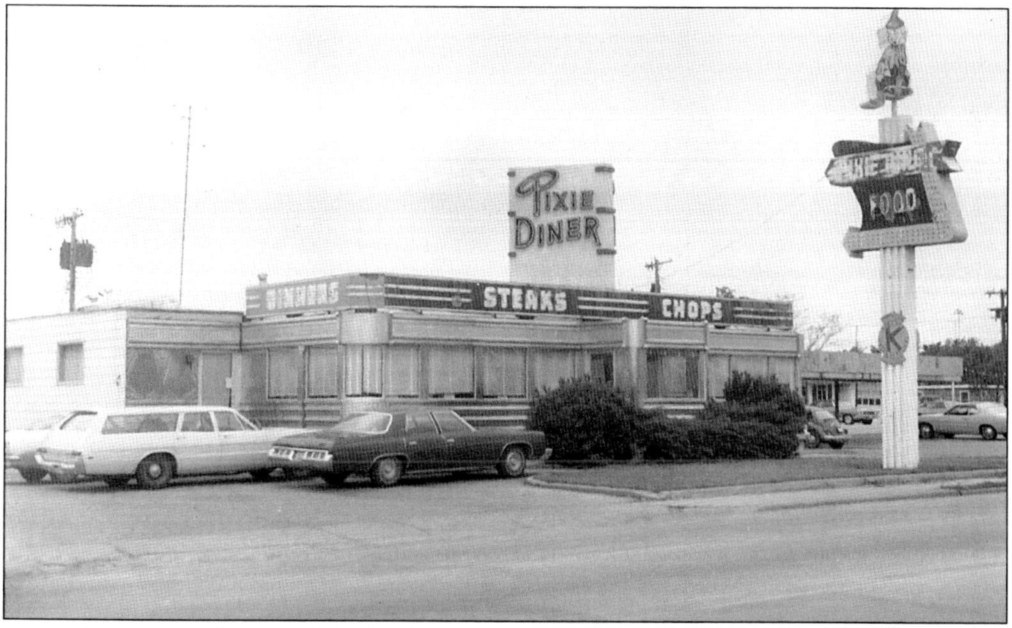

Before the advent of franchised food outlets, Munsonians enjoyed eating at local restaurants which had distinctive names and reputations. The Pixie Diner was one such restaurant. (BSUA-SG.)

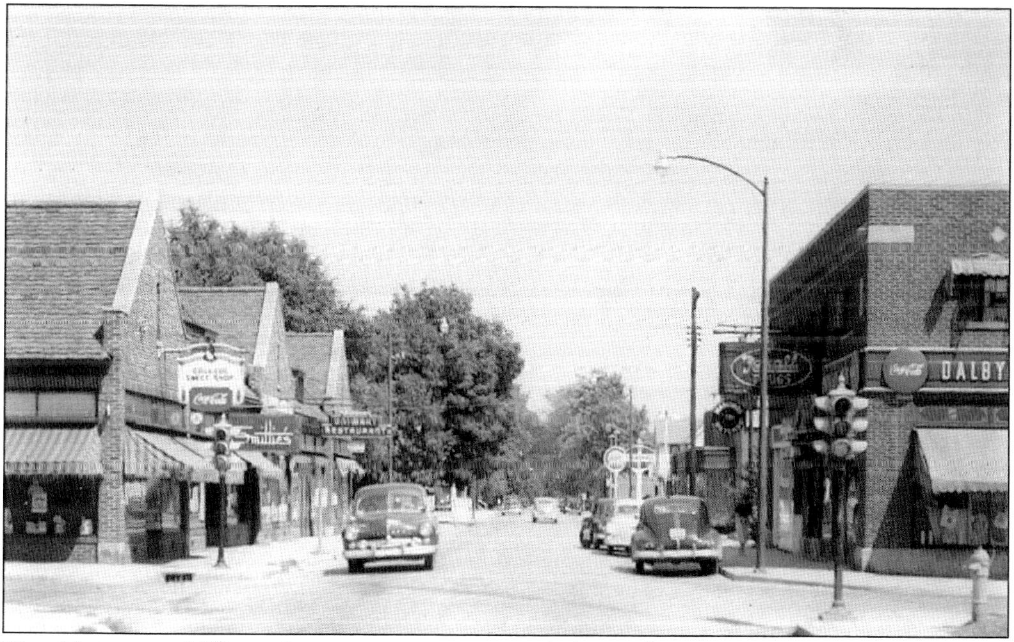

The University Village shopping center, east of the Ball State campus, emerged during the 1930s as a viable commercial district, thanks in part to spending by college students. (BSUA- Jeff Koenker Collection.)

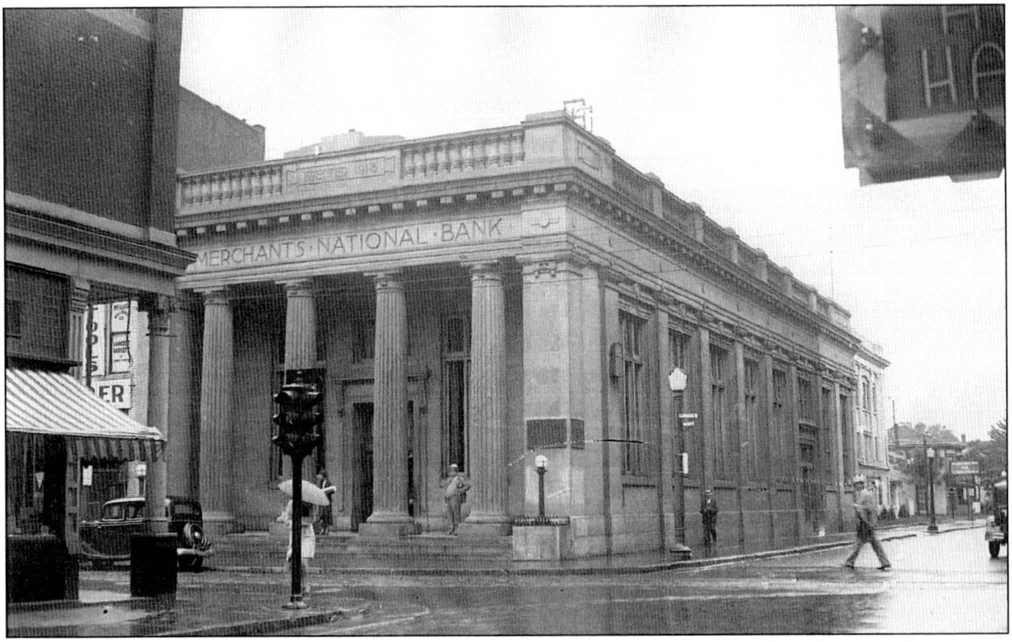

The Merchants National Bank, founded in 1893, built its first modern building in downtown Muncie in 1913. The bank's impressive structure symbolized finance and banking in Muncie throughout much of the 20th century. (BSUA-SG.)

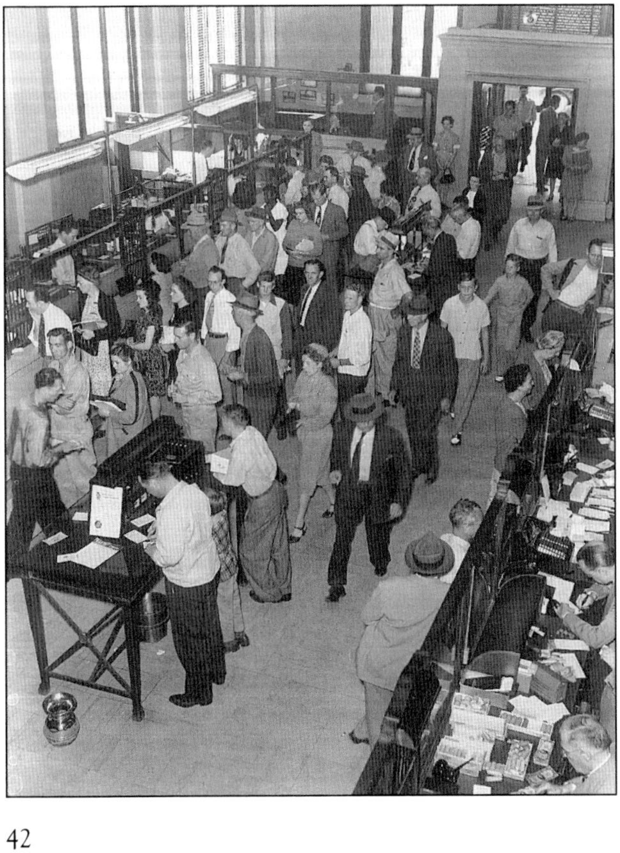

The lobby of Merchants National Bank was an especially busy place on payday as customers came in to cash their paychecks. (First Merchants Corporation.)

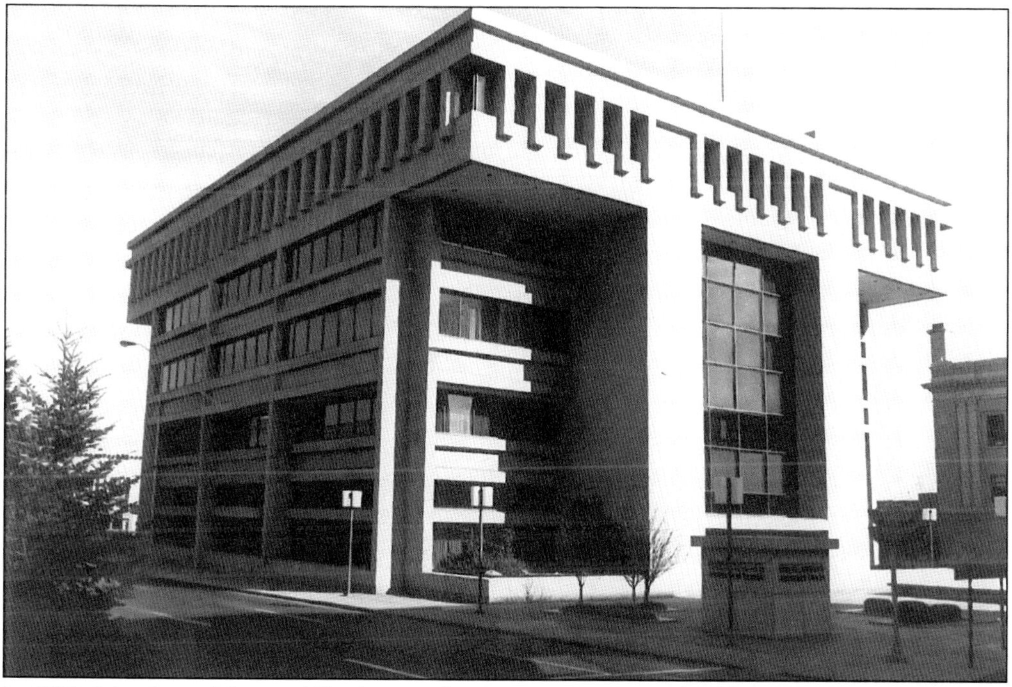

In 1972, Merchants National Bank moved to an impressive new building on East Jackson Street in Muncie. (First Merchants Corporation.)

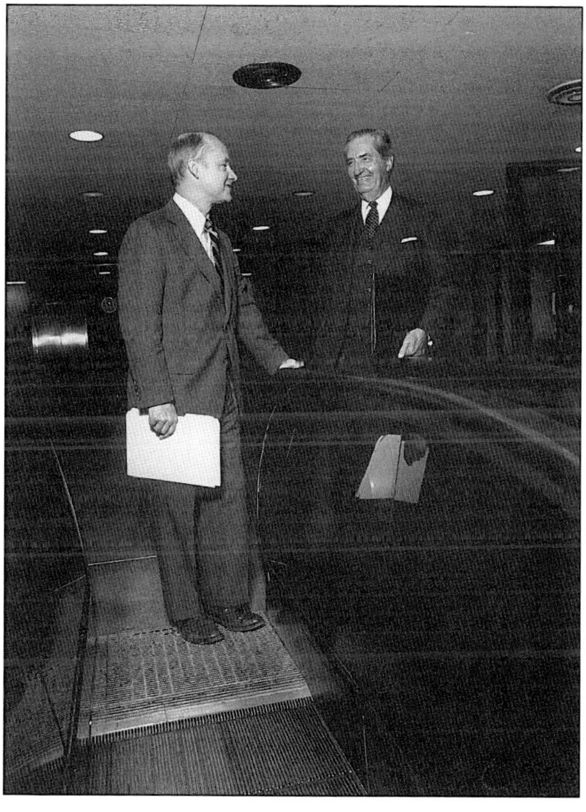

Stefan S. Anderson (left) and William P. Givens (right) were the leaders behind the growth of Merchants National Bank during the last half of the 20th century. Givens was president of Merchants National Bank from 1958–1979 and became one of the leaders of the community banking movement in Indiana. Anderson was president of Merchants National Bank from 1979 to 1999, and guided it into its present status as a holding corporation for other community banks in east central Indiana. (First Merchants Corporation.)

FAMILY ENTERPRISE

In *Middletown in Transition* (p. 23), the Lynds wrote about the presence of a "small business" culture in Muncie. In Muncie, so the Lynds argued, most businessmen thought of themselves as "small businessmen," either as proprietors or managers of enterprises with a relatively small number of employees whose purpose was to serve the local community. Many of the small businesses of the Lynd era eventually grew to become large operations in the years after World War II. Many of Muncie's small businesses were family enterprises, owned or managed by successive generations of a particular family. Lynd noticed within the Muncie community an idealization of the "small business;" he may also have noticed a similar idealization of the "family business."

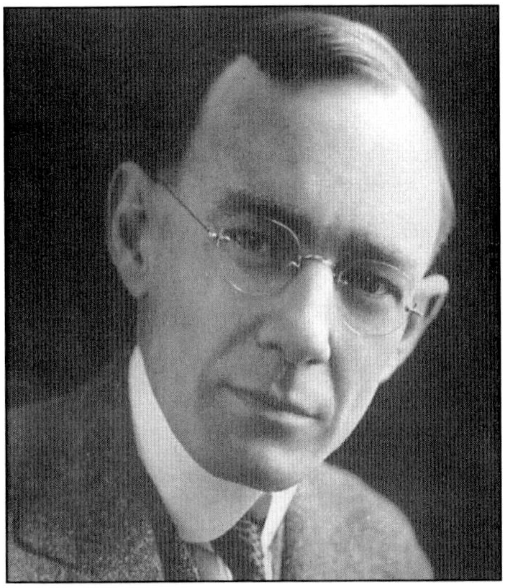

The Boyce and Galliher families provided ownership and leadership for one of Muncie's centennial businesses, A.E. Boyce and Company. The founder of the company was Arthur Earl Boyce. The business specialized in printing forms for recordkeeping used in businesses, schools, and government offices. The company also sold several lines of commercial stationary products. (Boyce Forms Systems.)

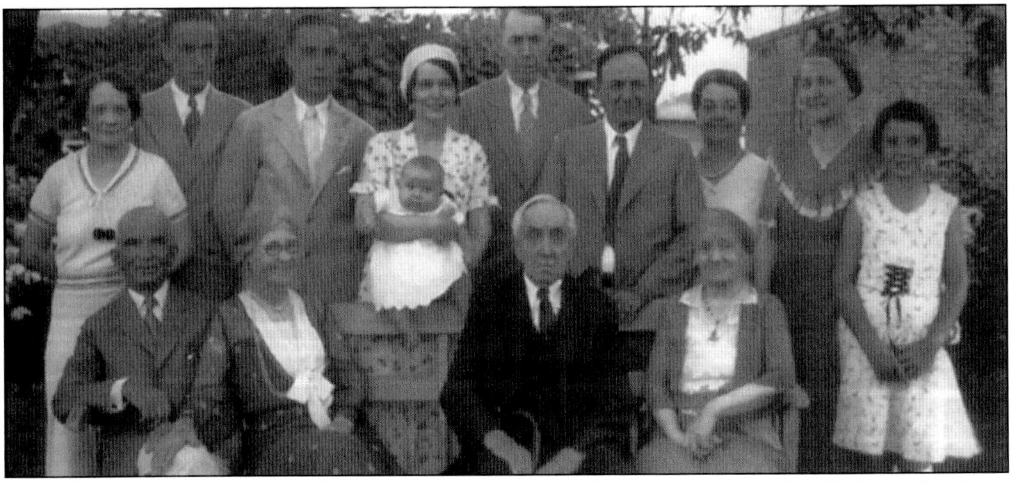

Taken in 1933, this photograph shows a reunion of the Boyce family and the Galliher family. The two families became related in 1926 when Harriet Boyce, daughter of Arthur Earl Boyce, married Robert J. Galliher. The Galliher family traces its roots back to the late 1830s in Muncie, and the Gallihers owned and managed several local business enterprises. Pictured here, from left to right, are: (seated) George N. Patterson, Hattie Patterson, Martin J. Galliher, Margaret Mohler Boyce; (top row) Jane J. Galliher, David M. Galliher, Robert J. Galliher, Harriet Boyce Galliher (holding Robert B. Galliher), Delbert M. Galliher, Arthur E. Boyce, Georgia Patterson Boyce, Etta Taylor (sister of Margaret Boyce), and Marjorie Galliher. (Boyce Forms Systems.)

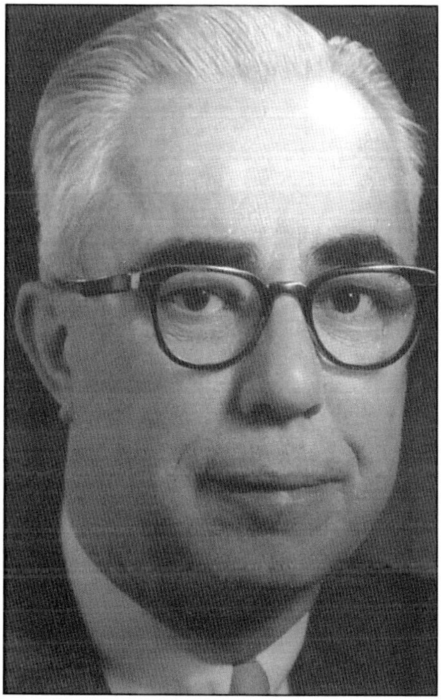

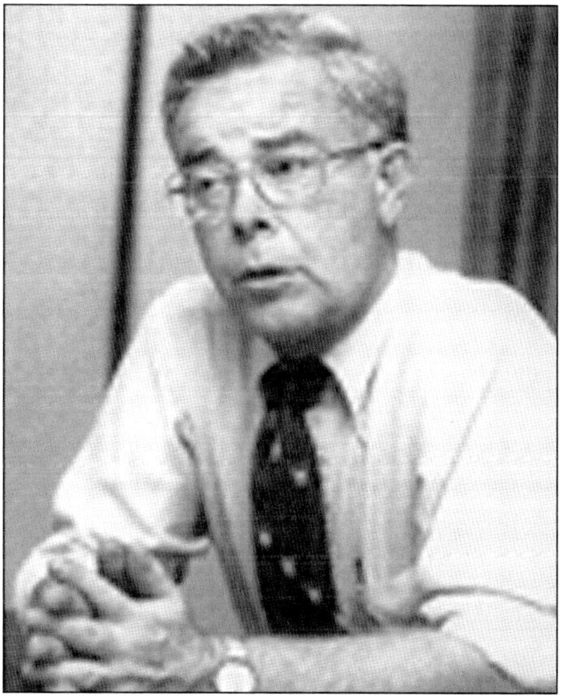

Robert J. Galliher (on left), son-in-law of Arthur E. Boyce, successfully managed both the A.E. Boyce Company and the Morrison-Galliher insurance agency during the 1950s and 1960s. David A. Galliher (on right), a grandson of A.E. Boyce, oversaw the expansion of the A.E. Boyce Company from the mid-1950s through the 1980s. (Boyce Forms Systems.)

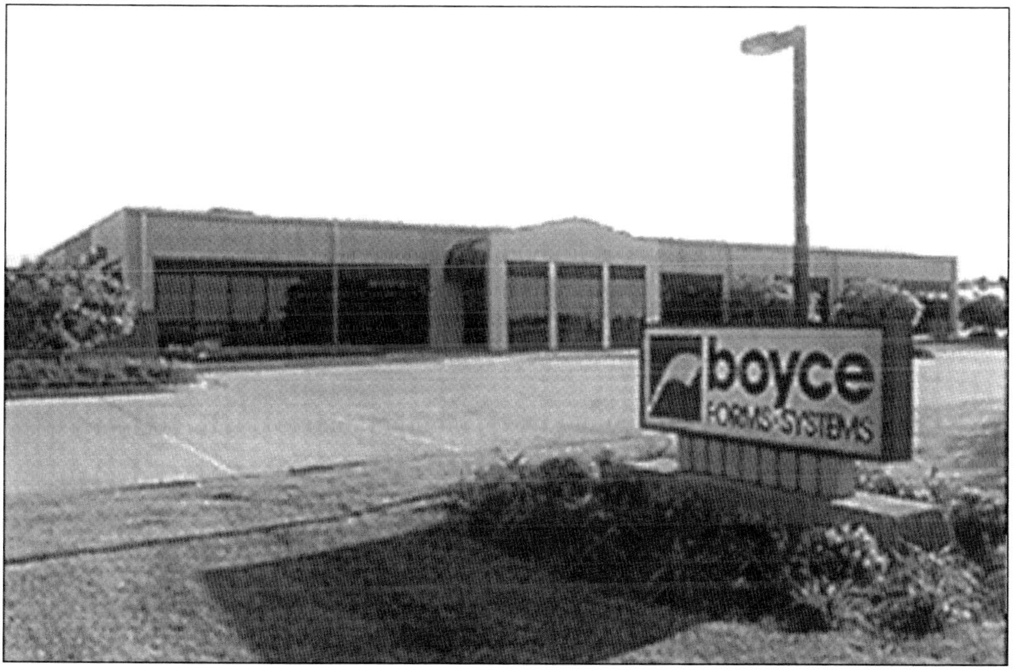

The Boyce enterprise was one of the first in Muncie to be located at the new Air Park industrial center.

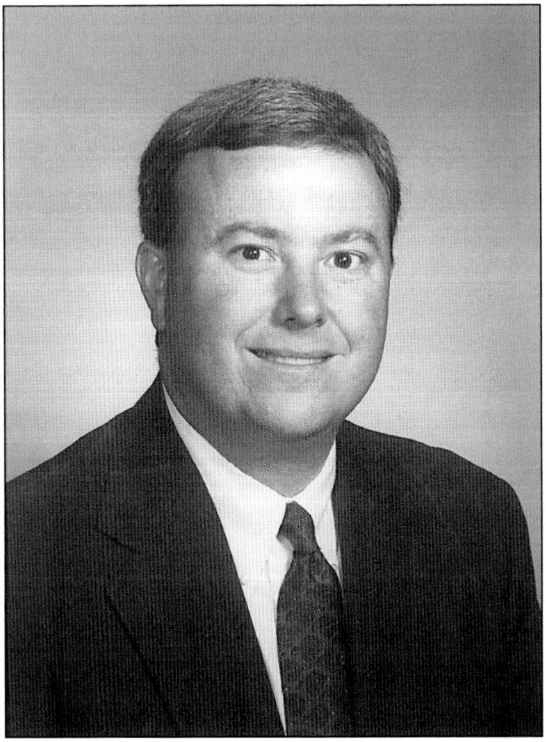

Michael B. Galliher, son of David A. Galliher, represented the family's fourth consecutive generation of management. Under his leadership, the Boyce Company expanded its position in the continuous forms market and also entered the software field for the use of forms required by the Indiana State Board of Accounts. (Boyce Forms Systems.)

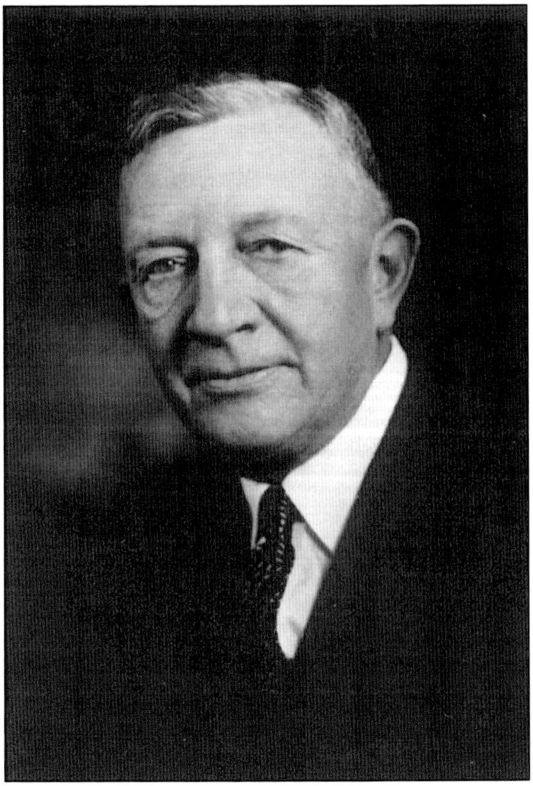

Harry R. (H.R.) Maxon, along with his two brothers John H. Maxon and John J. (Jack) Maxon, formed the Maxon Premix Burner Company in 1916. The company specialized in the manufacture of burners and valves for the combustion products industry. (Maxon Corporation.)

Harry R. (Red) Maxon Jr., son of H.R. Maxon, was a dynamic industrialist who guided Maxon Corporation to industry leadership between 1930 and 1970, and moved the company into the international market. (Maxon Corporation.)

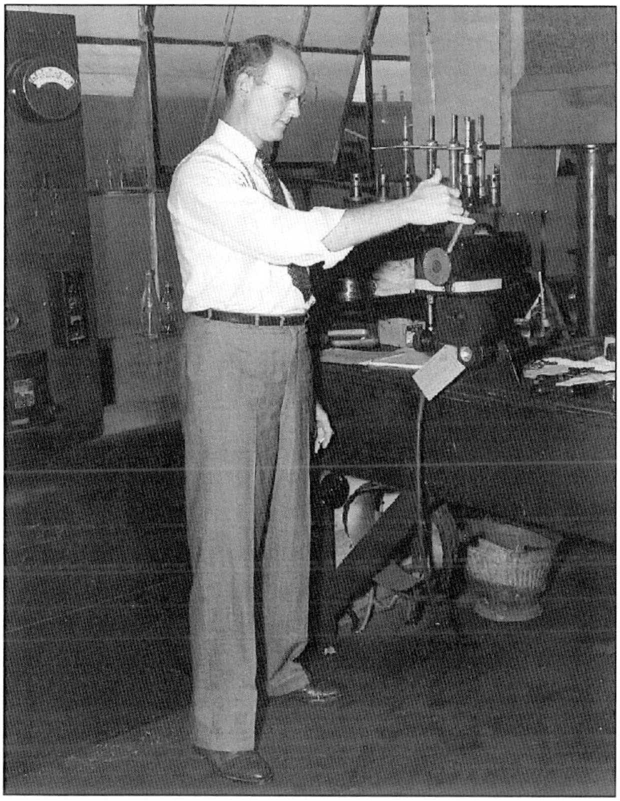

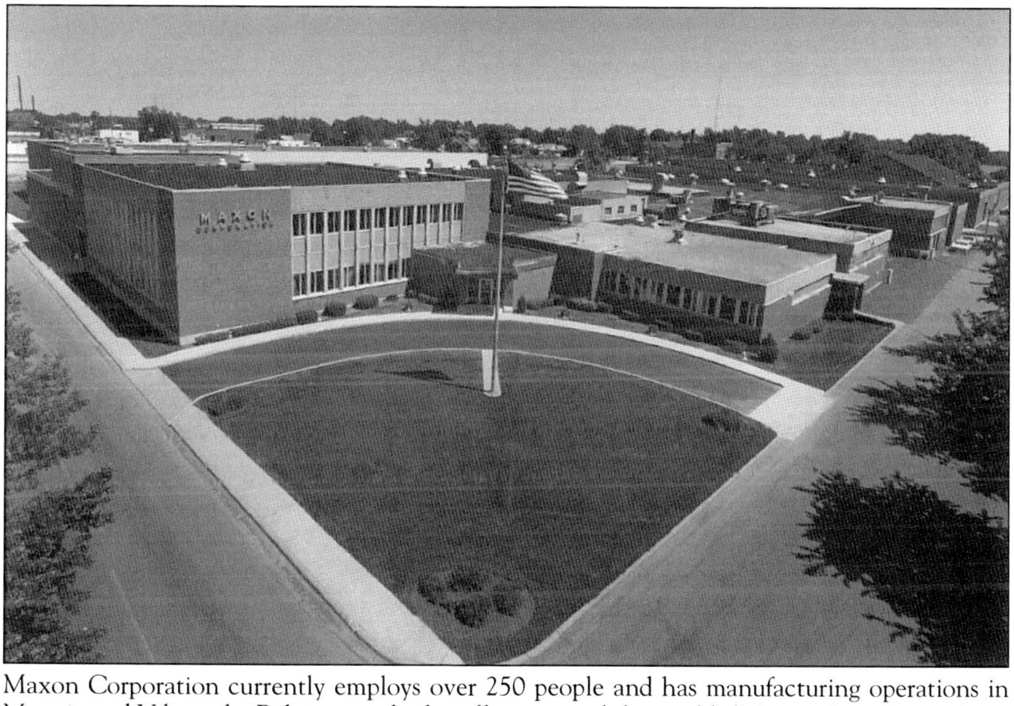

Maxon Corporation currently employs over 250 people and has manufacturing operations in Muncie and Vilvoorde, Belgium, and sales offices around the world. (Maxon Corporation.)

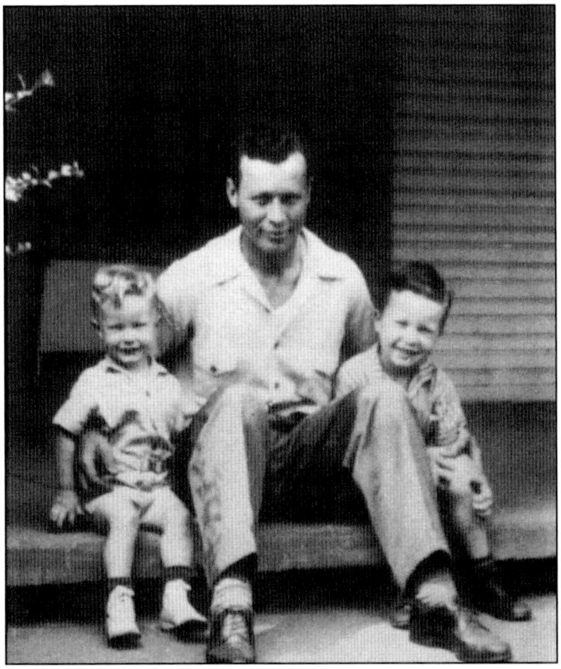

Marsh Supermarkets, Incorporated, one of Indiana's largest corporations, was established in Muncie in 1933 by Ermal Marsh, a recent graduate of Ball State Teachers College. Beginning in Muncie with a single grocery store, Marsh dreamed of establishing a statewide chain of groceries. He is shown in this early photo with his two sons, Alan (left) and Don (right). Both sons succeeded their father in the management of the Marsh enterprise. (Marsh Supermarkets, Incorporated.)

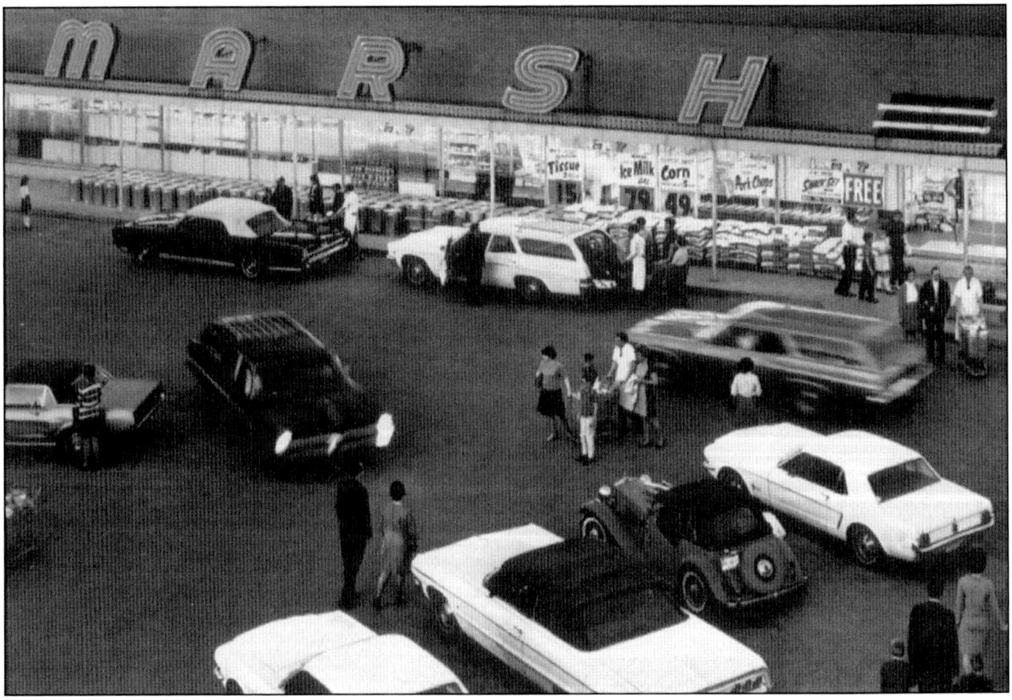

In 1947, Marsh built its first grocery with the superstore concept in Muncie. By the end of the 1950s, Marsh had perfected the supermarket concept and the concept of self-service. It had also added a modern warehouse and distribution facility in nearby Yorktown, Indiana. The corporation now operates almost 30 stores in central Indiana and western Ohio. (Marsh Supermarkets, Incorporated.)

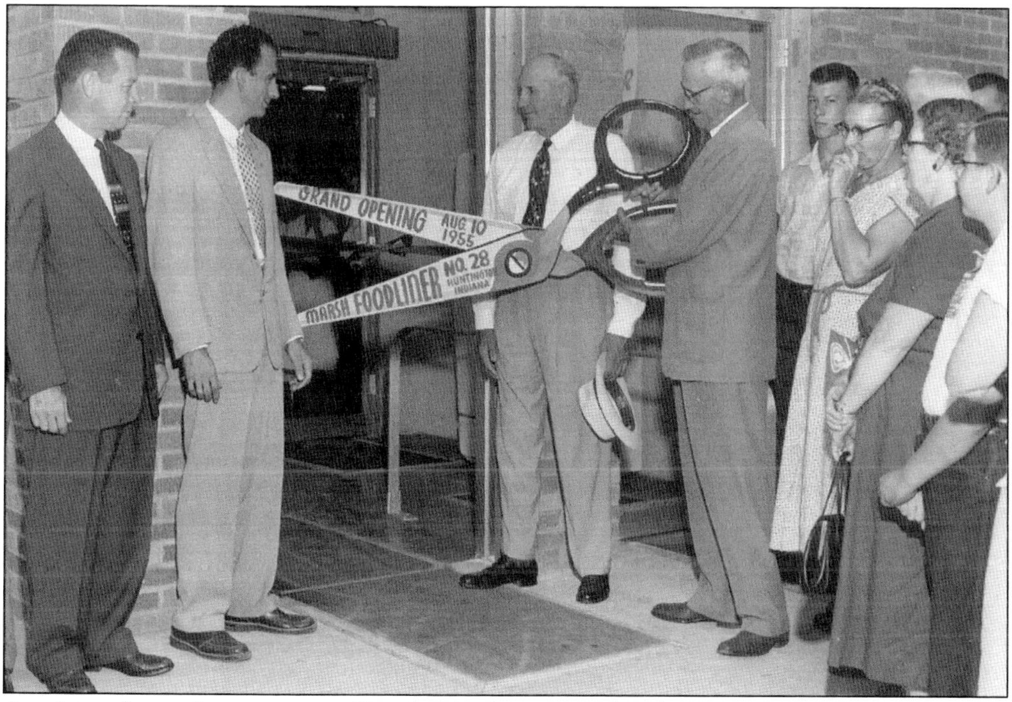

As this photo demonstrates, Ermal Marsh was a hands-on executive. He is shown here attending the opening of a Marsh store in Huntington, Indiana, in 1957. (Marsh Supermarkets, Incorporated.)

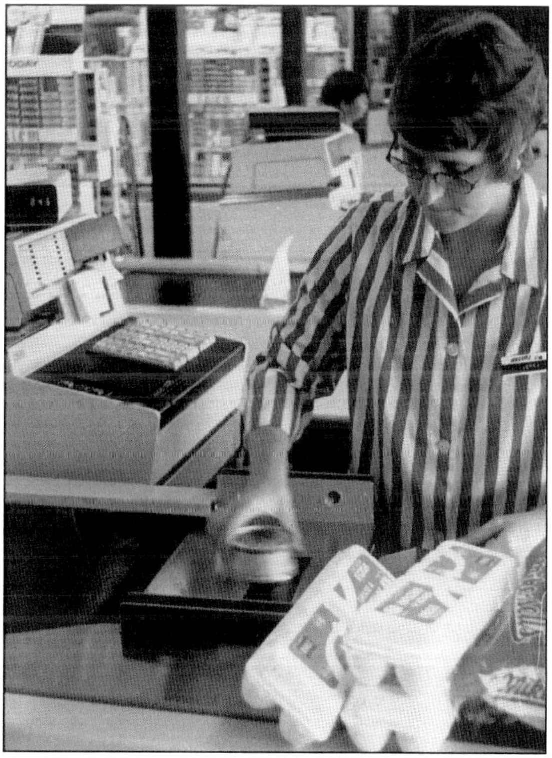

The Marsh organization was a pioneer in the introduction of many improvements in the food distribution industry. Among these innovations was the use of optical scanning technology by its cashiers in 1974. In 1991, Marsh Supermarkets, Incorporated moved its headquarters from Yorktown to Fishers, Indiana. (Marsh Supermarkets, Incorporated.)

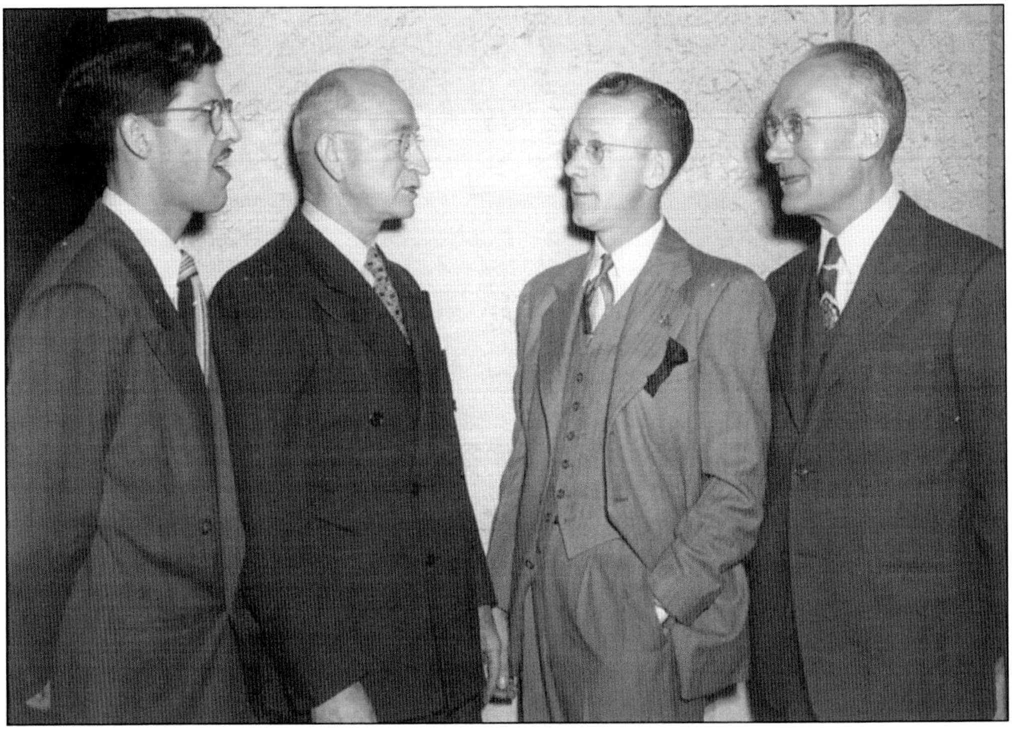

A.L. Ross and Sons was established in the 1920s as a corner grocery and general store. During its first quarter-century, the business expanded its number of stores in Muncie and became a fixture in the local grocery trade. Garland Ross (second from right) succeeded his father, A.L. Ross, in the management of the business. Others in the photo, from left to right, are: John Doolittle, a Ross employee; Myron Cromer, local agricultural extension agent; and Chester Wingate, president of Merchants National Bank. (Ross Supermarkets, Incorporated.)

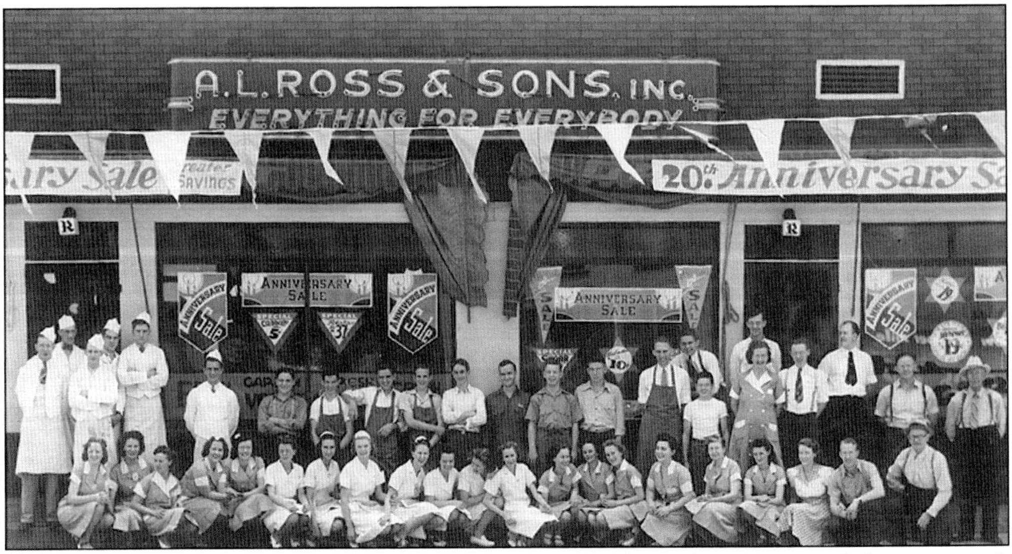

Employees of Ross Supermarkets gathered for a photograph on the occasion of the company's 20th anniversary in 1940. (Ross Supermarkets, Incorporated.)

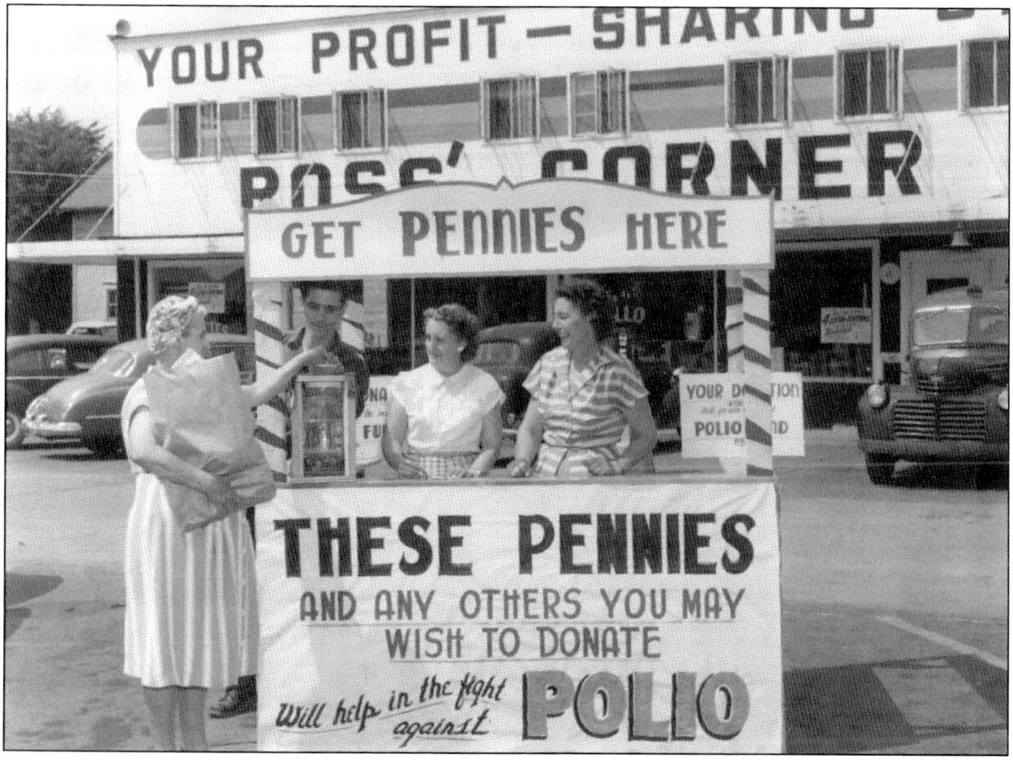

The Ross organization helped in local drives to raise money for the research and development of a vaccine for the dreaded disease of polio. In the late 1940s, Muncie experienced a serious polio epidemic. (Ross Supermarkets, Incorporated.)

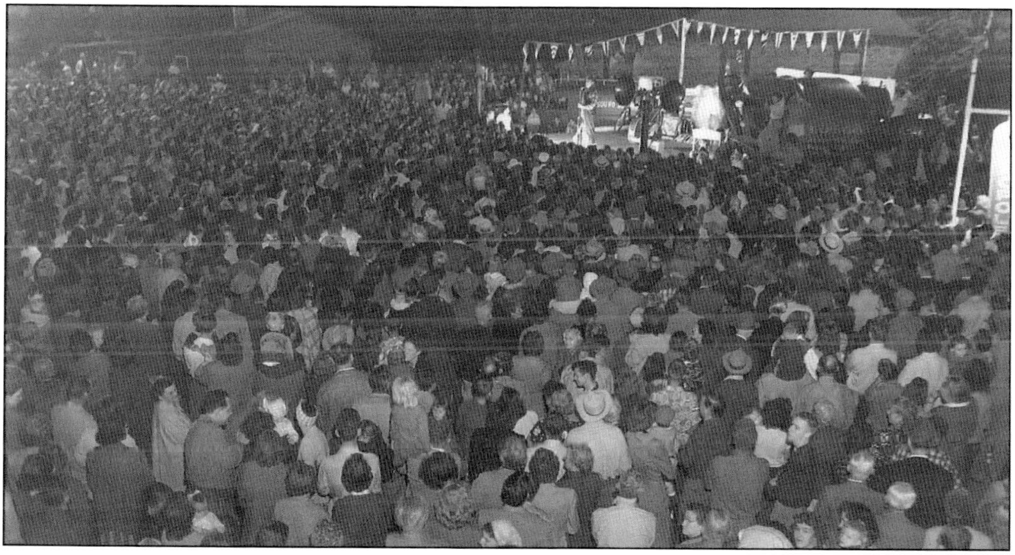

The Ross headquarters at Memorial Drive and Hoyt Avenue in Muncie became known as "Ross Corner." The company sponsored frequent events, combined with promotions, at Ross Corner, which were attended by thousands of Munsonians from the local neighborhoods. Seen in this photo is an open-air concert with music provided by a local band. (Ross Supermarkets, Incorporated.)

A Labor Community

In *Middletown*, the Lynds gave little attention to the importance of organized labor in Muncie during the 1920s. By the 1930s, however, organized labor had become increasingly prominent as workers sought the protection of unionization to deal with the economic uncertainties created by the Depression. By the early 1930s, the major industries of Muncie, auto parts manufacturing and glass production, had become targets of union efforts for organization. In *Middletown in Transition* (p. 32–33), the Lynds wrote about the growth of labor sentiment in the community and how union leaders were becoming part of the decision-making process in the economic life of Muncie.

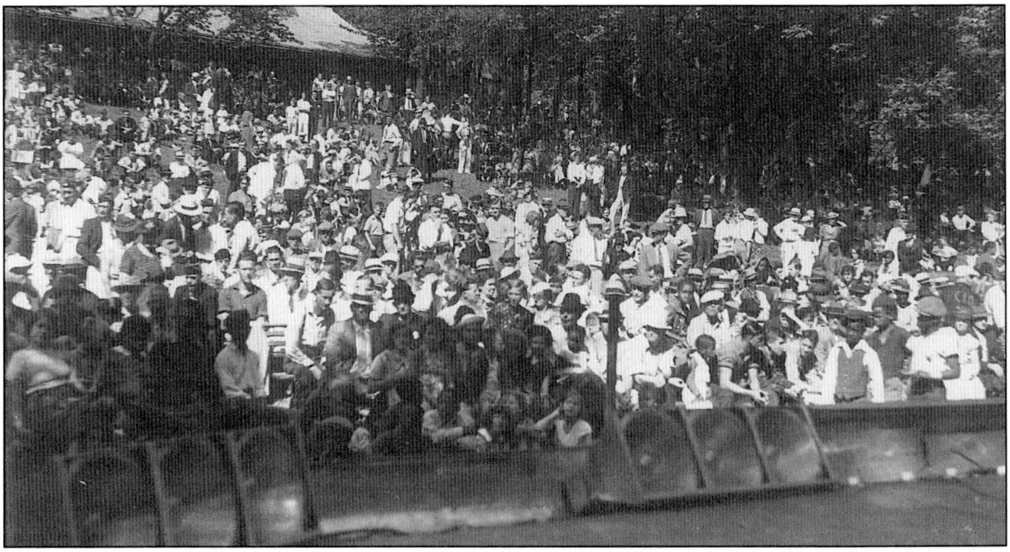

As an industrial community, Muncie experienced a rise in unionization throughout much of the 20th century. This photo, taken by photographer Carl Duffey, shows a rally for Local 459, United Auto Workers (UAW) at McCulloch Park in Muncie. Judging from the number of children in the photo, the rally was obviously a family event. (BSUA-SG.)

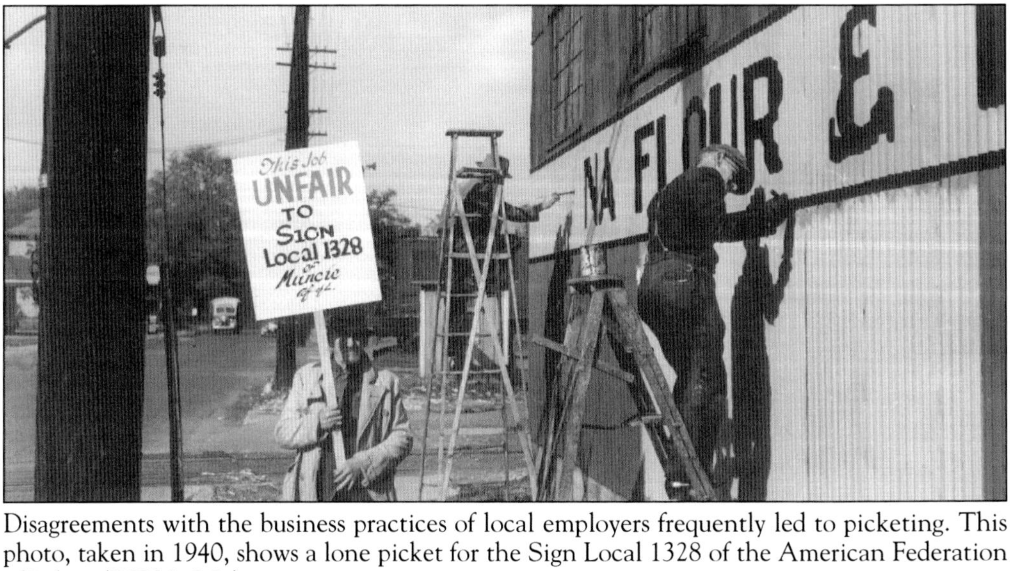

Disagreements with the business practices of local employers frequently led to picketing. This photo, taken in 1940, shows a lone picket for the Sign Local 1328 of the American Federation of Labor. (BSUA-SG.)

Frank J. Nelson came to Muncie from West Virginia in the 1930s. He was one of the first African Americans in Muncie to become a leader in local organized labor. Nelson was employed at the Muncie Malleable Foundry Company and belonged to local 532 of the UAW. (Hurley C. Goodall.)

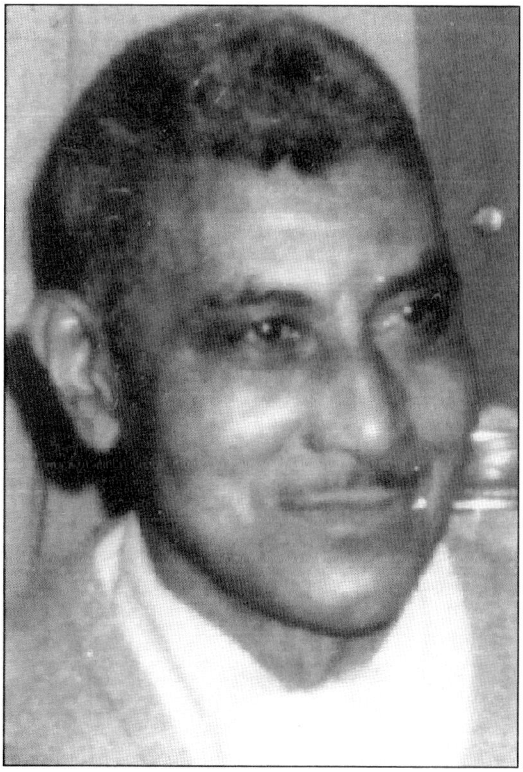

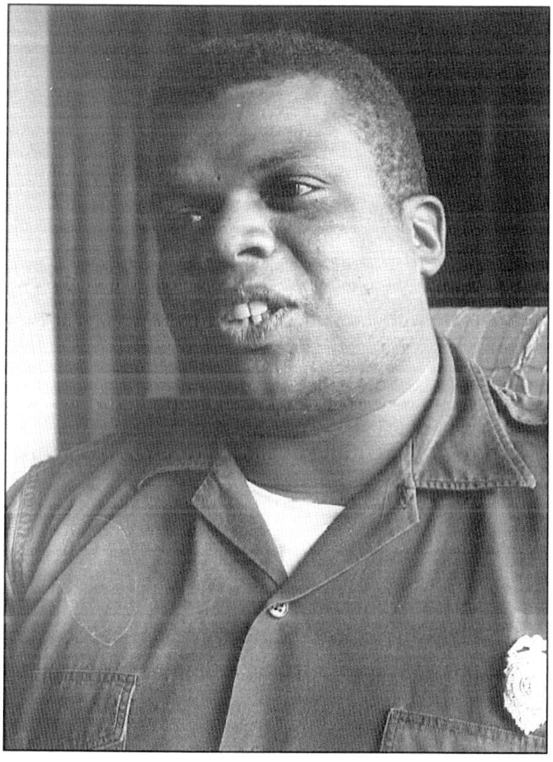

Hurley C. Goodall became an active labor leader in Muncie following his return from service in the United States Army after World War II. He became a leader in the UAW and then was one of the first African Americans in Muncie to be appointed to the fire department. He became an active leader in the Fire Fighters Union and later was the first African American from Muncie to win election to the local board of education. In 1978, he was elected to the Indiana House of Representatives where he served successive terms until his retirement in 1992. (Hurley C. Goodall.)

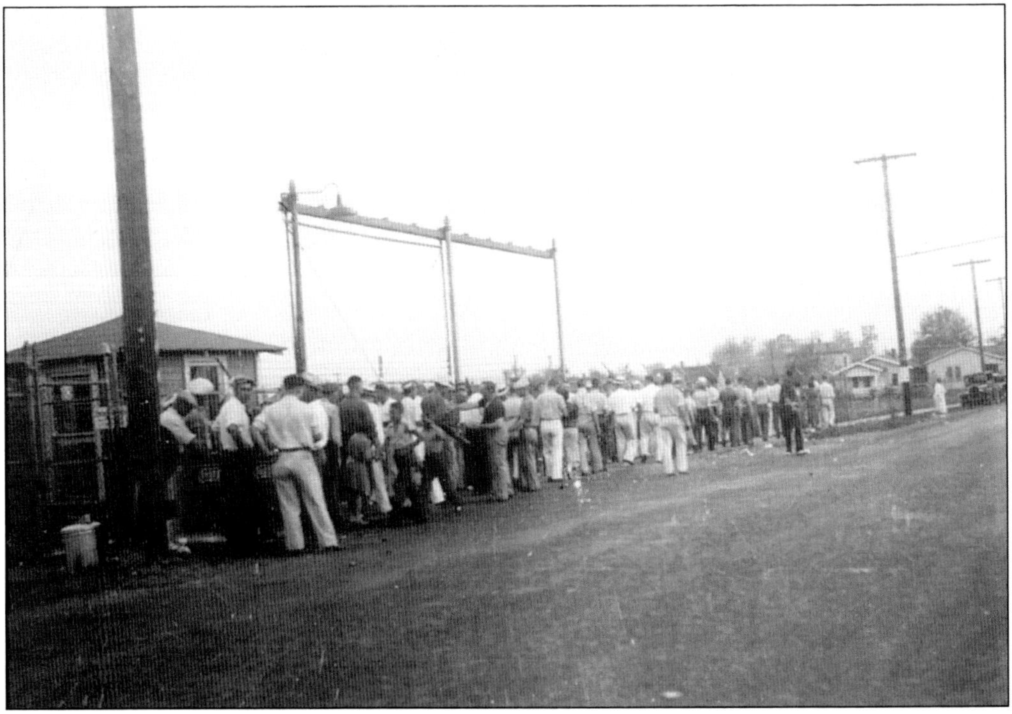

This photo shows a picket line of striking workers at Muncie's Acme-Lee Company in 1937. (BSUA-SG.)

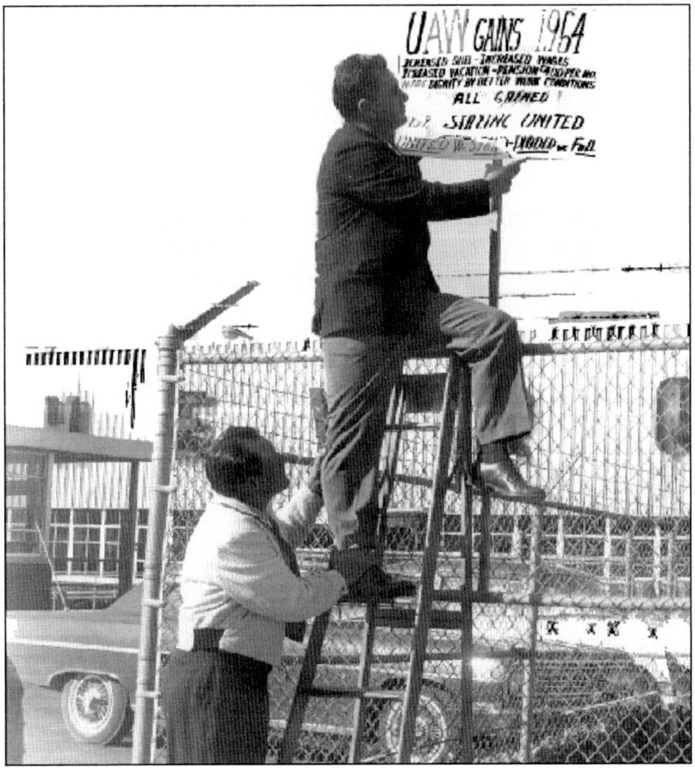

UAW officials hung a poster outside the plant gates of Chevrolet-Muncie in 1964 during national collective bargaining negotiations between General Motors Corporation and the UAW. (BSUA-Everett Ferrill Collection.)

Three

Making a Home, Training the Young

In both *Middletown* and *Middletown in Transition*, the Lynds gave extensive discussion to the homes, families, neighborhoods, and domestic pastimes of Muncie's population. In the 1920s and 1930s, as it is today, Muncie was primarily a community of homeowners—single family dwellings in urban neighborhoods and suburban "additions." Likewise, family concerns, particularly as they related to child rearing and the quality of the local schools, were paramount concerns in the minds of most parents. As the Lynds wrote in *Middletown in Transition* (p. 204): "Middletown cares about its children. They symbolize to the parent generation a path of release from certain of life's frustrations and a large share of this generation's hope of the future." For that reason, the daily concerns of most Munsonians revolved around home, family, and school.

Contrasting Neighborhoods

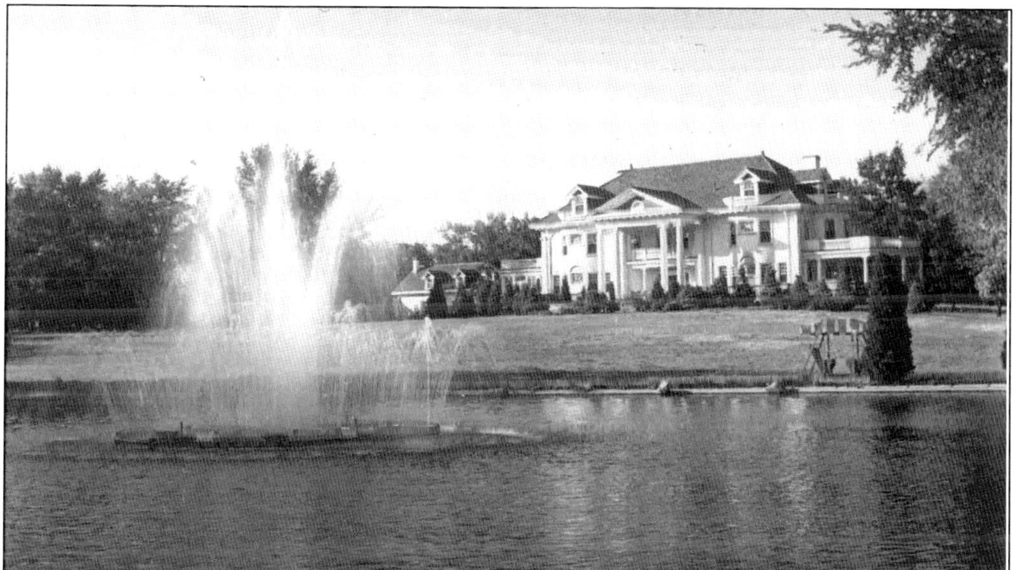

"Hazelwood," the home of Alva L. Kitselman, was a gracious mansion on University Avenue four blocks east of the Ball State campus. The property now belongs to Hazelwood Christian Church. (BSUA-SG.)

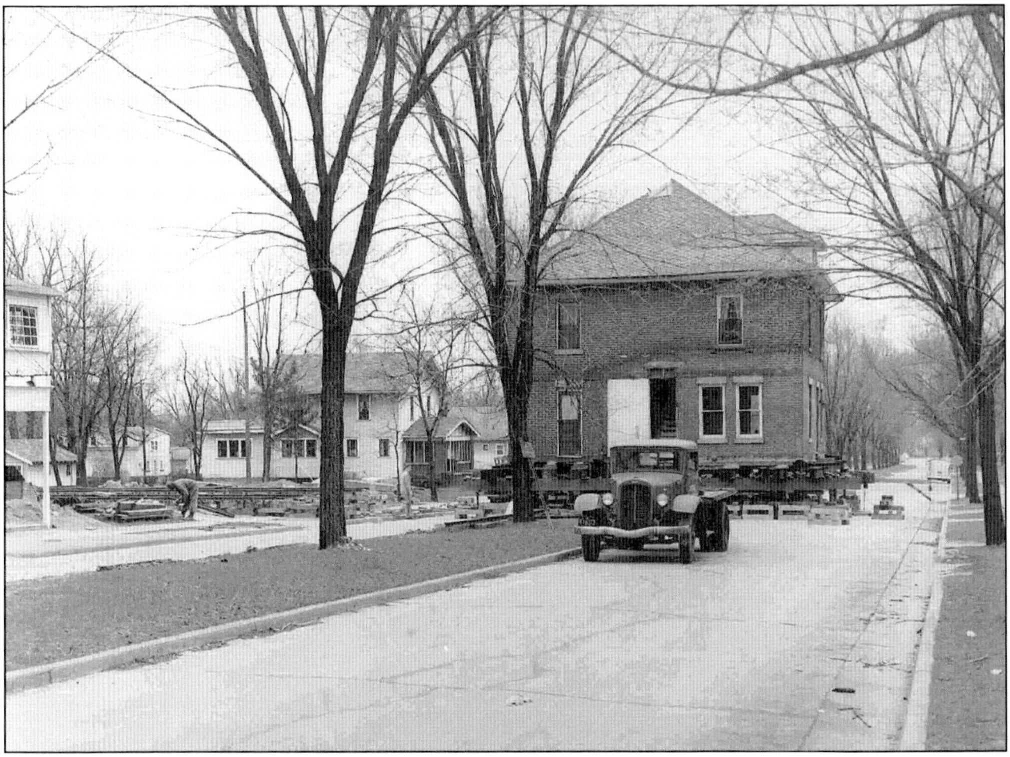

A frequent sight in the 1950s, workers move a house on College Avenue in a middle-class neighborhood adjacent to the Ball State campus. (BSUA-SG.)

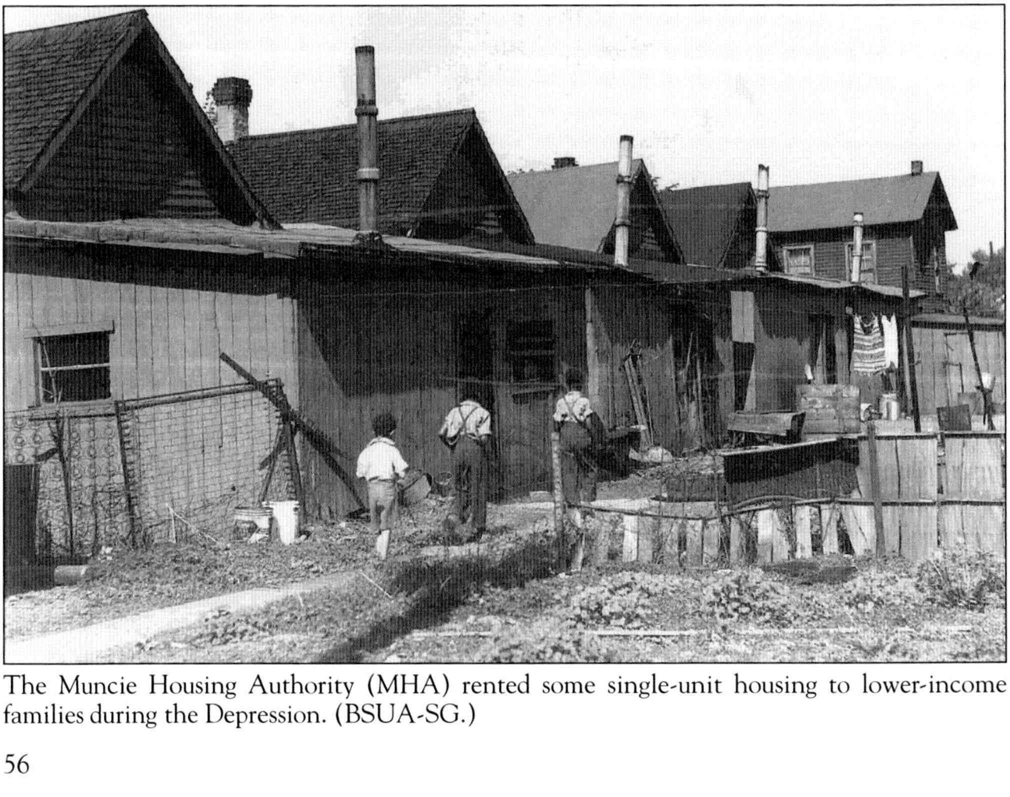

The Muncie Housing Authority (MHA) rented some single-unit housing to lower-income families during the Depression. (BSUA-SG.)

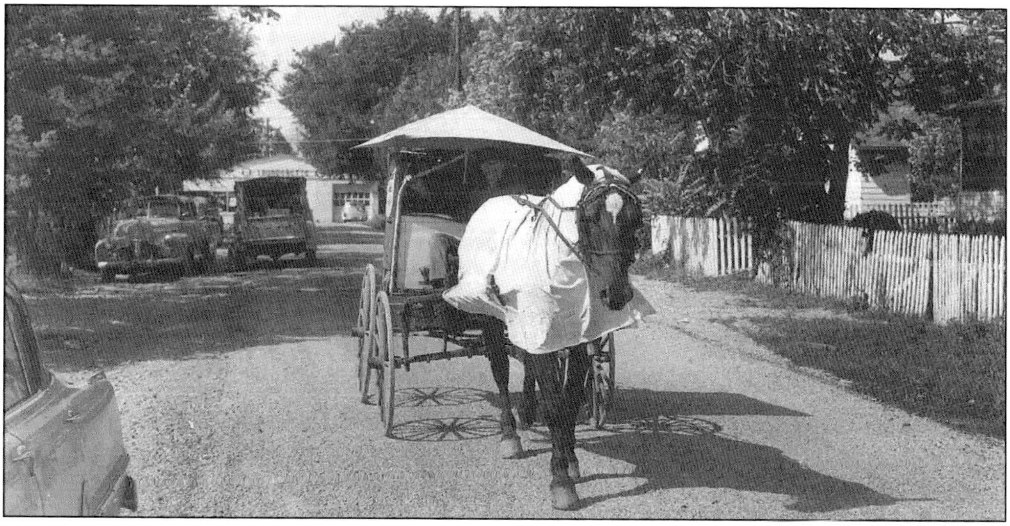

As late as the mid-1950s, ice cream salesmen in horse-drawn wagons sold their products throughout the city's neighborhoods. (BSUA-SG.)

Students, Teachers, and Schools

The data that the Lynds compiled on schools and school attendance was voluminous. Most of Muncie's children attended public schools, either in the city school corporation or outside in rural (sometimes referred to as "county") schools. Moreover, the Lynds were quick to note that education was considered a route to upward social mobility for the families of Muncie. As stated in *Middletown* (p. 187): "If education is oftentimes taken for granted by the business class, it is no exaggeration to say that it evokes a fervor of a religion, a means of salvation, among a large section of the working class."

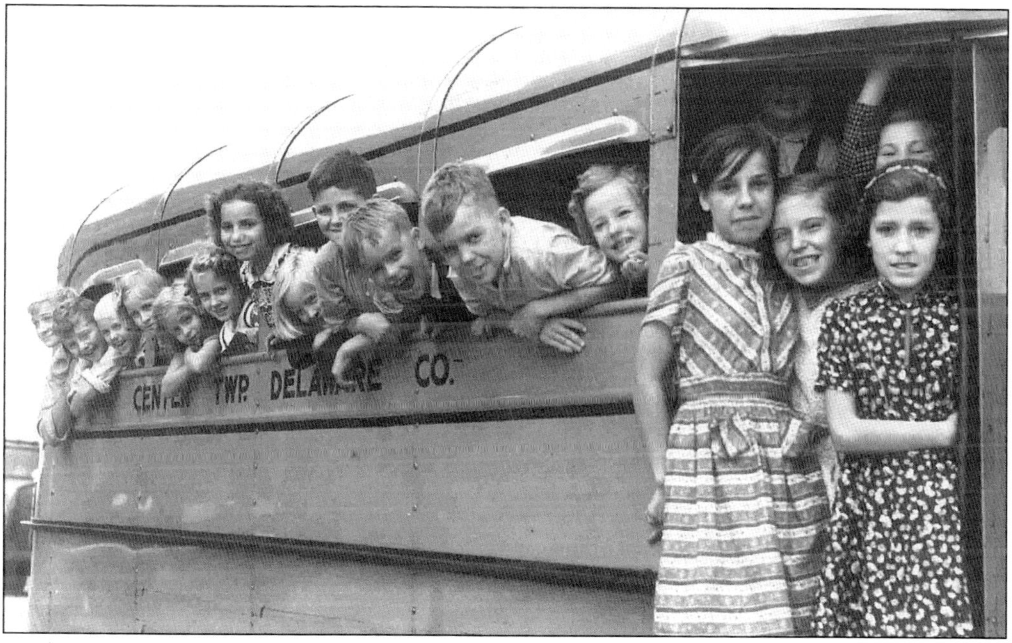

Students who attended rural schools, such as Center Township, rode the familiar yellow bus to school. (BSUA-SG.)

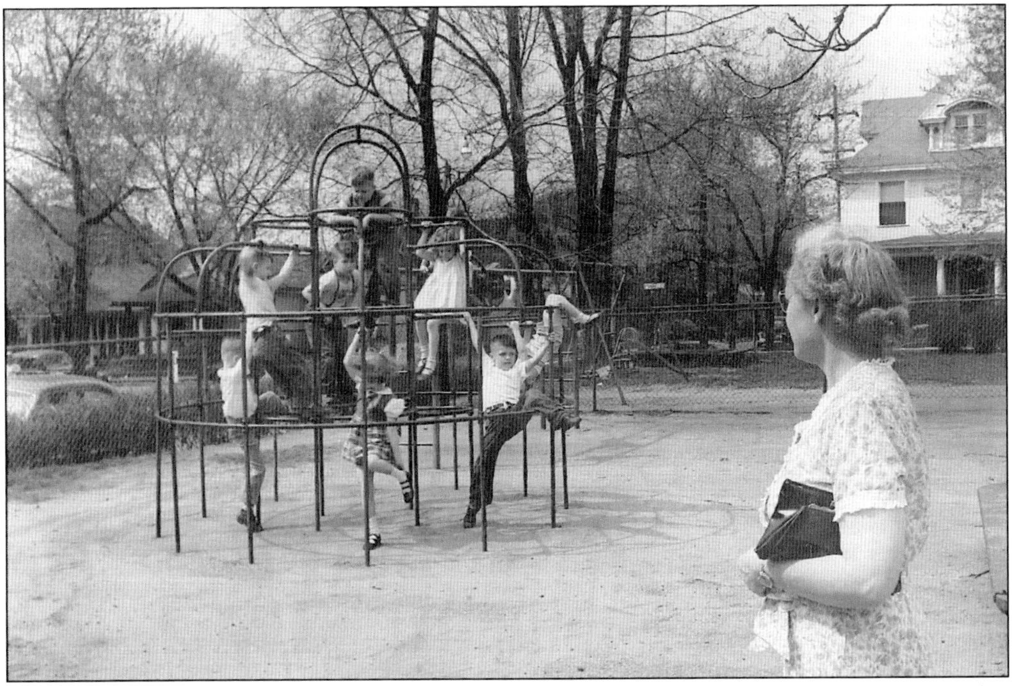

A playtime attraction for these children at a local day school was the "monkey bars." This popular piece of playground equipment belongs to a bygone era, given current concerns about child safety. (Minnetrista Cultural Center.)

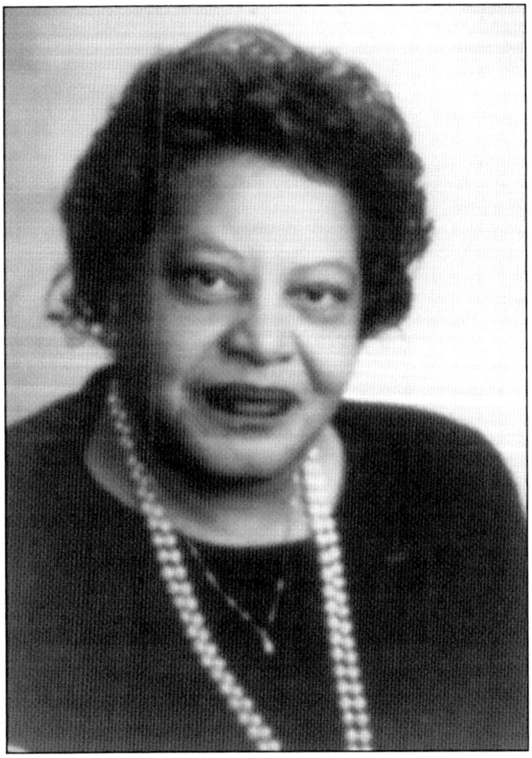

Doris Faulkner Stewart was one of the first African American women to teach in the Muncie community schools. A gifted performer and music educator, she later became the director of music for the entire school corporation. She also directed the community's annual Christmas sing at the Muncie Fieldhouse for many years. (BSUA-SG.)

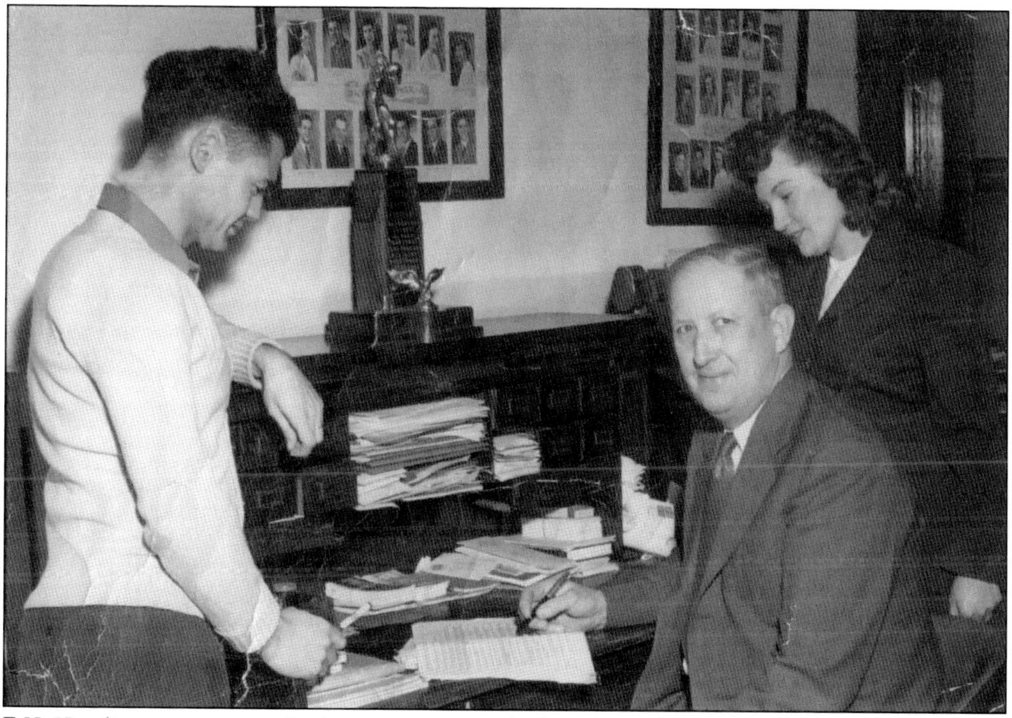

E.K. Keesling, center, was the longtime principal of Center School. In this picture he is flanked by two teachers, Lloyd Frasier and Mary Moore. (BSUA-Center School Collection.)

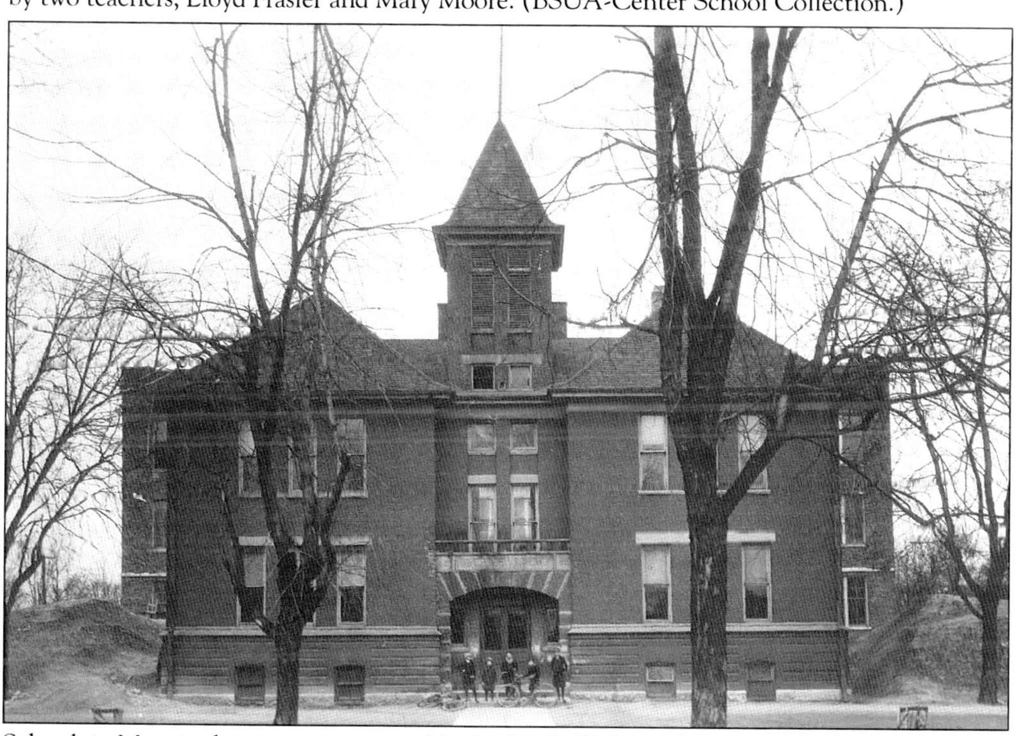

Schools in Muncie that were constructed in the first half of the 20th century had an architectural similarity. Pictured above is Riverside School. (BSUA-SG.)

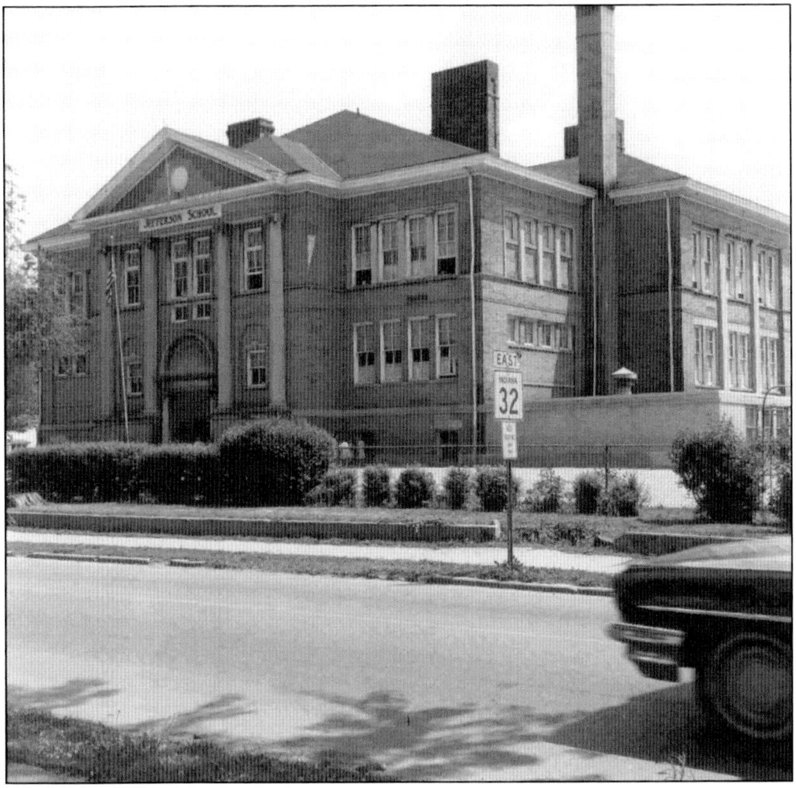

Pictured is Jefferson School in central Muncie. (BSUA-SG.)

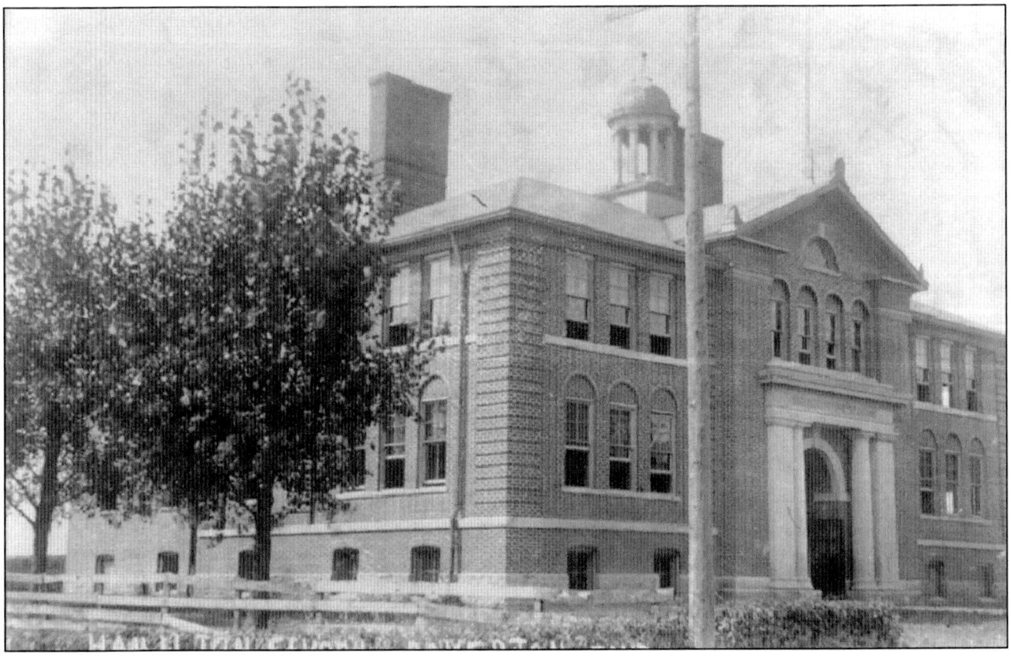

Shown here is Hamilton Township School in Royerton in the northern part of Delaware County. (BSUA.)

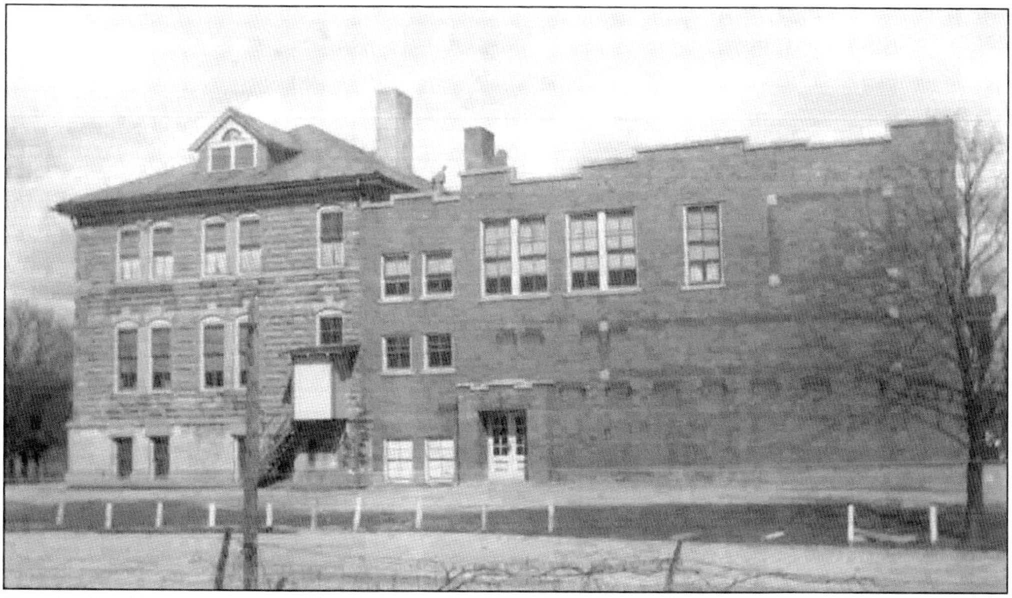

Rural schools sometimes suffered from a lack of architectural imagination when they chose to expand their buildings. One such case was the Center School, whose expansion failed the test when it came to matching up aesthetically with the design of the original school. (BSUA-Center School Collection.)

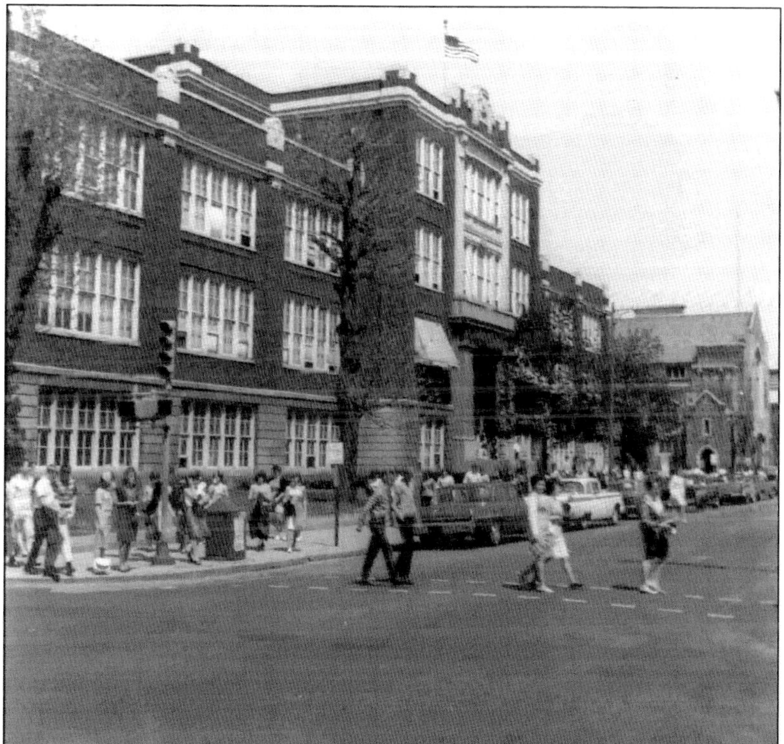

Muncie Central High School is pictured in the 1960s. (BSUA-SG.)

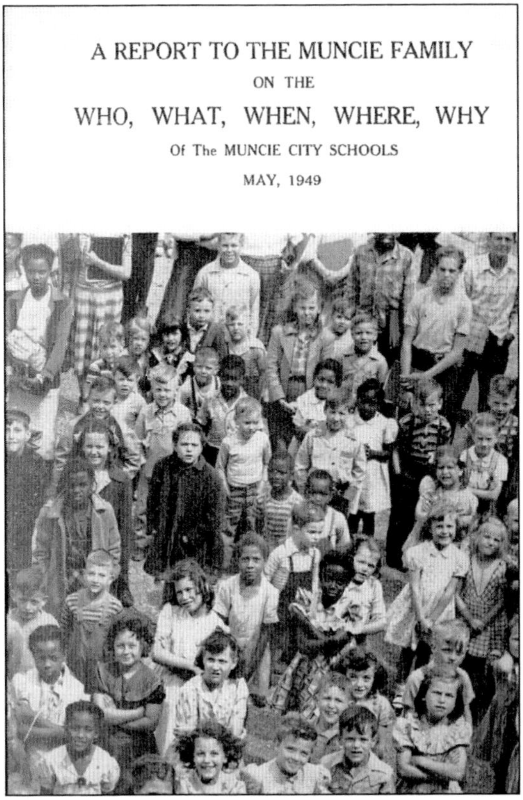
A REPORT TO THE MUNCIE FAMILY
ON THE
WHO, WHAT, WHEN, WHERE, WHY
Of The MUNCIE CITY SCHOOLS
MAY, 1949

The Muncie City Schools published an annual "Report to the Muncie Family" during the 1940s. The cover of the report shows the diversity of students being served by the local schools. (Minnetrista Cultural Center.)

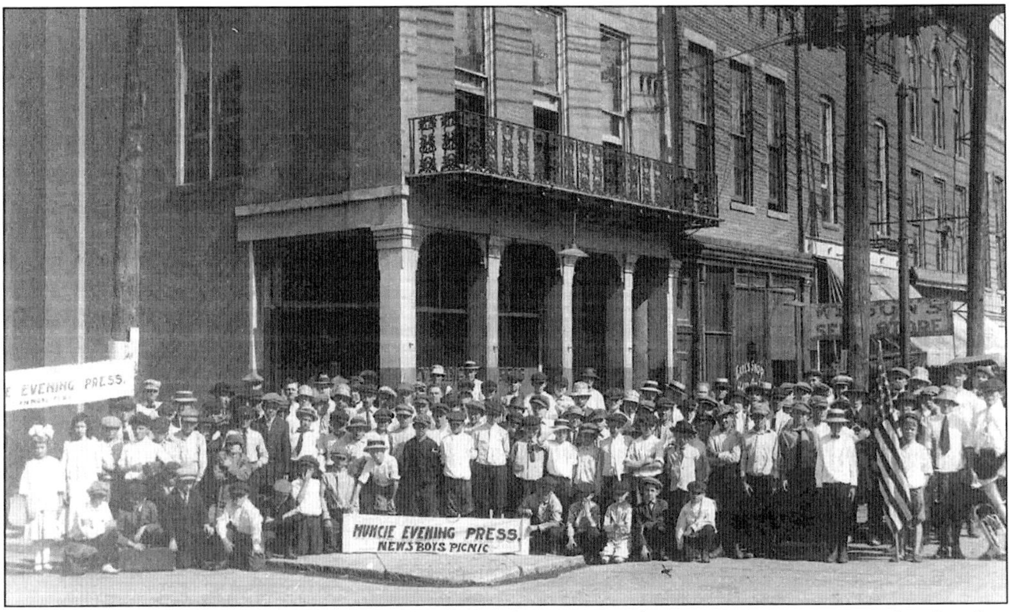

Delivering newspapers provided employment for many of Muncie's young people. In this photo, newspaper boys assemble for a photo at the *Muncie Evening Press*'s annual newsboy picnic. (BSUA-SG.)

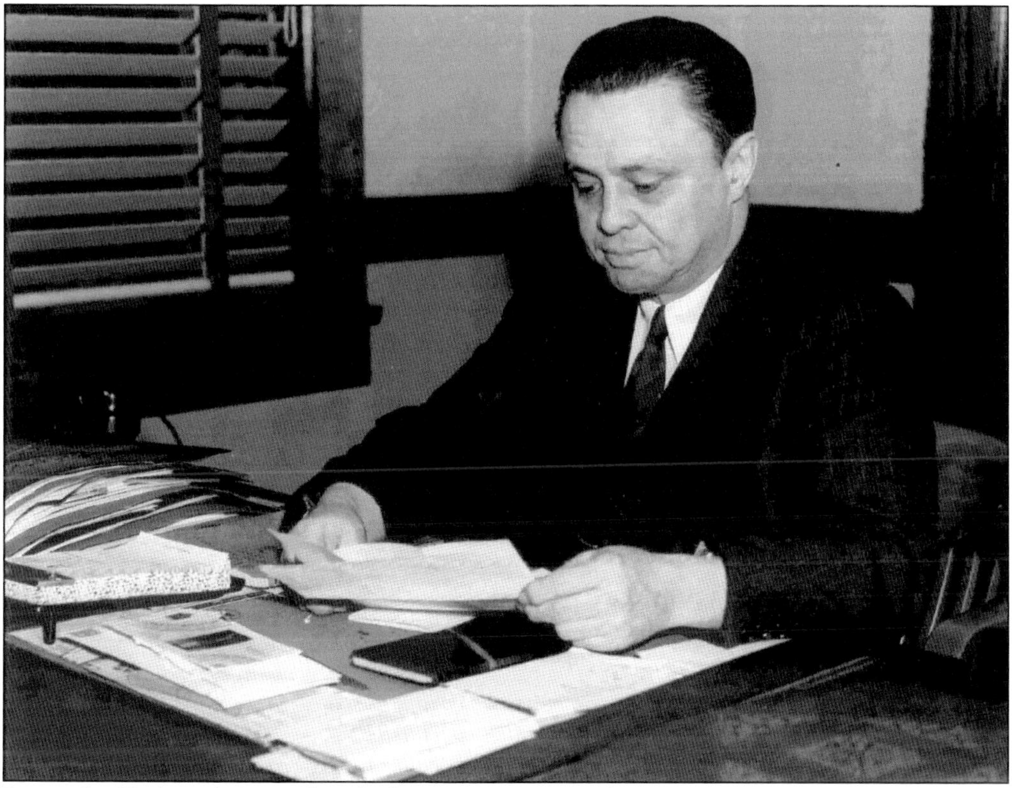

Pictured is Herbert A. Pettijohn, the longtime secretary of Muncie's YMCA. Pettijohn organized youth activities for thousands of children during his long career. (BSUA-SG.)

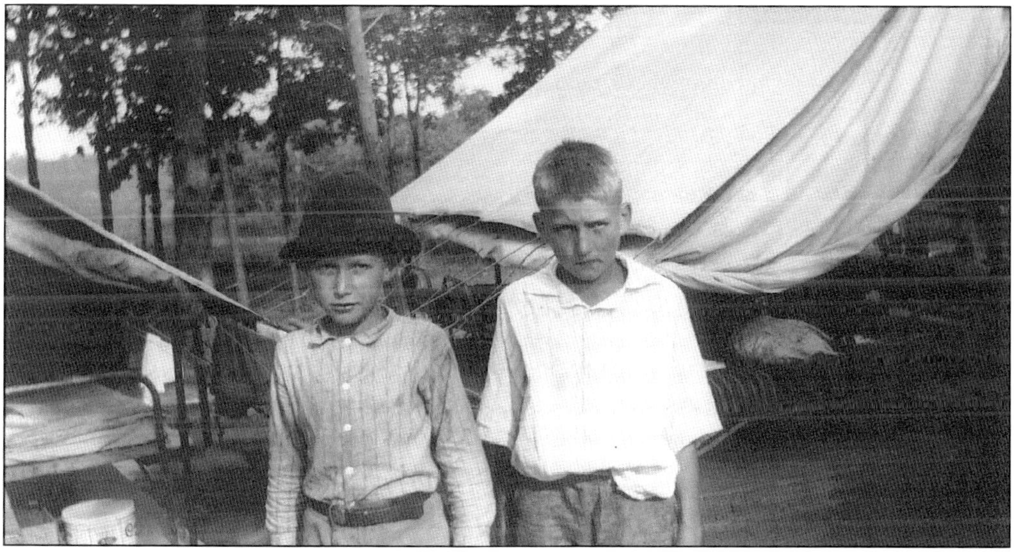

Two Muncie boys pose for a photograph in 1925 at Camp Crosley, a camp operated by the Muncie YMCA, on Lake Tippecanoe in northern Indiana. Camp Crosley was named in honor of Crosley Ball, the youngest son of Edmund and Bertha Ball, who died following complications from a tonsillectomy. (BSUA-SG.)

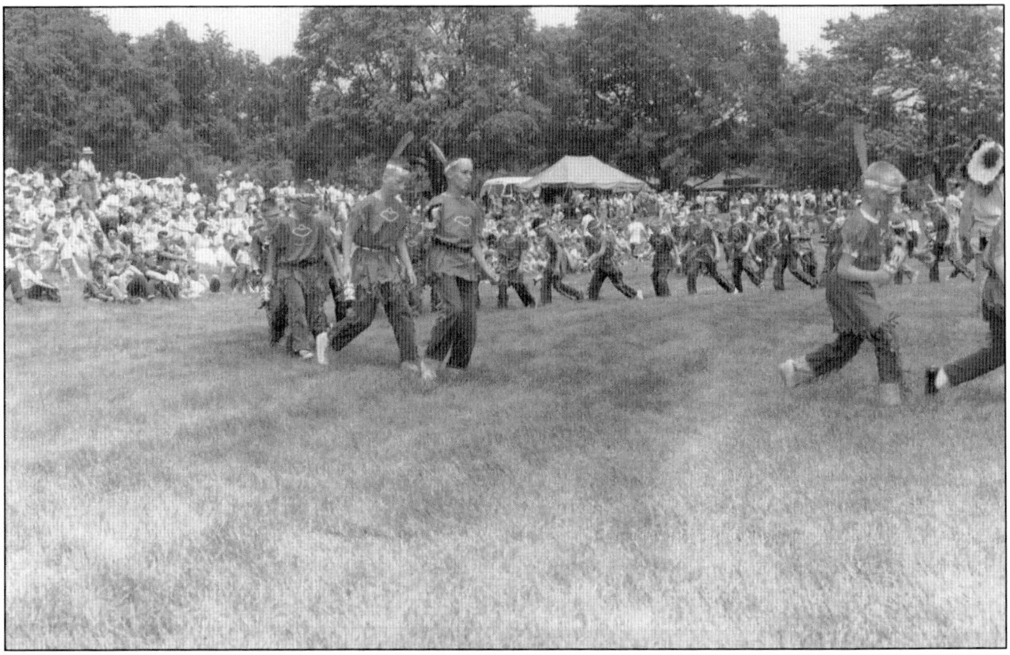

Scouting was a popular activity for both boys and girls in Muncie. In this photo, a Boy Scout troop is staging a Native American ceremony. (BSUA-SG.)

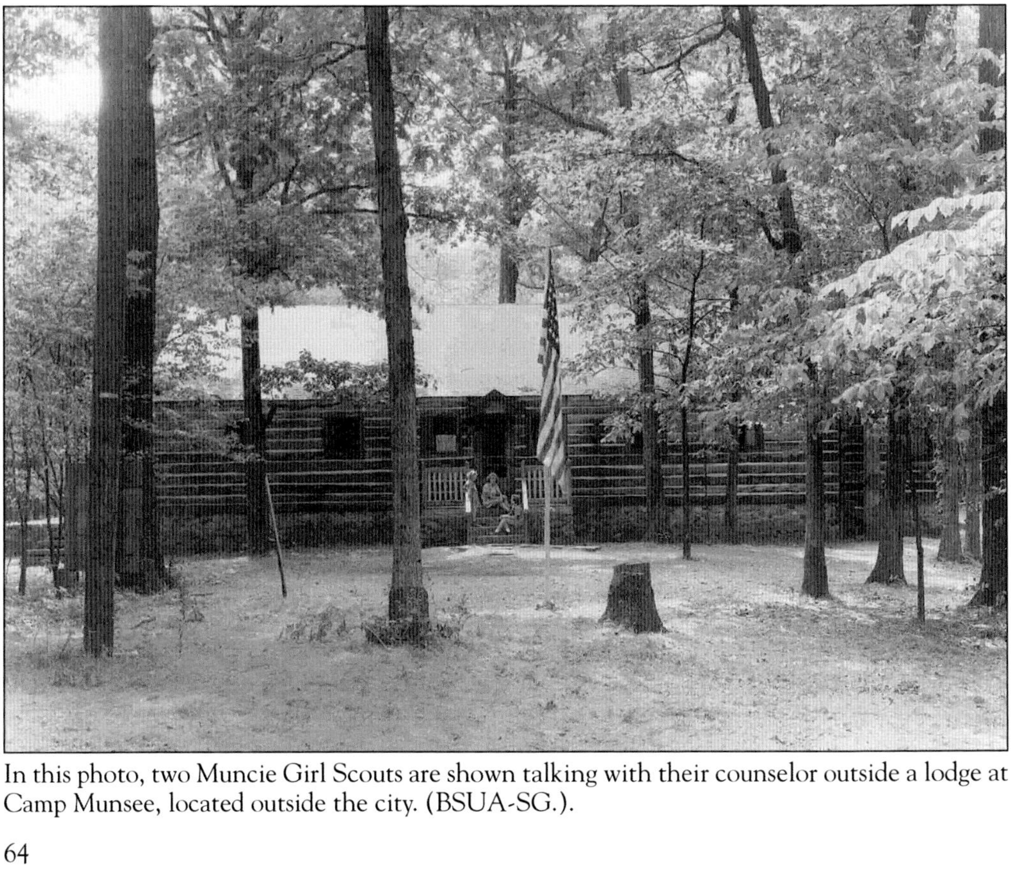

In this photo, two Muncie Girl Scouts are shown talking with their counselor outside a lodge at Camp Munsee, located outside the city. (BSUA-SG.).

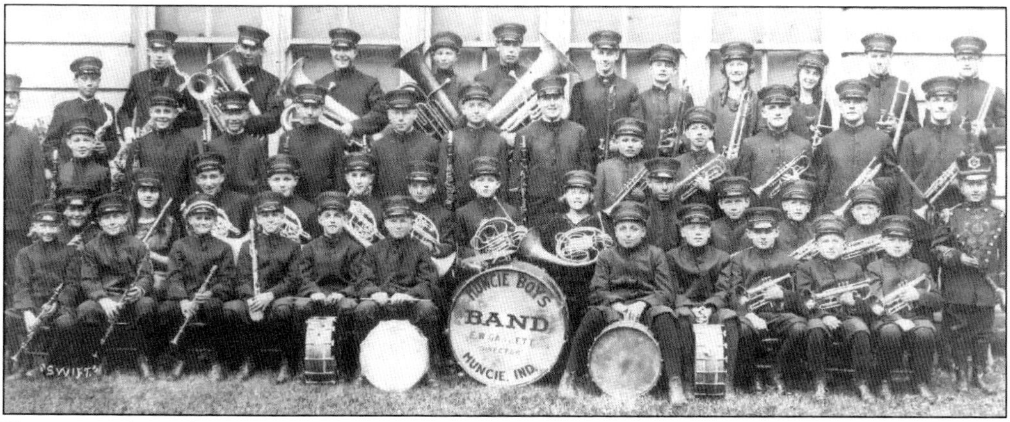

Young people with musical interests and talents were able to join E.W. Garrett's Muncie Boys Band. However, as the photo shows, not all members of the band were boys. (BSUA-SG.)

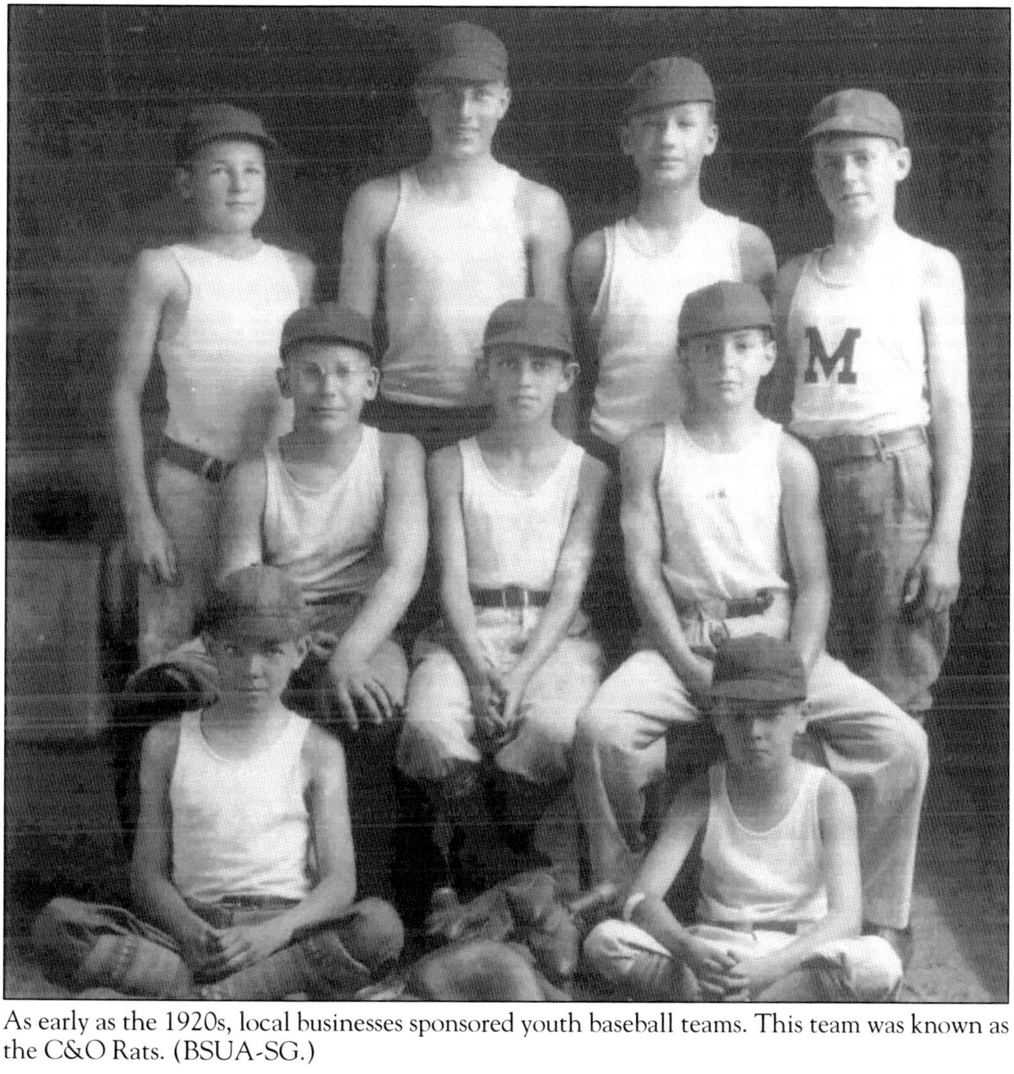

As early as the 1920s, local businesses sponsored youth baseball teams. This team was known as the C&O Rats. (BSUA-SG.)

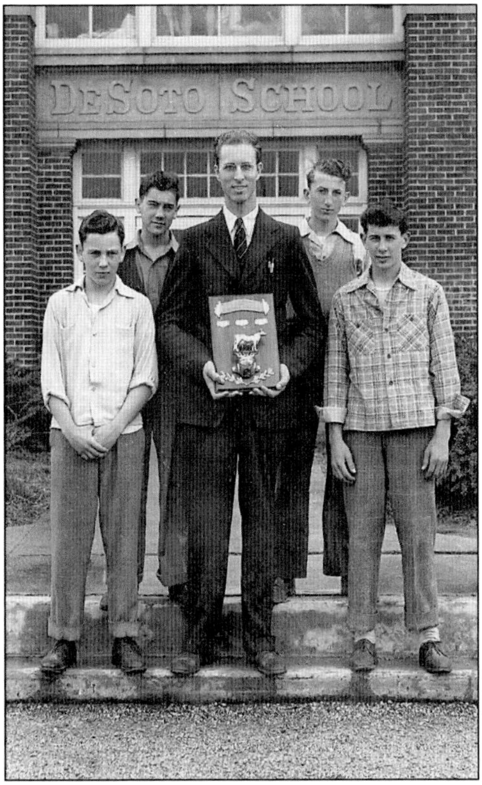

Agriculture provided numerous opportunities for involvement by local youth. This photo shows the winners of the local dairy-judging contest. The winners attended De Soto High School, a small county school northeast of the city. (Minnetrista Cultural Center.)

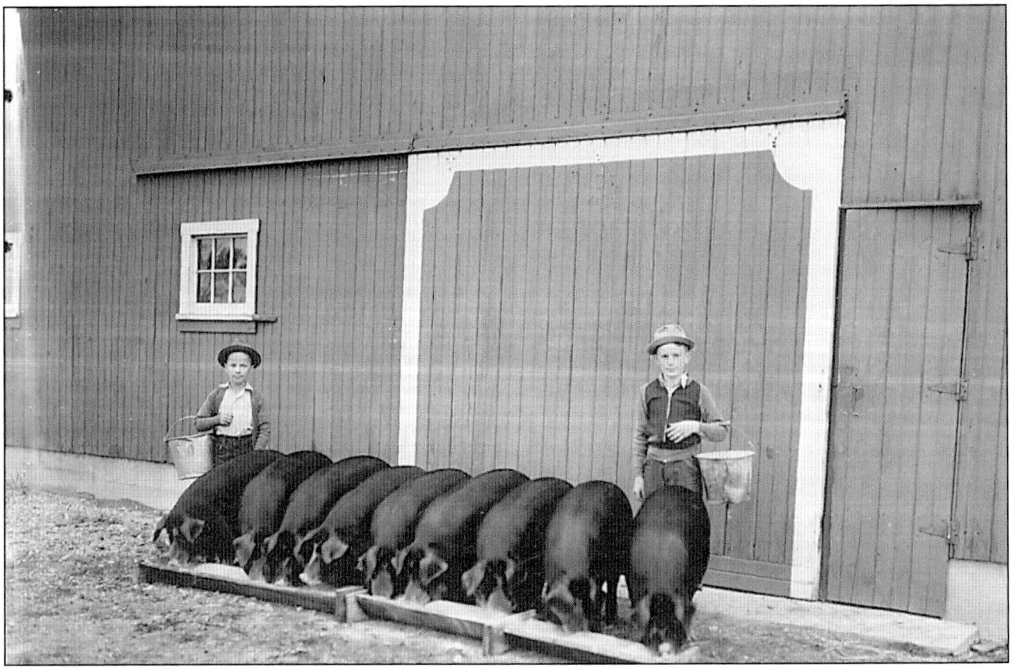

Chores on the farm were a daily ritual for many rural young people. In this photo, a young farmer tends to his herd of pigs. (Minnetrista Cultural Center.)

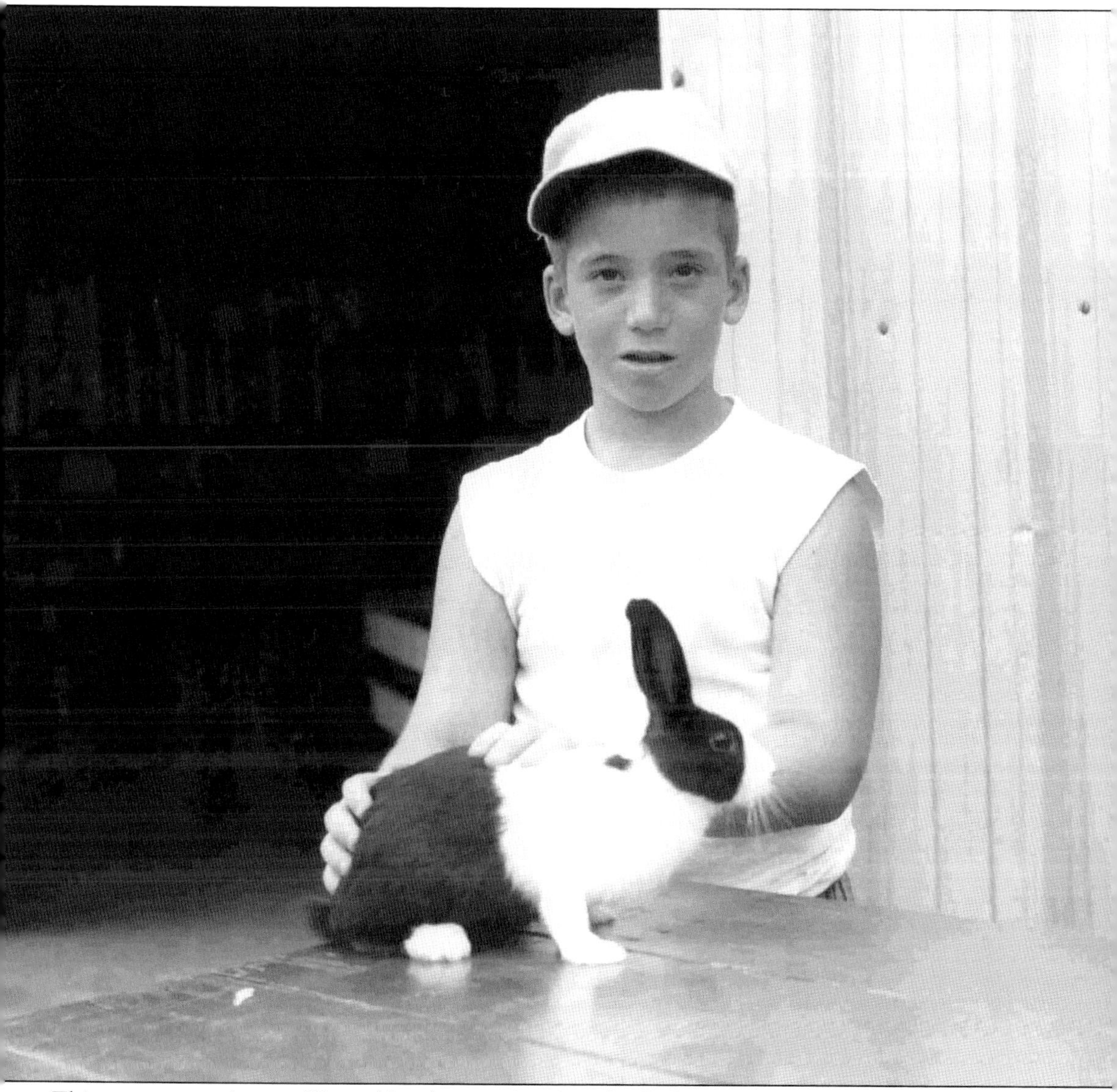

This young man shows off his rabbit during a break at the Delaware County Fair. (BSUA-SG.)

Hoosier Hysteria—Middletown Style

The sport of basketball, particularly high school basketball, was the paramount athletic interest in Muncie during the 20th century. Most of the community's attention was directed toward the Muncie Central High School Bearcats, winners of eight state championships, more than any other high school in Indiana history. Ironically, however, it was a defeat, rather than a victory which basketball connoisseurs associate with Muncie Central. In the final game of the 1954 state high school tournament, lowly Milan defeated Muncie Central, proving that "any school, no matter how small, can win a state tournament." Milan's defeat of Muncie Central was such a hallmark event that it provided the story line for the film *Hoosiers* in the 1980s.

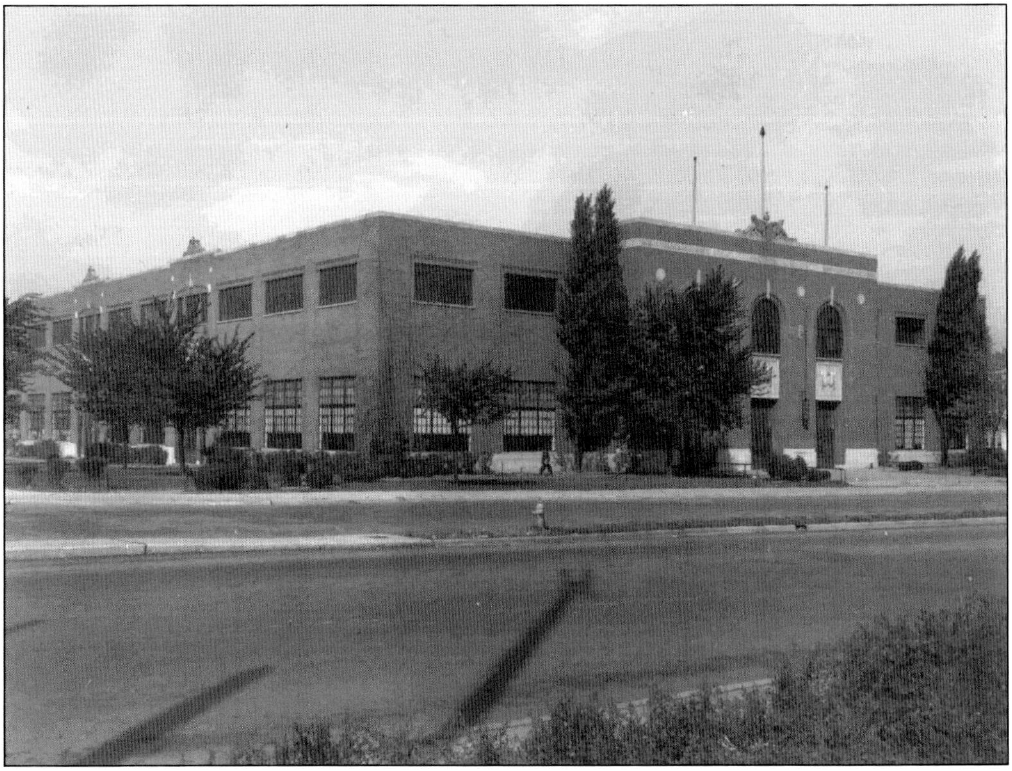

One of America's palaces for high school basketball, the North Walnut Street Fieldhouse, in Muncie, was completed in 1928. With a seating capacity of 7,500, it was the largest arena for high school basketball in the United States for nearly 40 years. (BSUA-SG.)

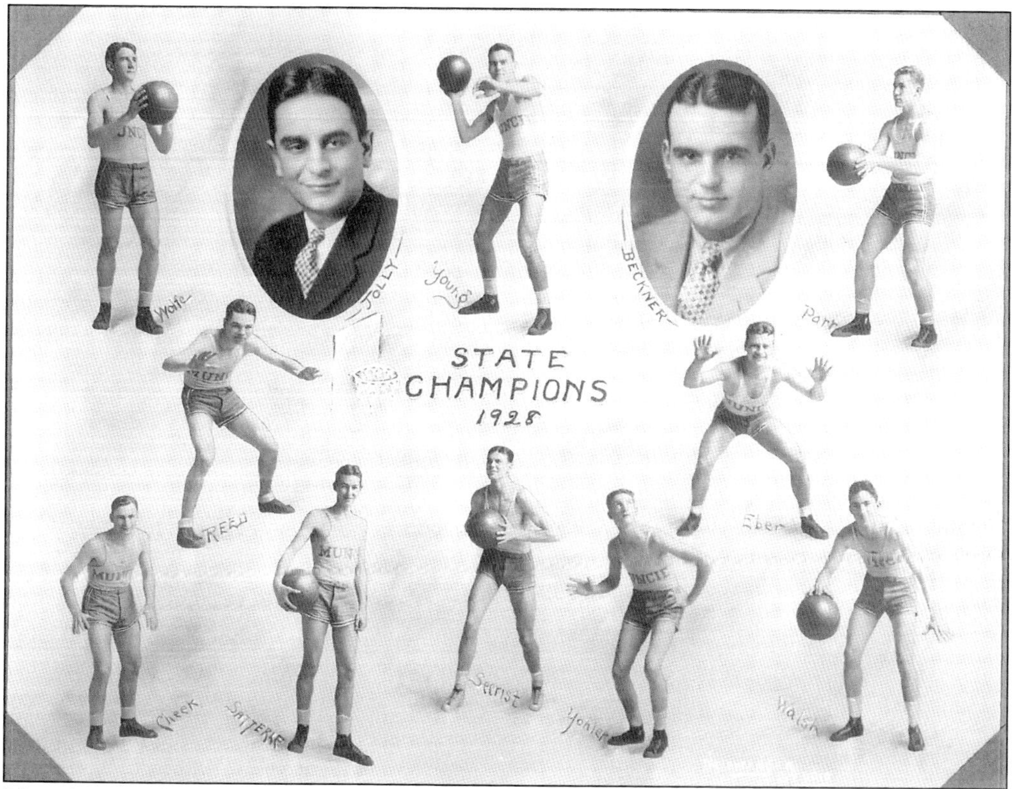

This photograph shows a composite of the players and coaches from the 1928 state championship team. Coached by Pete Jolly, the 1928 team was the first of eight state champions during the 20th century. (Minnetrista Cultural Center.)

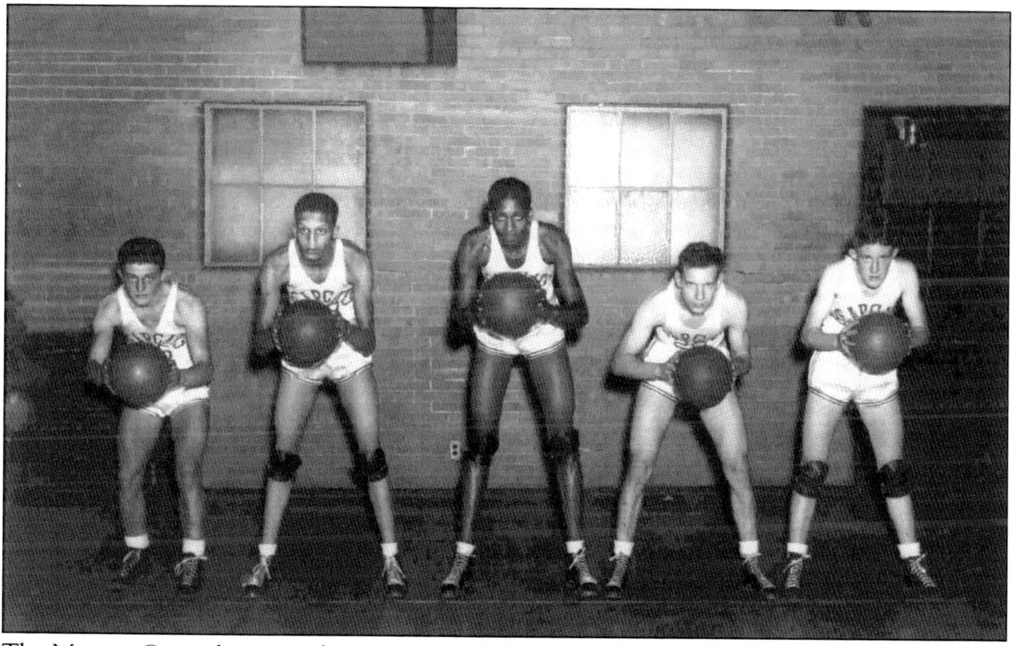

The Muncie Central starting five are pictured above, 1937–1938. (BSUA-SG.)

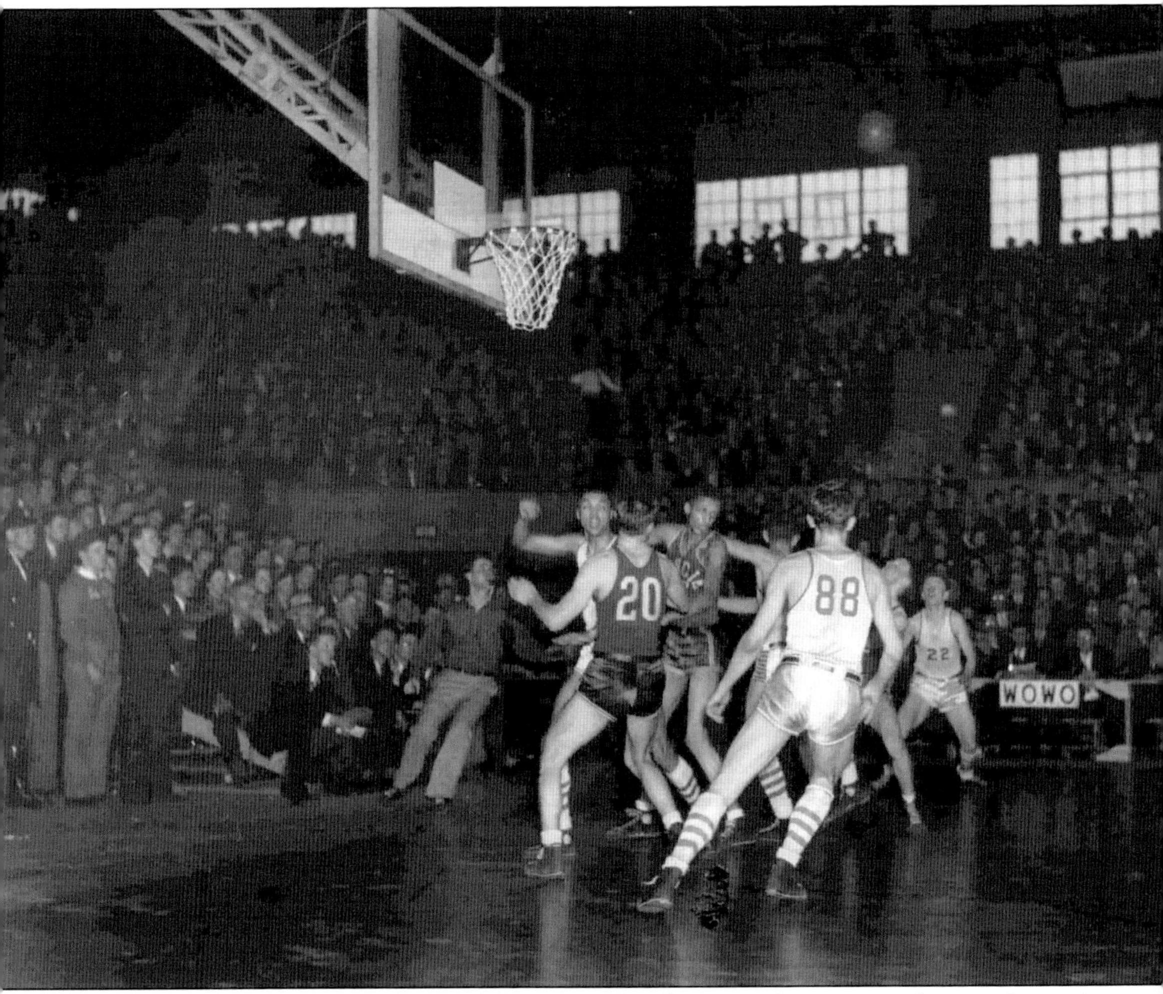

For decades, the Muncie Central Bearcats played to standing-room-only crowds at the Fieldhouse. (BSUA-SG.)

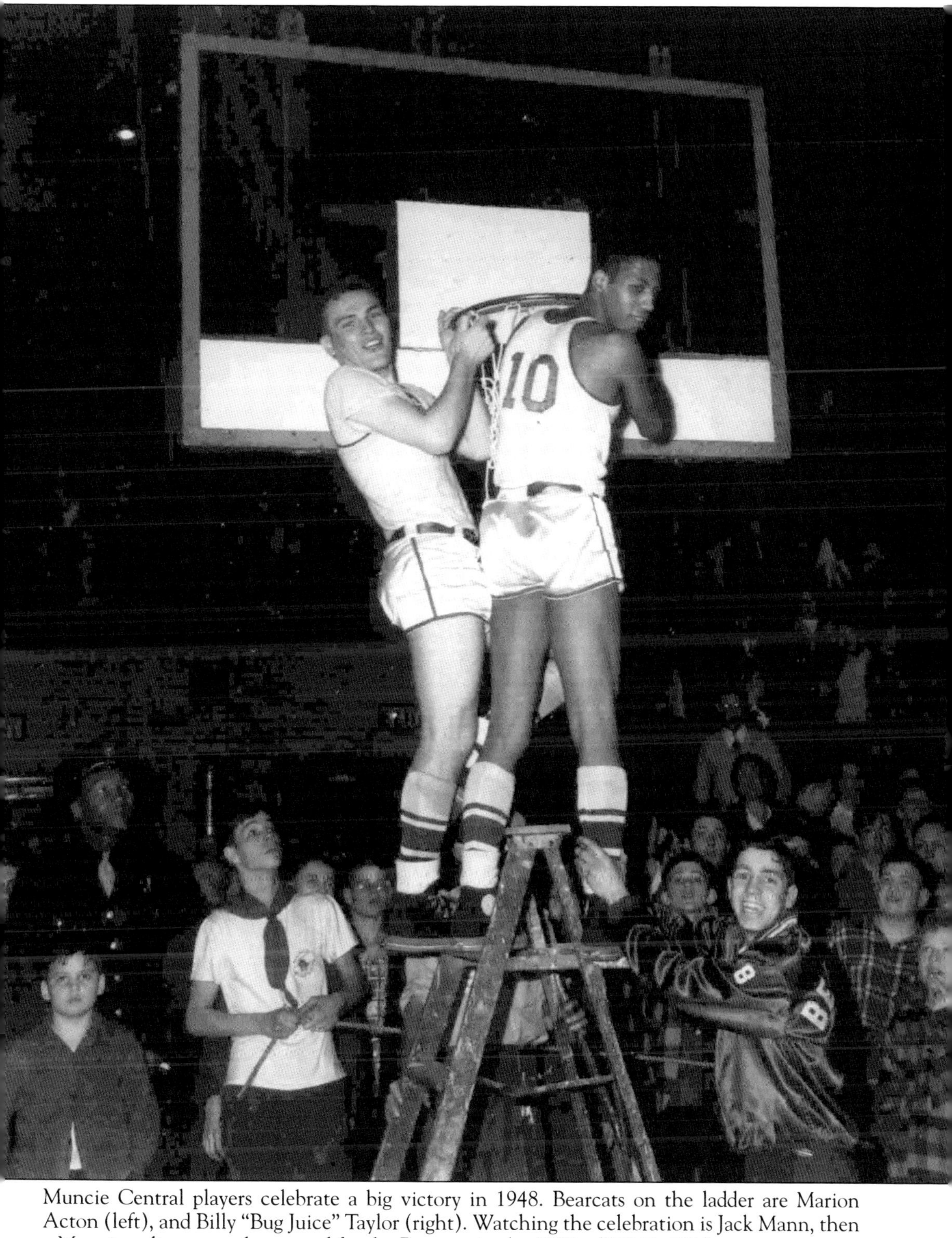

Muncie Central players celebrate a big victory in 1948. Bearcats on the ladder are Marion Acton (left), and Billy "Bug Juice" Taylor (right). Watching the celebration is Jack Mann, then a Muncie policeman, who started for the Bearcats in the 1930s. (BSUA-SG.)

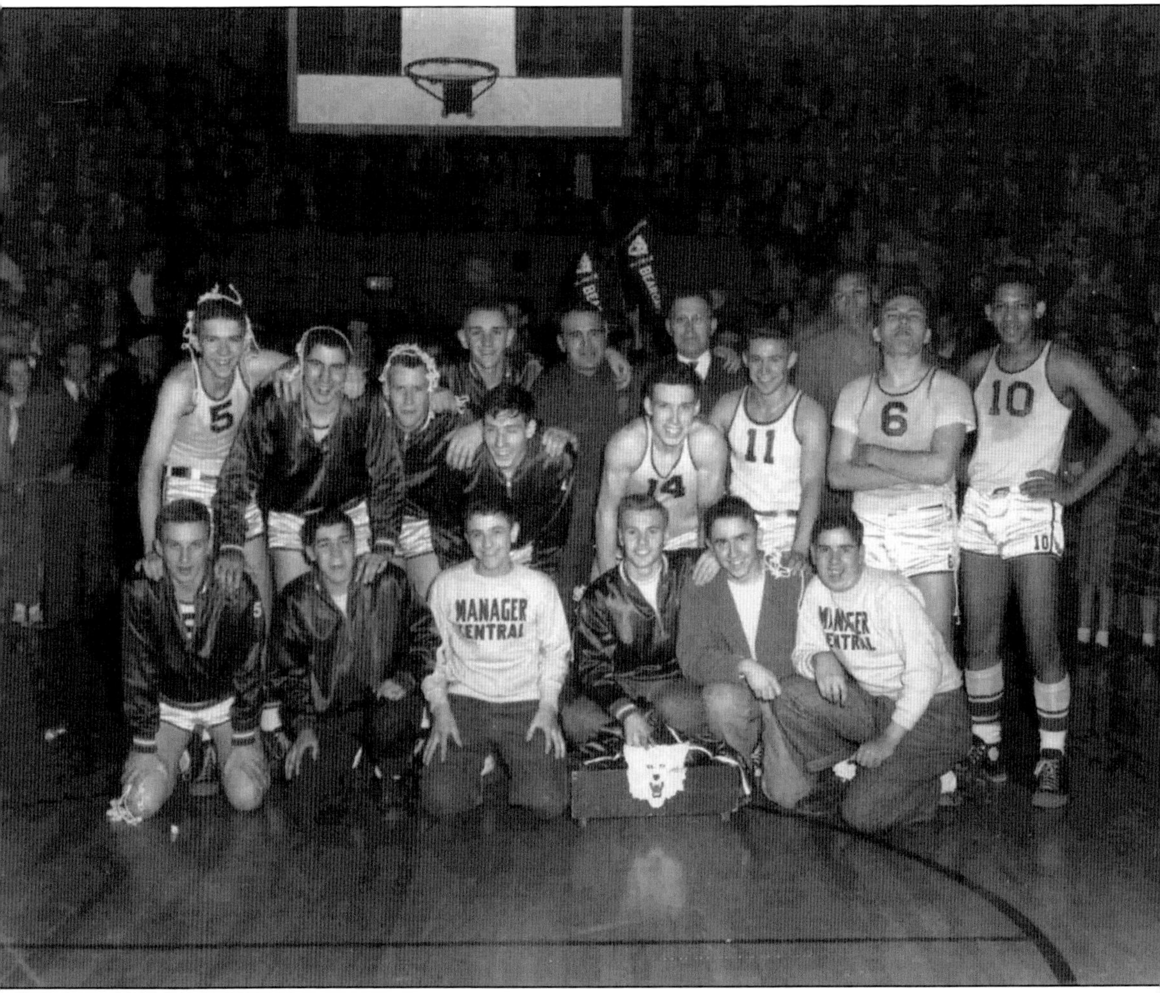

Following a victory in 1948, a Bearcat team photo was in order, with coaches and student managers included. (BSUA-SG.)

Lending A Hand

Natural disasters, such as floods and tornados, have afflicted Muncie from time to time. This set of photos shows the extent of damage caused by a tornado that struck a rural area northwest of Muncie in 1948. These disasters resulted in emergency relief efforts by the Red Cross and civil defense volunteers.

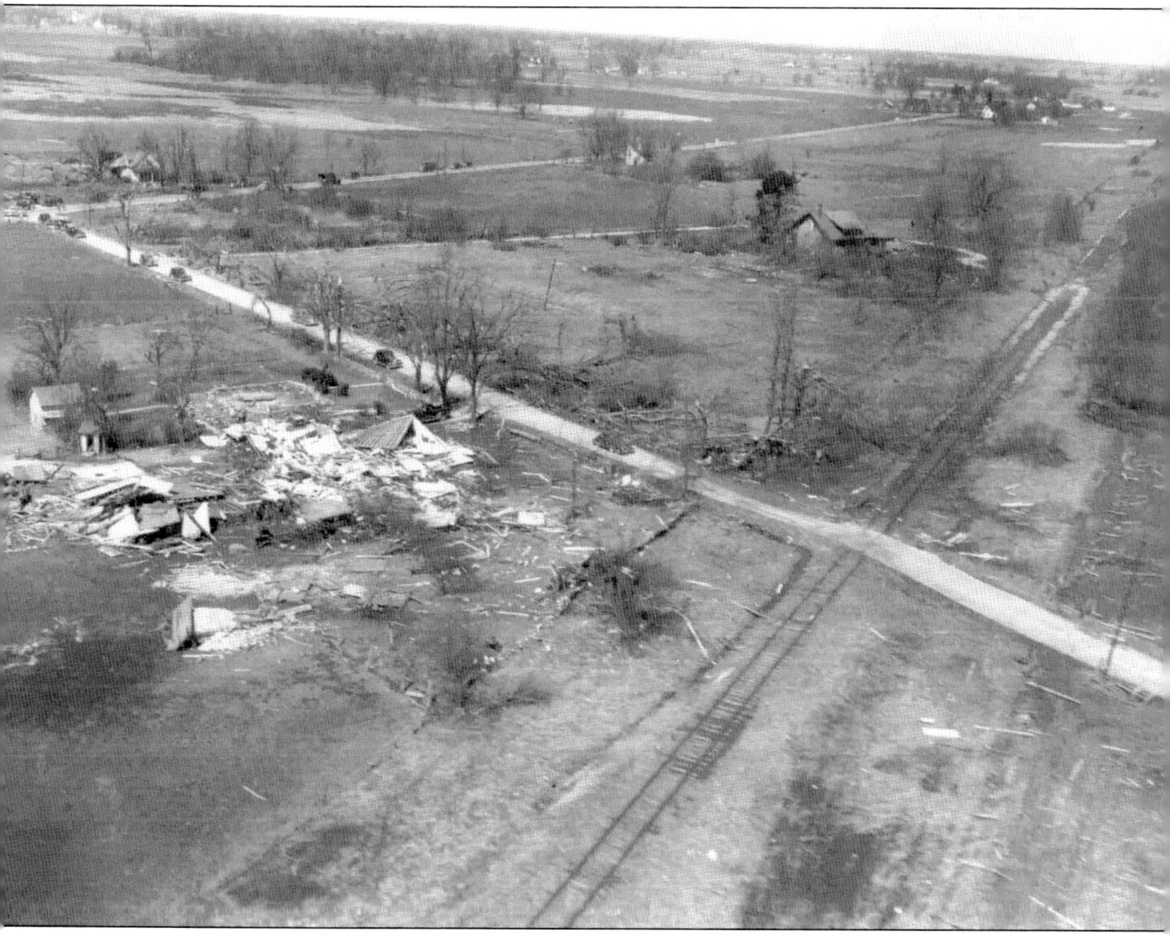

This is an aerial view of the devastating tornado that struck an area near Gaston, Indiana, northwest of Muncie, in April 1948. (BSUA-SG.)

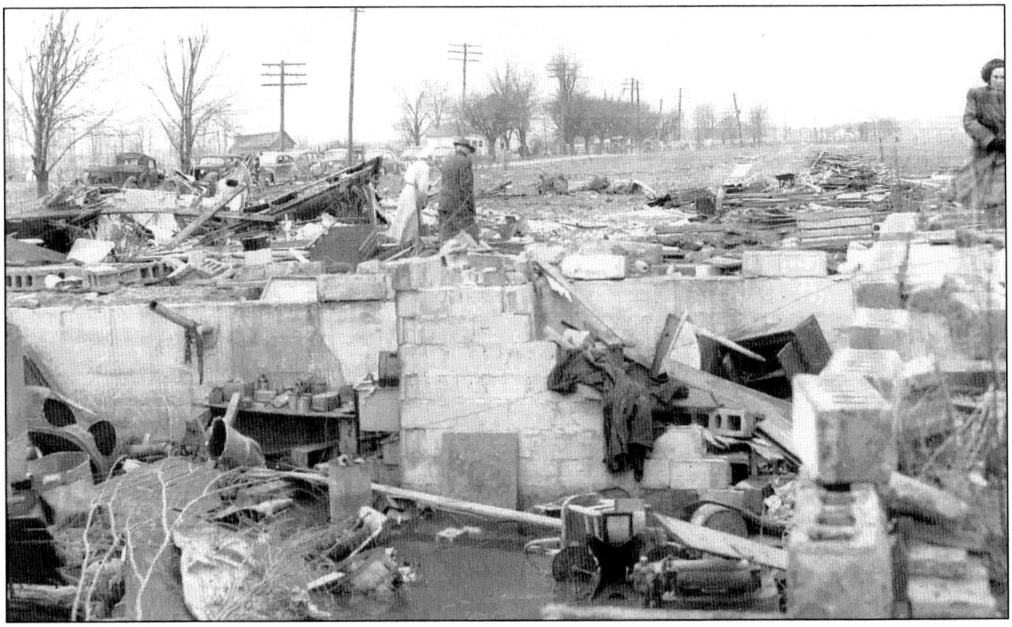

Residents assessed the extent of damage to their property. (BSUA-SG.)

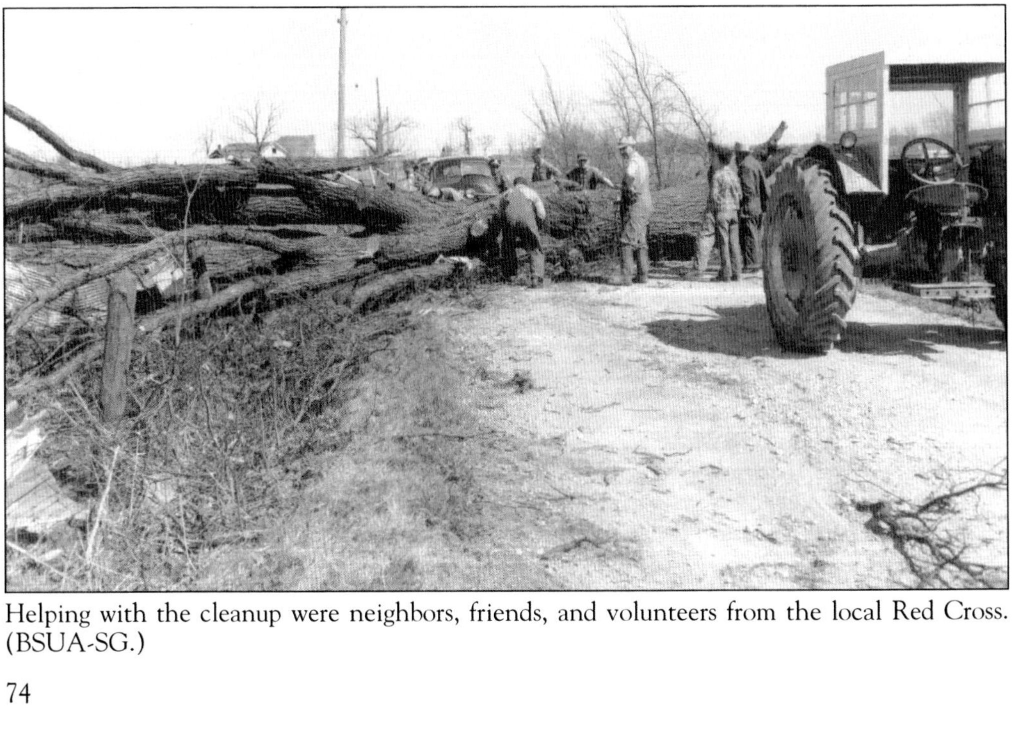

Helping with the cleanup were neighbors, friends, and volunteers from the local Red Cross. (BSUA-SG.)

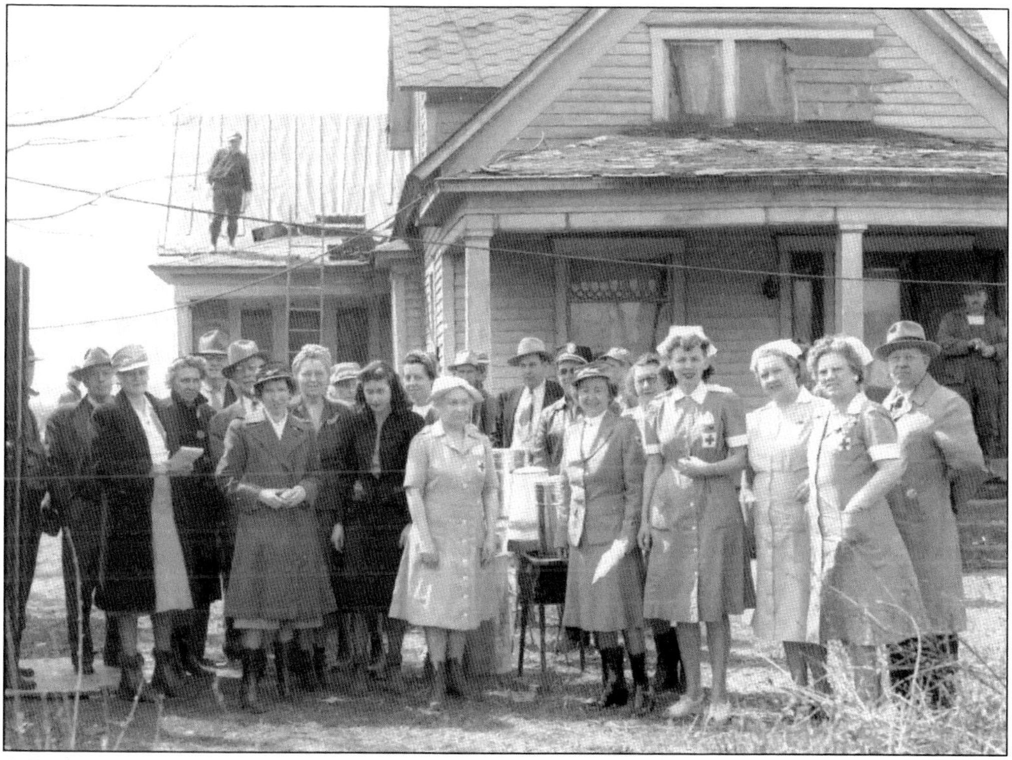

A Red Cross volunteer provided refreshments to those helping in the clean-up effort. (BSUA-SG.)

ATTRACTIONS, DIVERSIONS, AND OCCASIONAL DIFFICULTIES

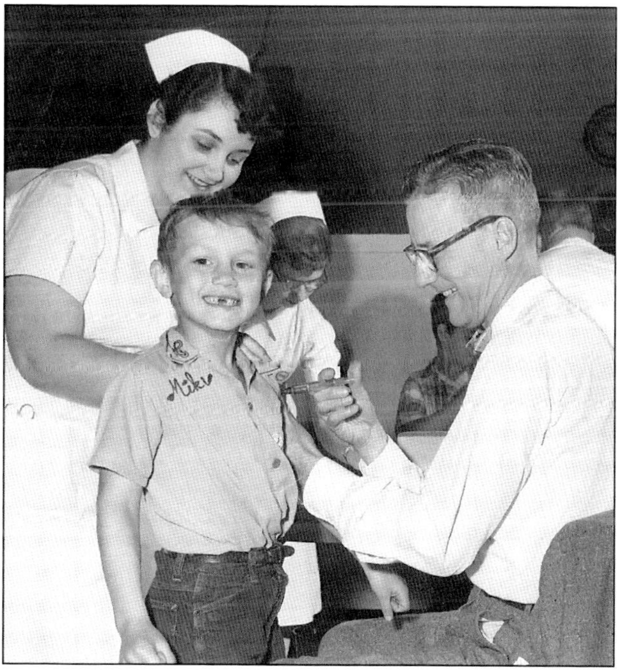

A common experience for Muncie's school children was receiving their "shots" before attending school. Administering the procedure was Forrest Kirshman, M.D., one of Muncie's longtime general practitioners. (Minnetrista Cultural Center.)

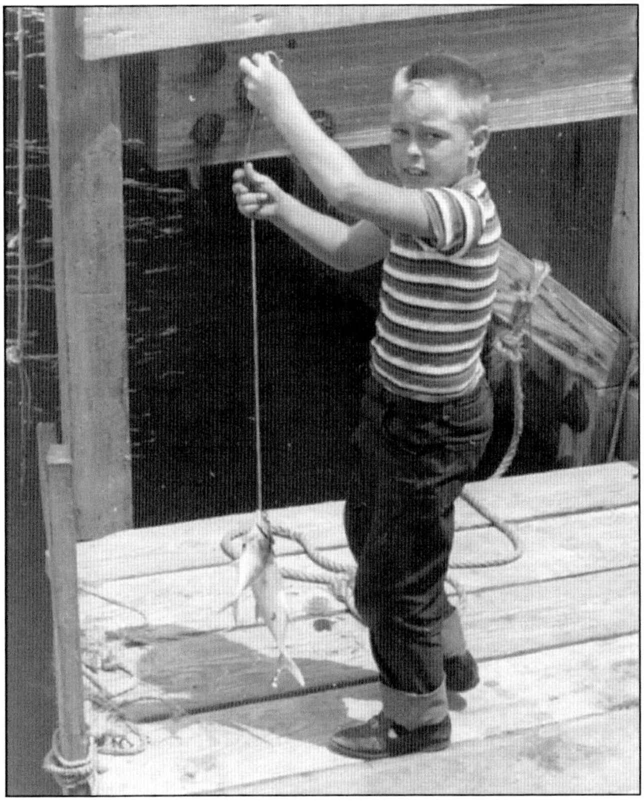

Taken in the mid-1950s, this photo shows one of Muncie's successful young fishermen. (BSUA-Ozbun Collection.)

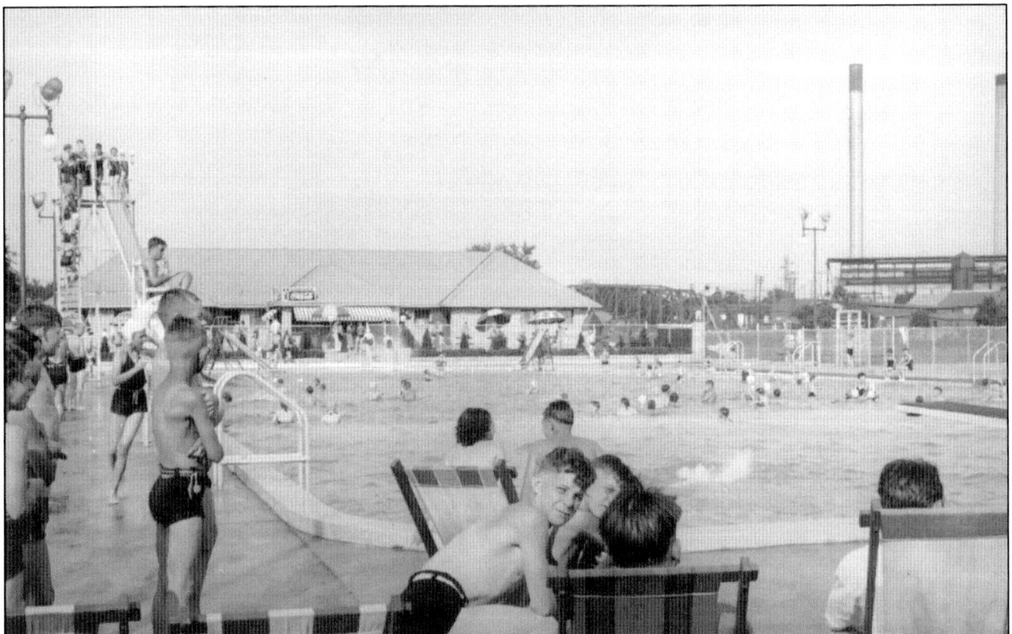

Many a warm summer afternoon was spent swimming at Tuhey Pool, the city's municipal pool. (BSUA-Ozbun Collection.)

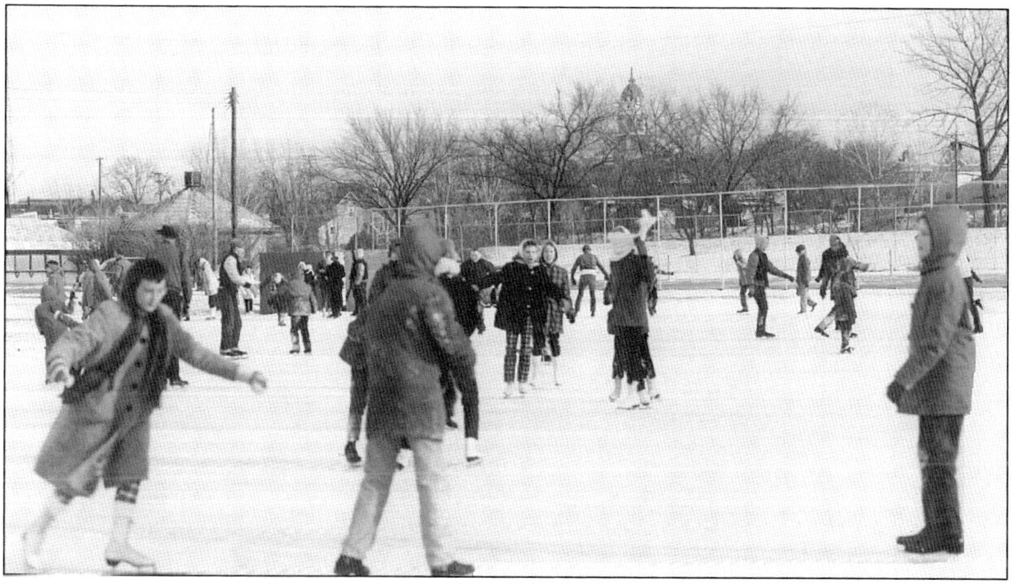

In wintertime, an ice rink was maintained outside Tuhey Pool for the enjoyment of youthful skaters. (BSUA-Ozbun Collection.)

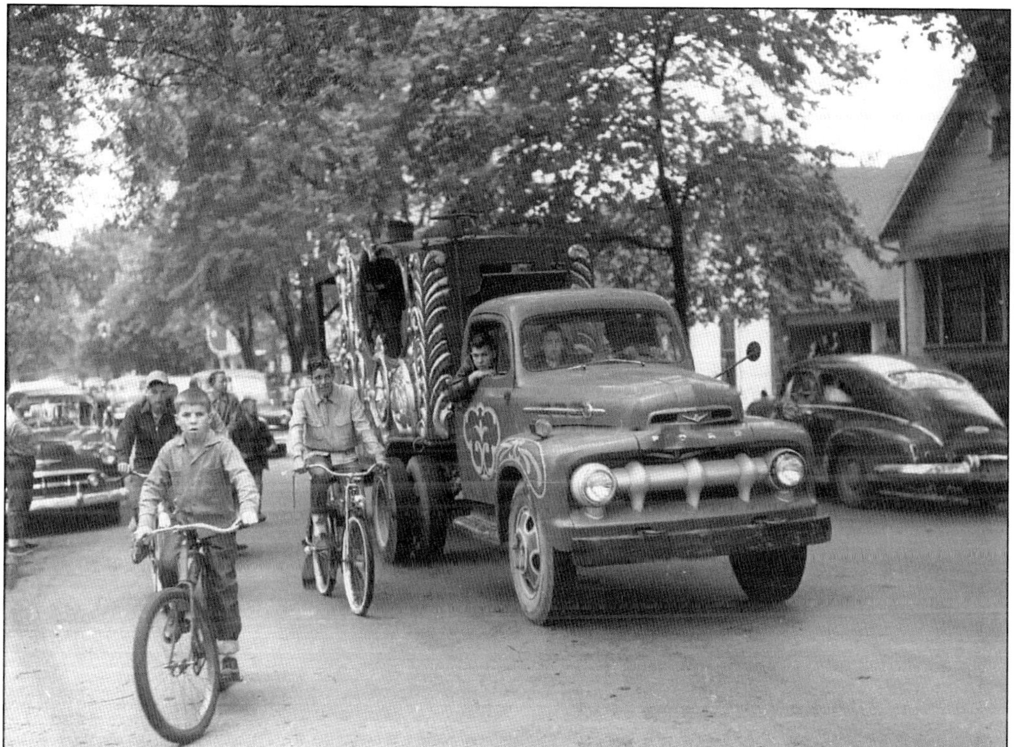

A memorable event from the 1950s occurred when the King Brothers Circus visited Muncie. Circus acts and performers often toured Muncie's neighborhoods to promote their program before the circus officially opened. (BSUA-SG.)

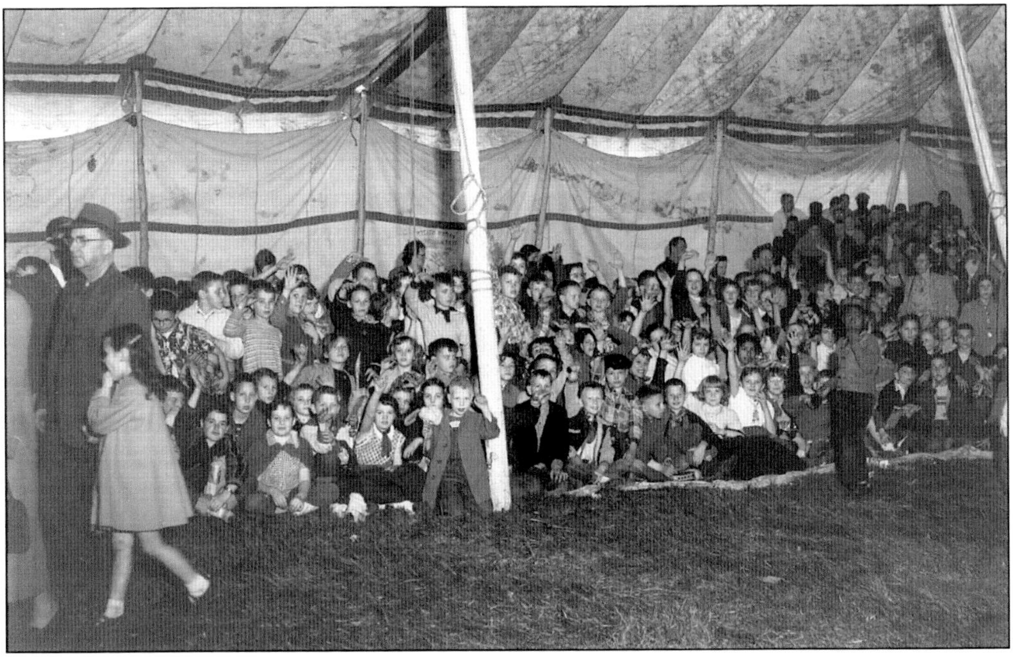

Taken in 1953, this photo shows children jammed into the circus tent to see a performance of the Mills Brothers Circus. (BSUA-SG.)

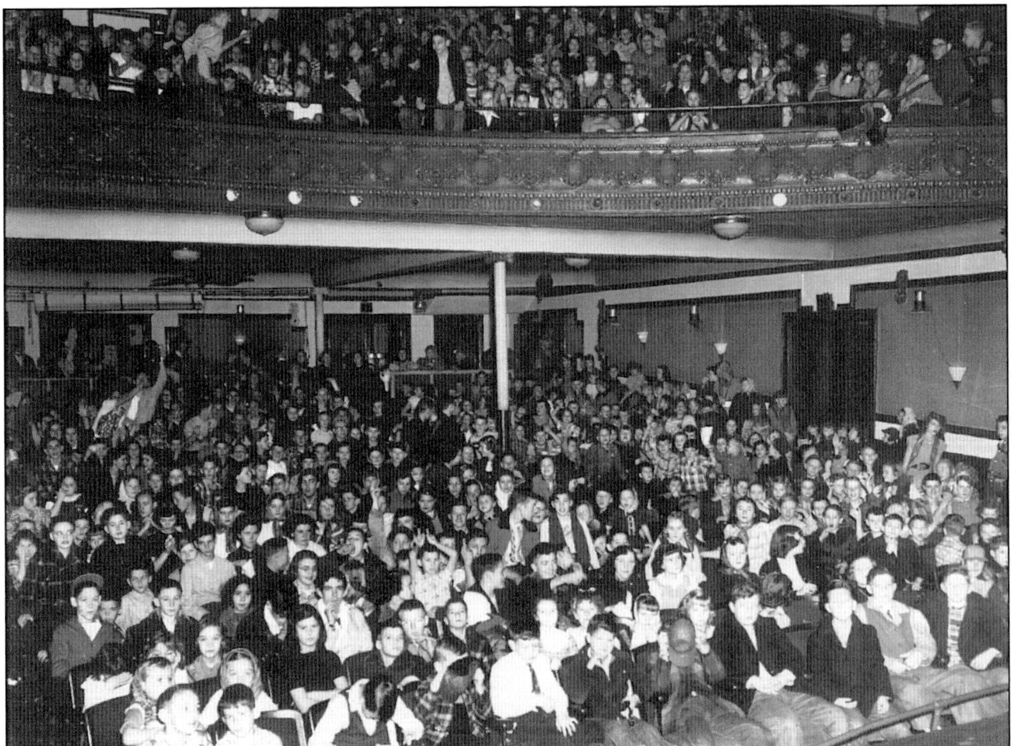

Like their parents, Muncie's children enjoyed a trip to the "show." Taken in 1951, this photo shows a crowd of children posing for the photographer at the Hoosier Theater. (BSUA.)

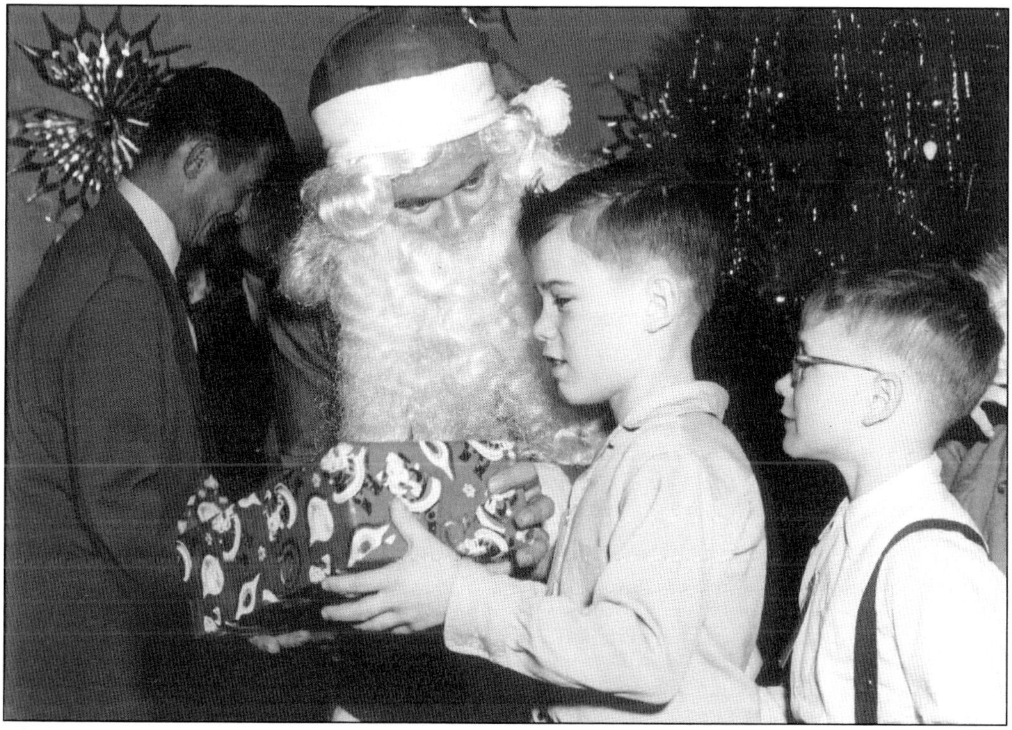

Children of Muncie, like children everywhere, enjoyed annual visits to see Santa Claus. (BSUA-Ozbun Collection.)

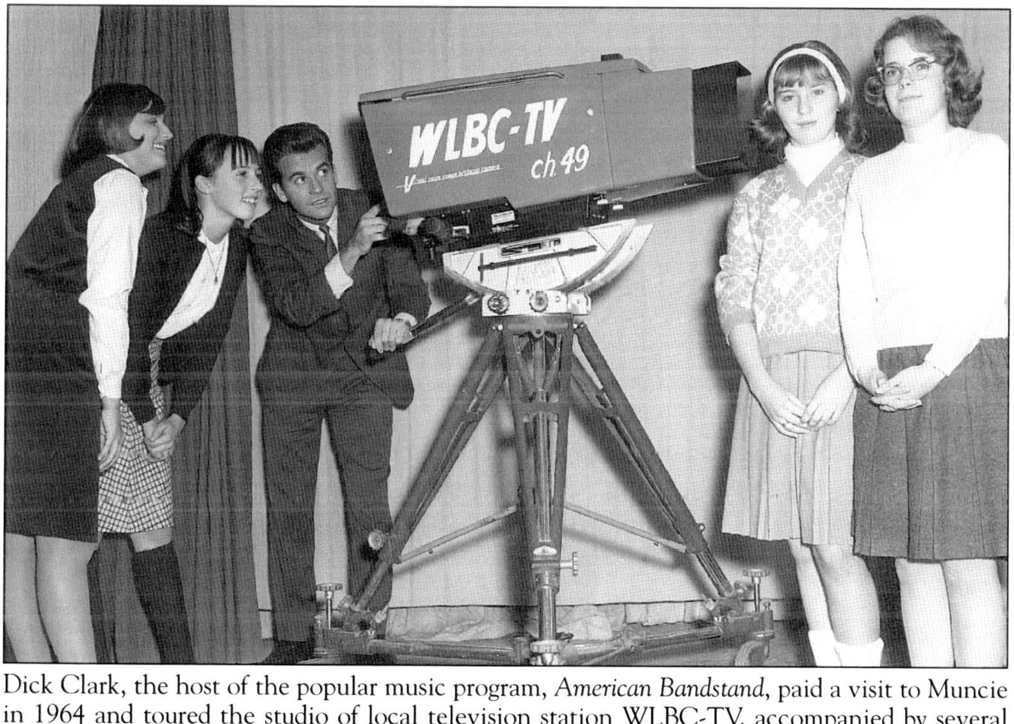

Dick Clark, the host of the popular music program, *American Bandstand*, paid a visit to Muncie in 1964 and toured the studio of local television station WLBC-TV, accompanied by several high school students. (BSUA-Ozbun Collection.)

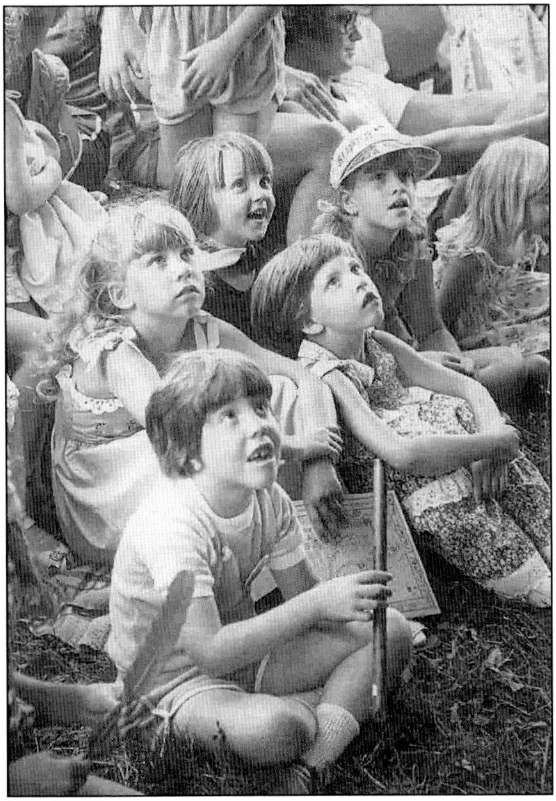

Muncie children sit engrossed as a storyteller recounts a tale during the Renaissance Fair in 1980. (BSUA-Renaissance Fair Collection.)

BALL STATE: FROM TEACHERS COLLEGE TO UNIVERSITY

When the Lynds set about to write *Middletown in Transition*_(p. 215), they conceded that they had underestimated the importance of Ball State to the community. In fact, they referred to it as "an inconspicuous institution out in the edge of the cornfields, on the margin of the city's consciousness." For the next 50 years, however, Ball State continued to grow. From less than one thousand students in 1945, the college's total enrollment surpassed ten thousand in 1965. During the 1970s, enrollment grew to over 18,000 students. Such growth added to the college's importance to the community, as one of its largest employers, as a provider of entertainment in the form of cultural and athletic events, and as a symbol of a community which had a variety of strengths. In 1965, the state legislature conferred university status upon the former Ball State Teachers College and the institution held a place as the third largest, behind Indiana University and Purdue University, of Indiana's state universities.

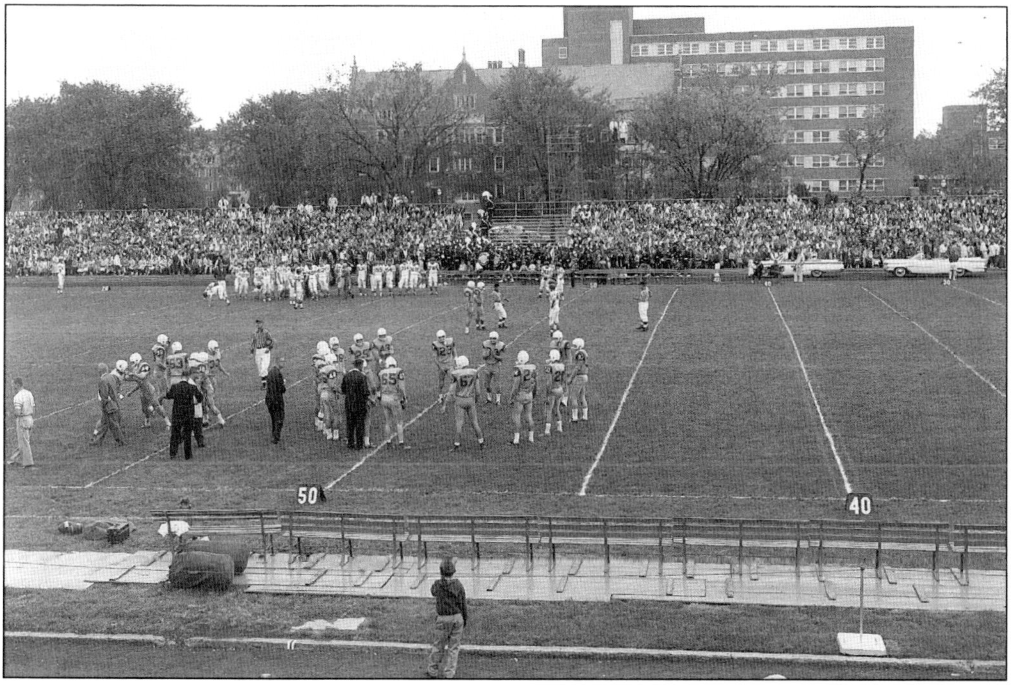

Ball State played its football games at Ball Field, along University Avenue across from Ball Memorial Hospital, from the 1920s to 1967. This photo shows players getting ready to play the Homecoming game in 1960. (BSUA.)

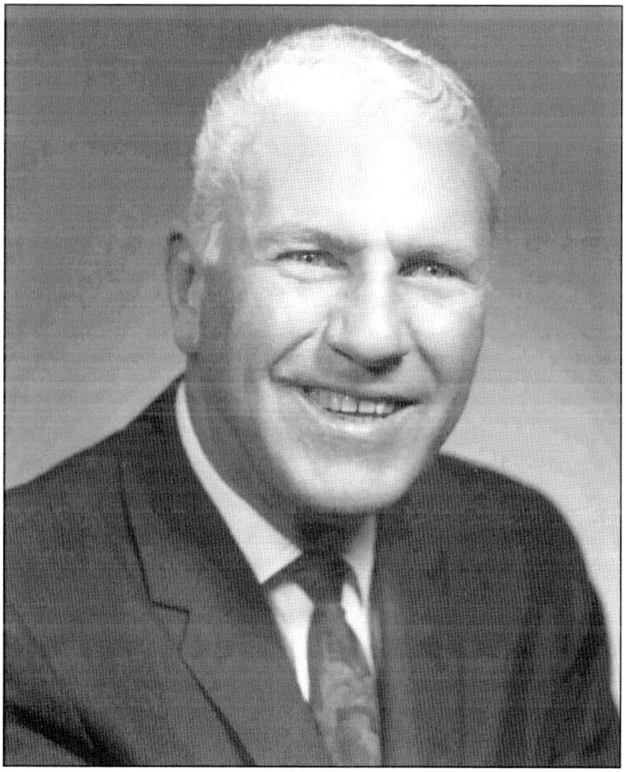

John R. (Jack) Emens served as president of Ball State from 1945 to 1968. Under his leadership, student enrollment grew from less than 1,000 to over 15,000. In 1965, Ball State Teachers College was officially renamed Ball State University in recognition of its growth in student enrollment and in its academic programs. (BSUA.)

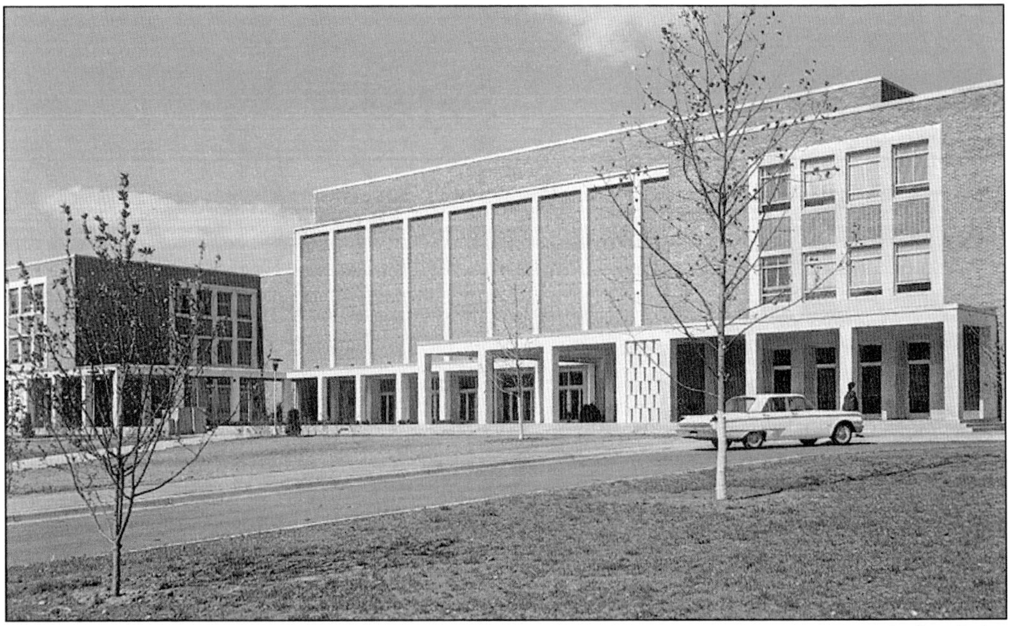

The John R. Emens College-Community Auditorium, which opened in 1964, symbolized the close relationship which existed between "Town and Gown". (BSUA.)

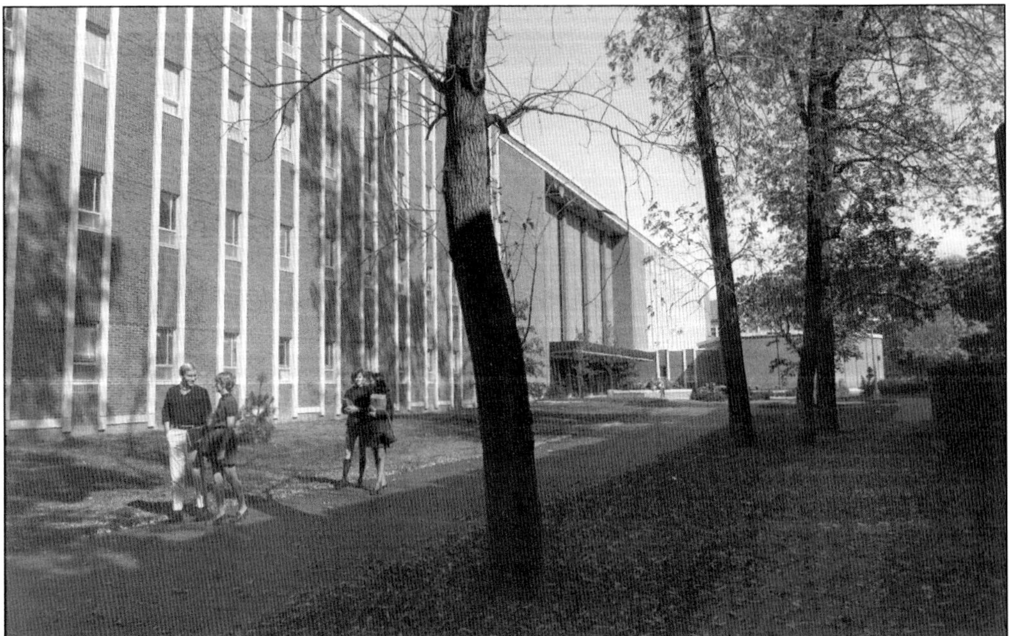

The Cooper Science Complex, named in honor of scientist/professor Robert Cooper, opened in 1970. The complex housed the departments of Biology, Chemistry, Physics, Physiology, Geography, Geology, and Mathematics as well as the University's Nursing School. (BSUA.)

Four

PRACTICING RELIGION

In both *Middletown* and *Middletown in Transition*, Robert and Helen Lynd gave considerable attention to the importance of religion in the life of the community. Some of this attention may be attributed to the fact that Robert Lynd had an extensive education and training in theology prior to undertaking his community studies in Muncie. Likewise, subsequent studies of Muncie, especially Theodore Caplow's *All Faithful People* (1983), have examined the role of religious practices, rituals, and observances throughout the community.

Dwight W. Hoover, in his essay, "From Simpson Chapel to Grace Baptist" from Caplow's *All Faithful People* (pp. 39–40), wrote: "The Lynds structured their study of religion around the role of the minister, the function of the church, the correlation of religious practices with social class, and the impact of industrialization on religious beliefs." During the 1920s and 1930s, the Lynds encountered a religious structure in Muncie that has largely remained true to form in the decades following. Like most mid-sized Midwestern communities, Muncie was a city where Protestant congregations predominated. It was a city characterized primarily by "mainline" Protestant congregations—Methodists, Baptists, Lutherans, and Presbyterians.

It is important to remember, however, that churches in other religious denominations and traditions also added vitality to the religious life of Muncie. Churches in the African-American community tended to be small but no less vibrant. The city's Roman Catholic parishes were smaller than those of some of the larger Protestant congregations, but were nevertheless active and self-supporting. Smaller congregations in the revivalist, evangelical tradition also existed.

In *Middletown* (p. 332), the Lynds summarized their findings about religion by noting a "division into 42 religious groups, almost all of them representing some branch of Christian faith, but each centering its worship in a separate building." The religious history of Muncie retains a distinct continuity with the conditions identified by the Lynds during the 1920s and 1930s.

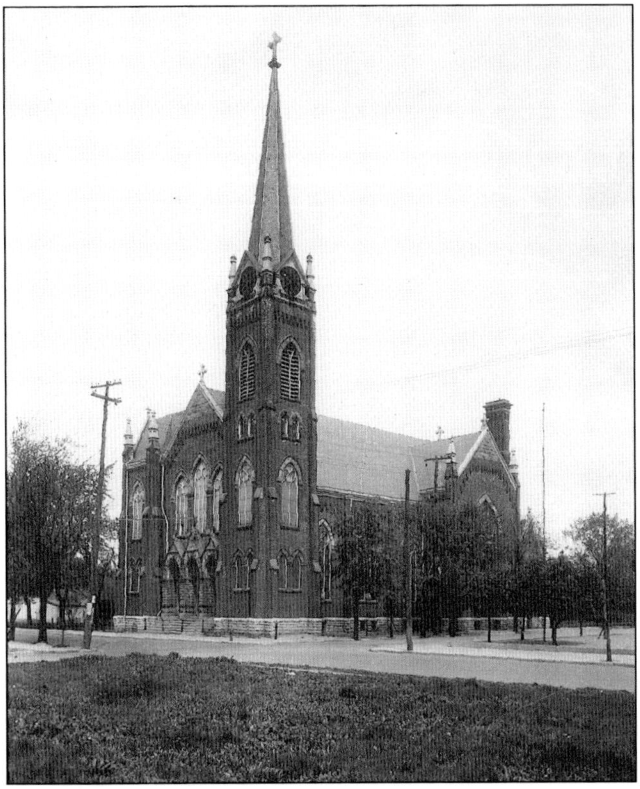

Pictured is St. Lawrence Catholic Church in east central Muncie. Built in 1893, St. Lawrence was an early pillar of the Roman Catholic community in Muncie. (BSUA-Sellers Collection.)

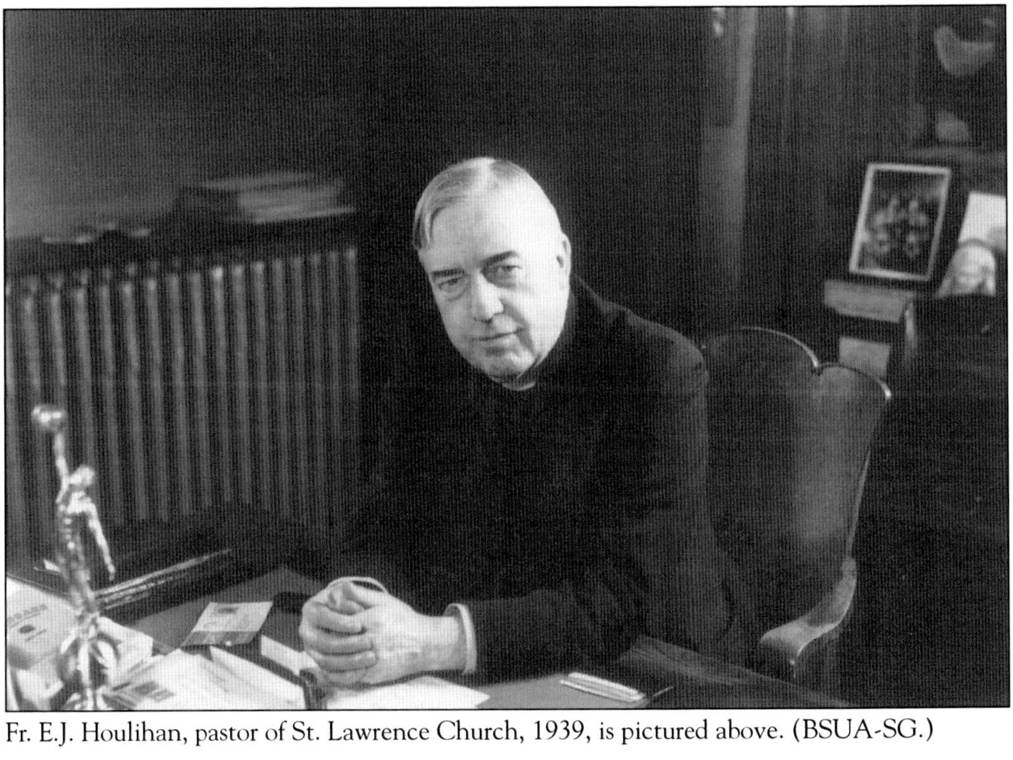

Fr. E.J. Houlihan, pastor of St. Lawrence Church, 1939, is pictured above. (BSUA-SG.)

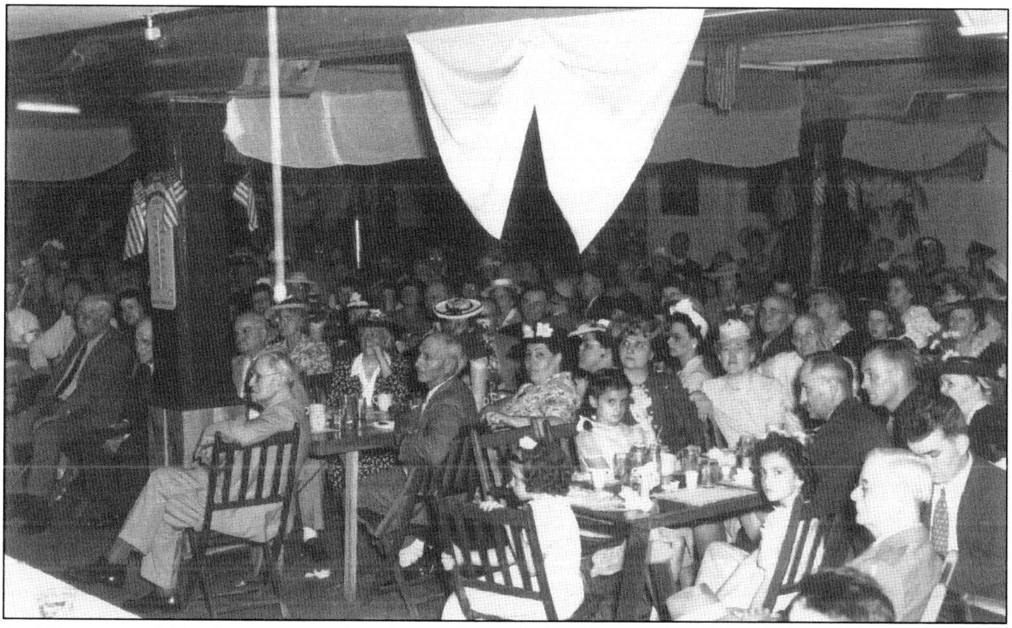

Parishioners of St. Lawrence Church celebrated the church building's 50th anniversary at a commemorative dinner in 1943. (BSUA-SG.)

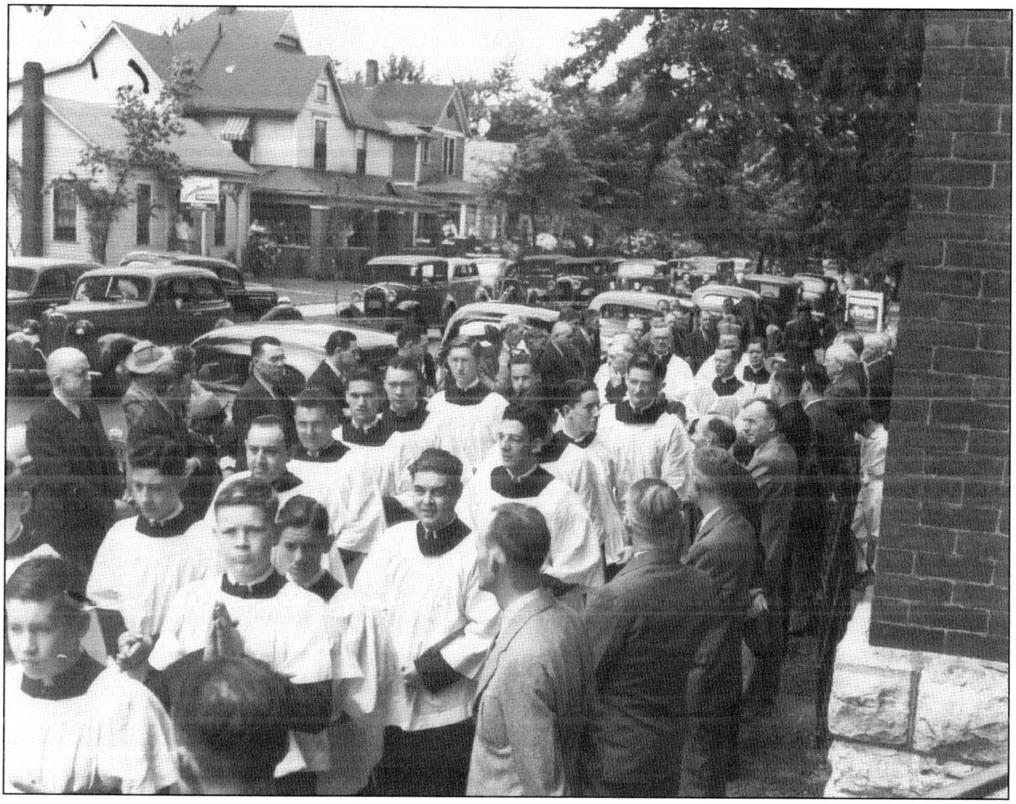

An assembly of worshippers gathers outside St. Lawrence Church in 1943. (BSUA-Greene Newspaper files.)

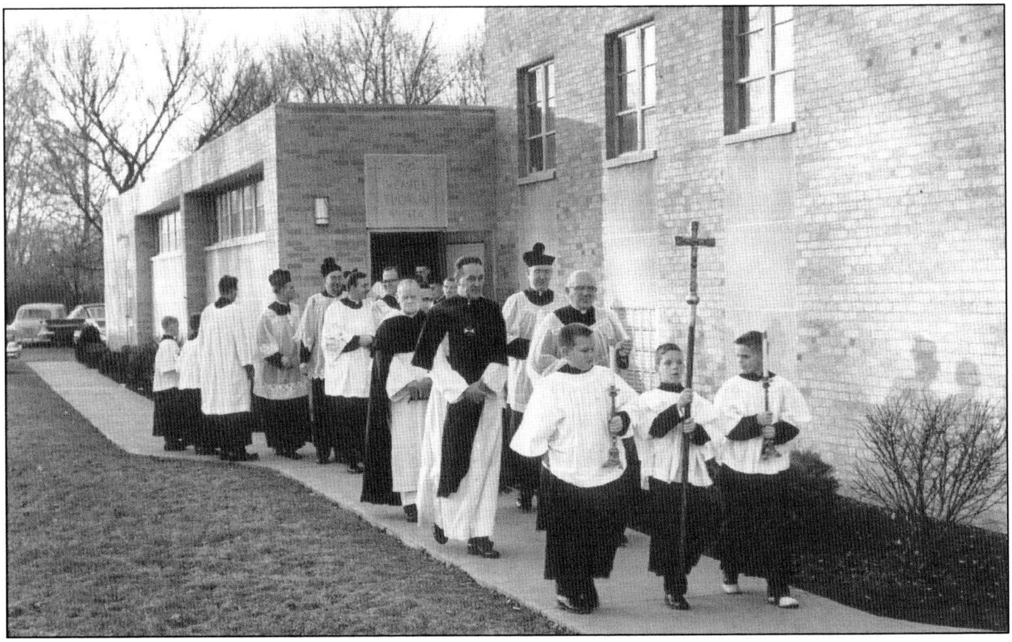

Children scheduled to participate in a mass assemble outside St. Mary's Church in 1959. St. Mary's Church was the second Roman Catholic congregation in the community, and it was located on West Jackson Street, one block south and west of the Ball State campus. Services began in 1930, but it was not until later that the parish moved into its present location. (BSUA-SG.)

The Church in the City

Churches of mainline Protestant denominations tended to construct their sanctuaries in the central part of the city. In that fashion, these congregations tended to be identified visibly with the character of the community.

The First Baptist Church of Muncie, located at Jefferson and Charles Streets, traces its roots back to the mid-1830s in Muncie. The building in the photo above was completed in the 1890s. (BSUA-SG.)

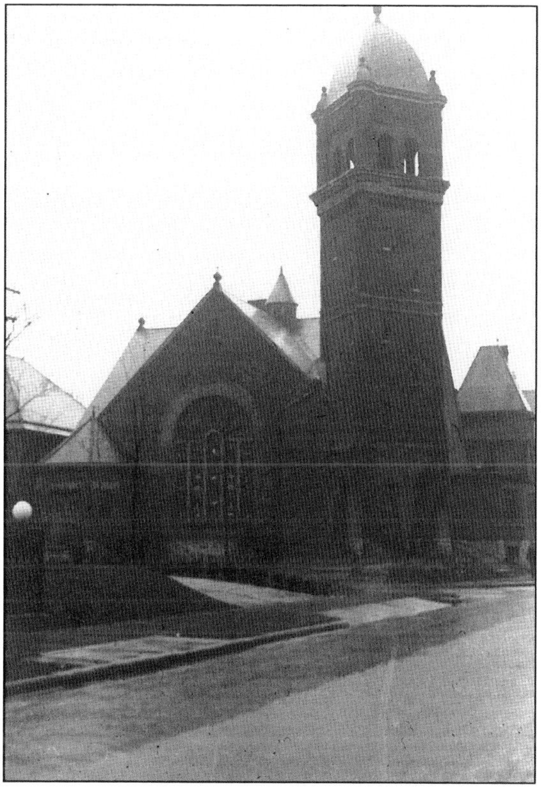

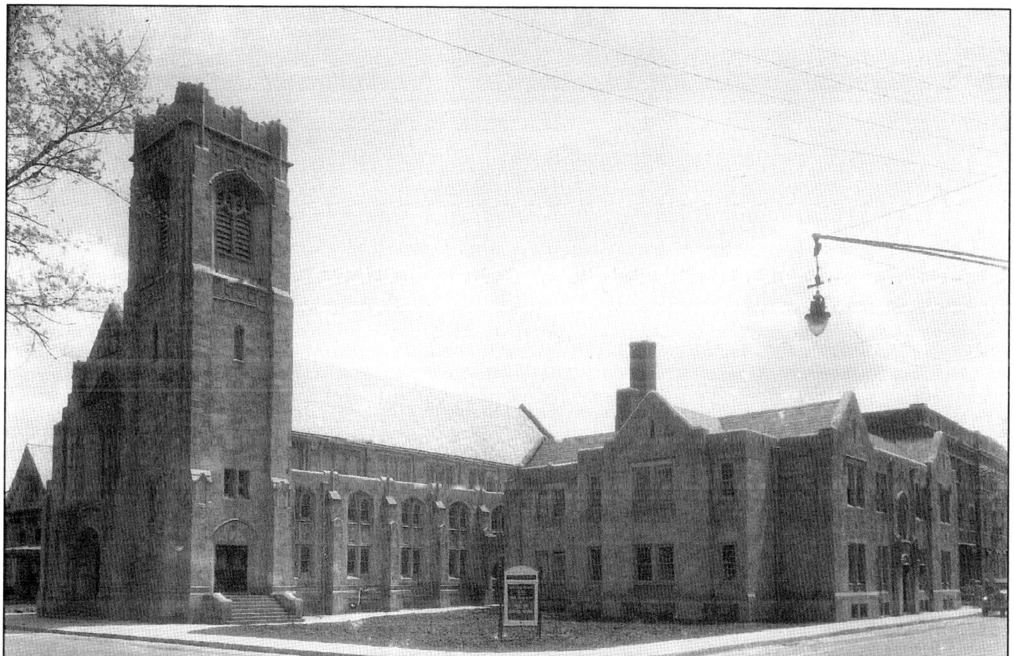

The First Baptist Church is shown here at its present location, Jefferson and Adams Streets. This building was completed in 1929. (BSUA-SG.)

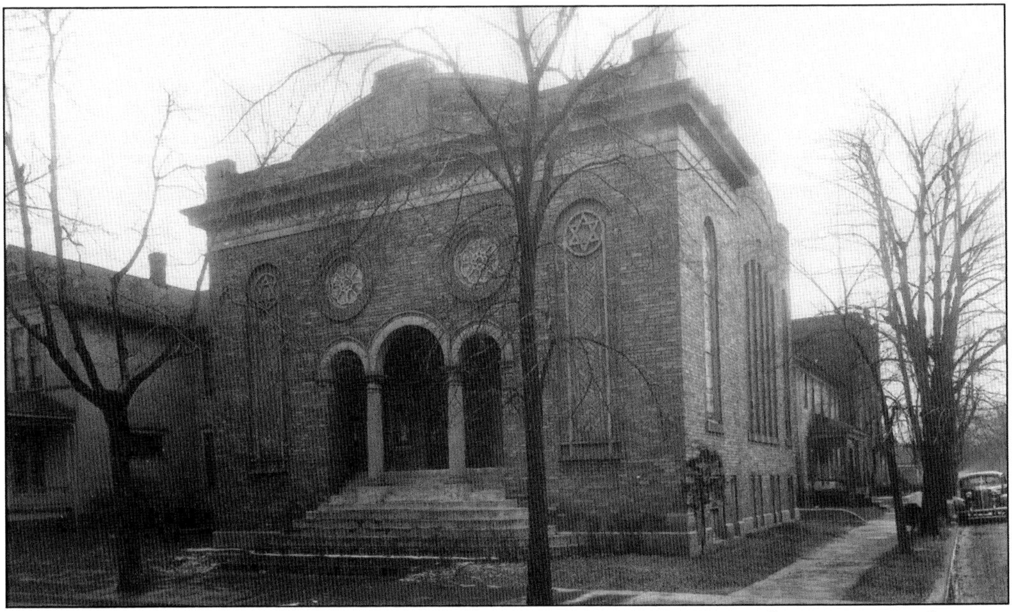

Pictured here is Temple Beth-El, the center of worship for Muncie's Jewish community. Services for Jewish worshippers were held in Muncie as early as 1891. Temple Beth-El was completed in 1922. A magnificent addition to the temple was finished and dedicated in 2000. (BSUA-SG.)

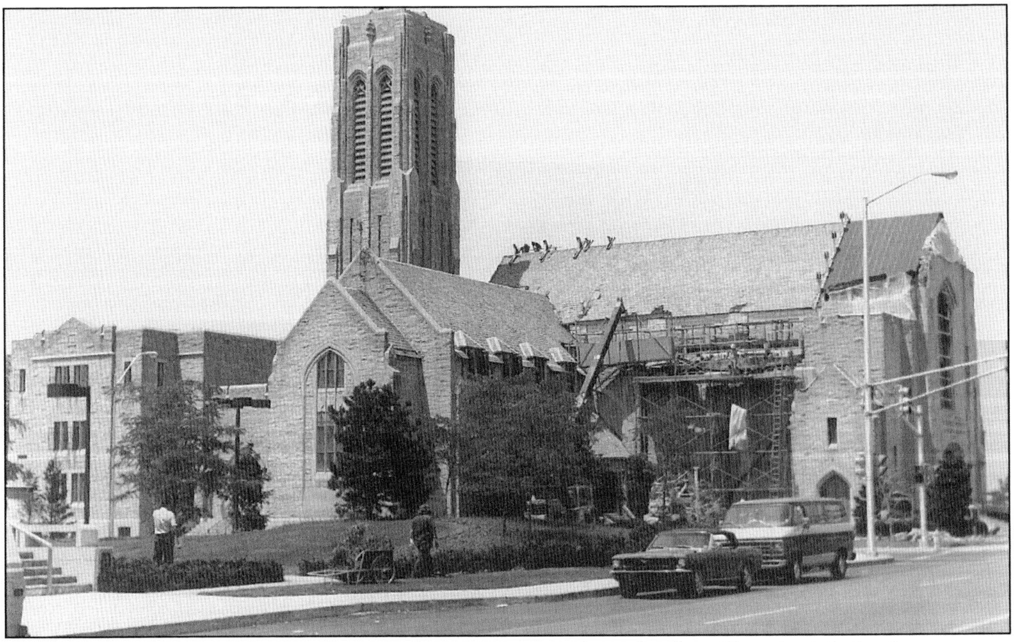

This is the venerable sanctuary of High Street United Methodist Church. Methodist services began in Muncie during the 1830s, and the High Street congregation became the pioneer church of the denomination in Muncie. At one time, the High Street Methodist Church was one of the largest Methodist congregations in the United States. The sanctuary was completed in 1930. This photo shows workers repairing damage to the church caused by a natural gas explosion and fire in the winter of 1978. (BSUA-SG.)

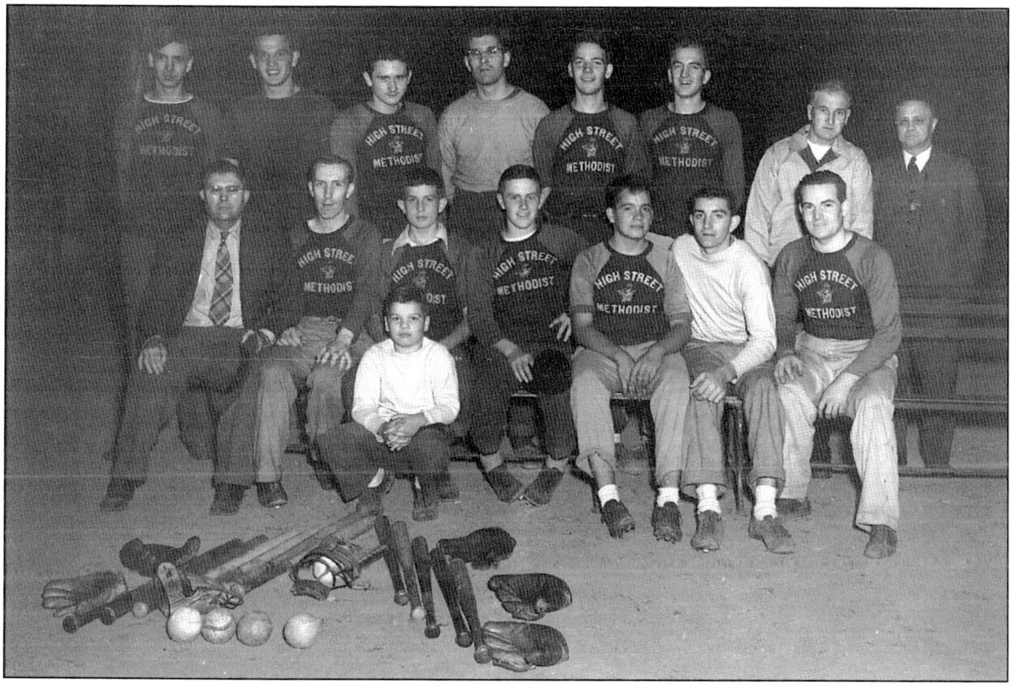

Muncie's churches have traditionally sponsored teams who participate in local church athletic leagues. This photo shows the men's softball team from High Street United Methodist Church.(BSUA-SG.)

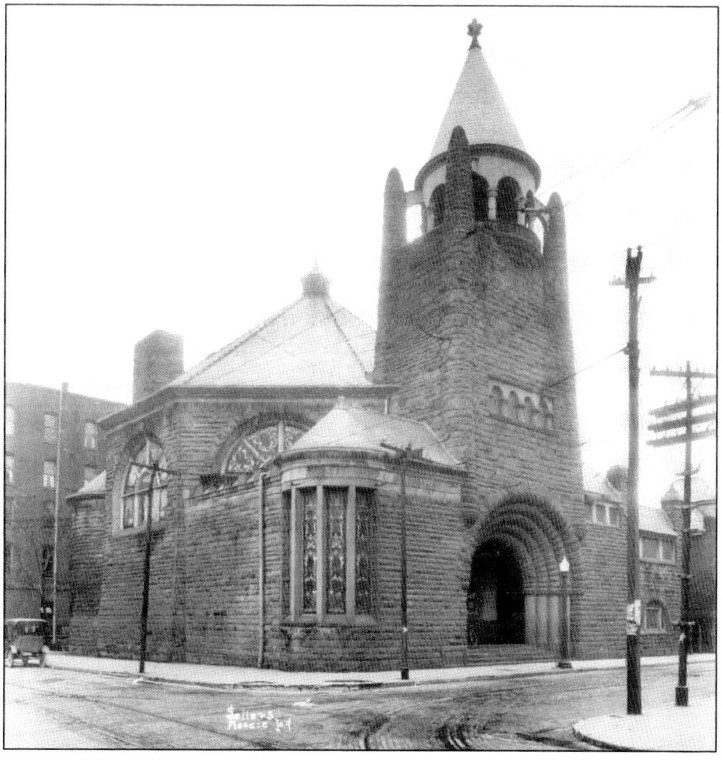

The First Presbyterian Church (PCUSA) originally held its services in an impressive sanctuary on the corner of Mulberry and Charles Streets in central Muncie. Presbyterian services began in the late 1830s. First Presbyterian Church held its services at this location from 1843 to 1955. (BSUA-Richard Greene Collection.)

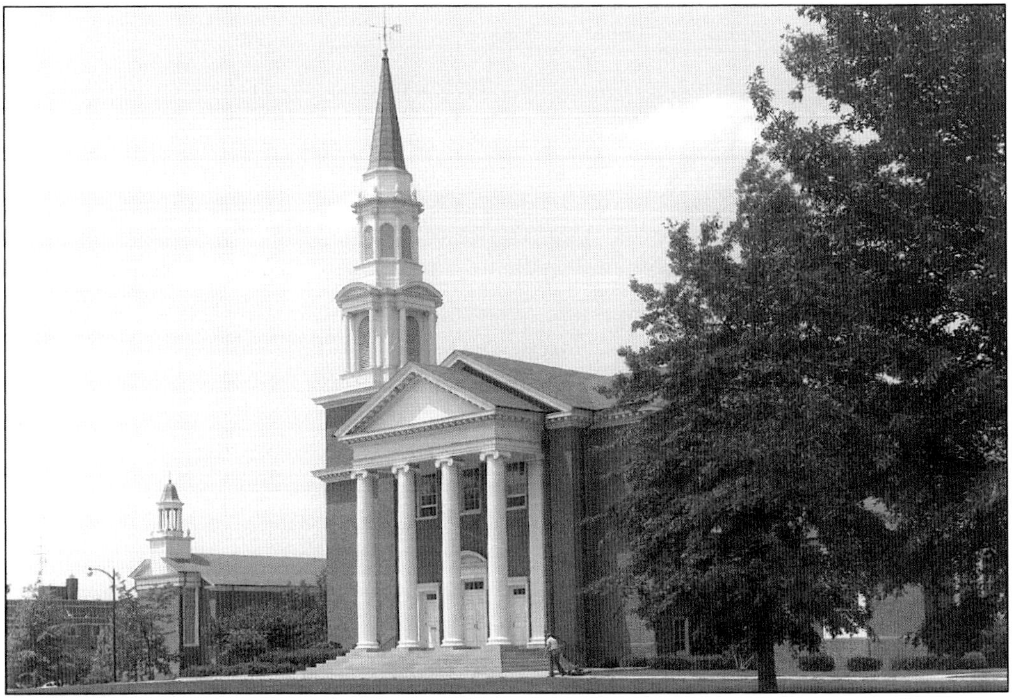

In 1955, First Presbyterian Church moved to an impressive new sanctuary on the corner of New York and Riverside Avenues, slightly to the south and east of the Ball State campus. (BSUA-SG.)

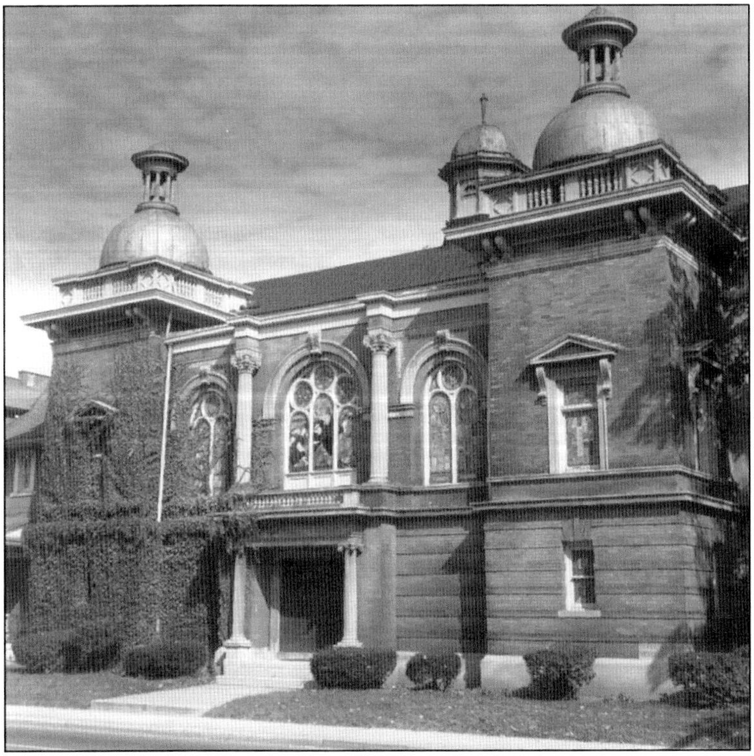

Pictured is St. John's Universalist Church in downtown Muncie. Muncie's Universalist congregation began worshipping in 1859. The church underwent several name changes. It originally was known as the First Universalist Church. In 1913, the church was renamed St. John's Universalist Church. In 1954, the church again changed its name back to the First Universalist Church. (BSUA-SG.)

One of Muncie's best known ministers, Rev. Arthur McDavitt was the pastor of the Universalist Church from 1924 to 1953. (BSUA.)

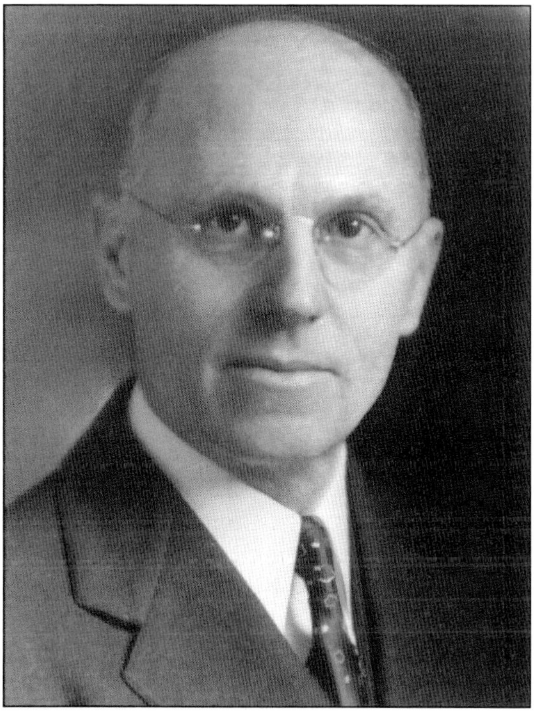

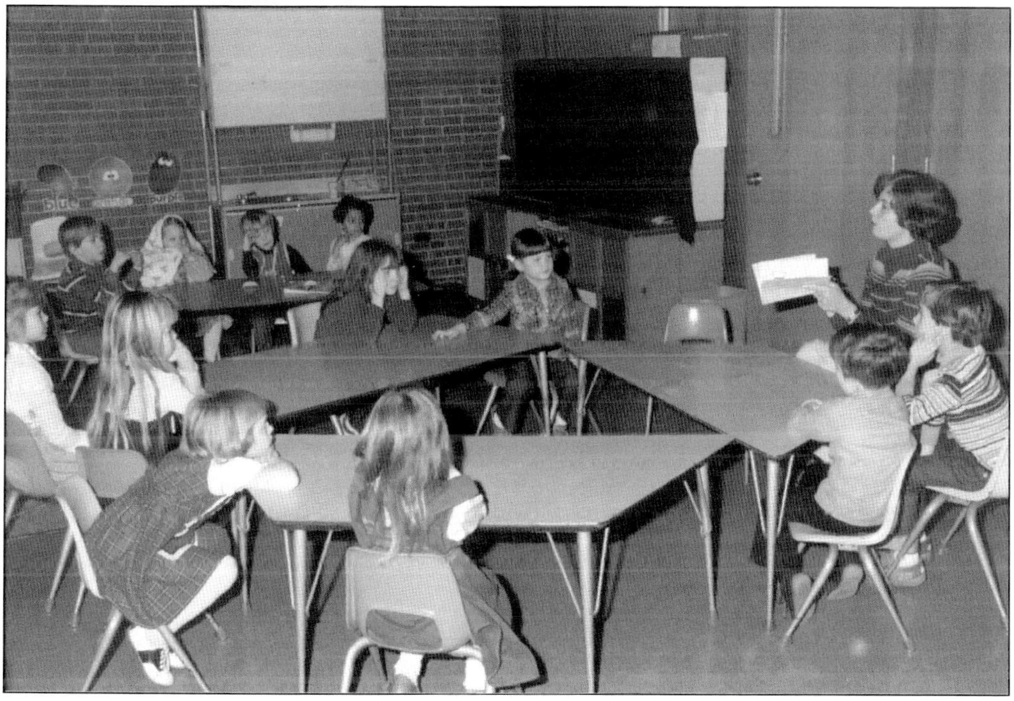

This is a scene from a church school class at the Unitarian-Universalist church in 1980. The Universalist and Unitarian denominations merged in 1961. Melinda Thornburg is the teacher for this class of children. The church moved to a new location in northwest Muncie in the mid-1960s. (BSUA.)

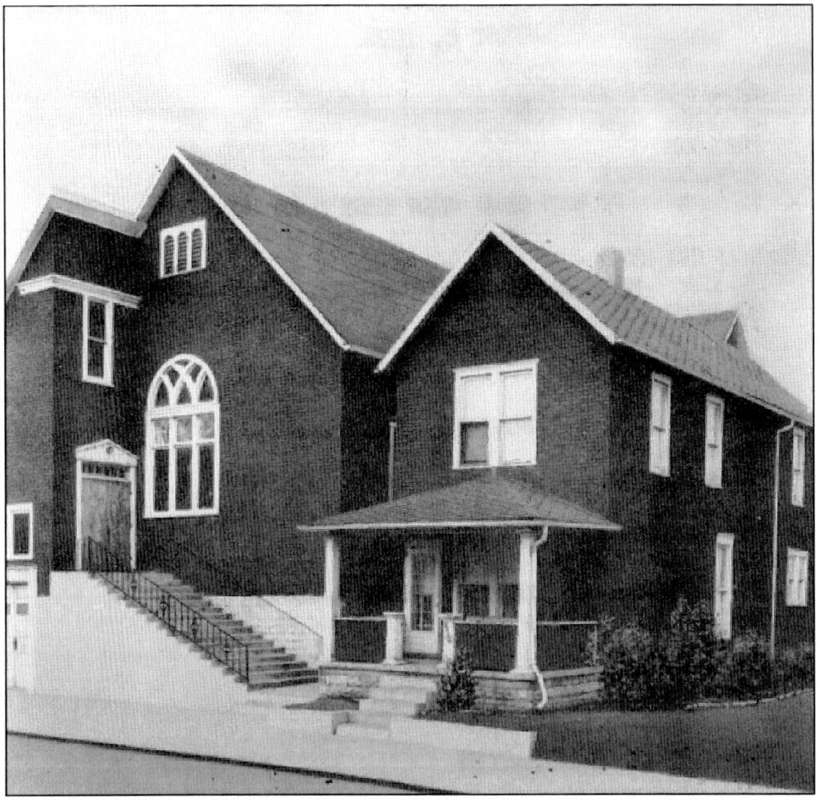

The Bethel A.M.E. Church in Muncie was established in 1868. Taken in 1914, this photo shows the church's second building. (Hurley C. Goodall.)

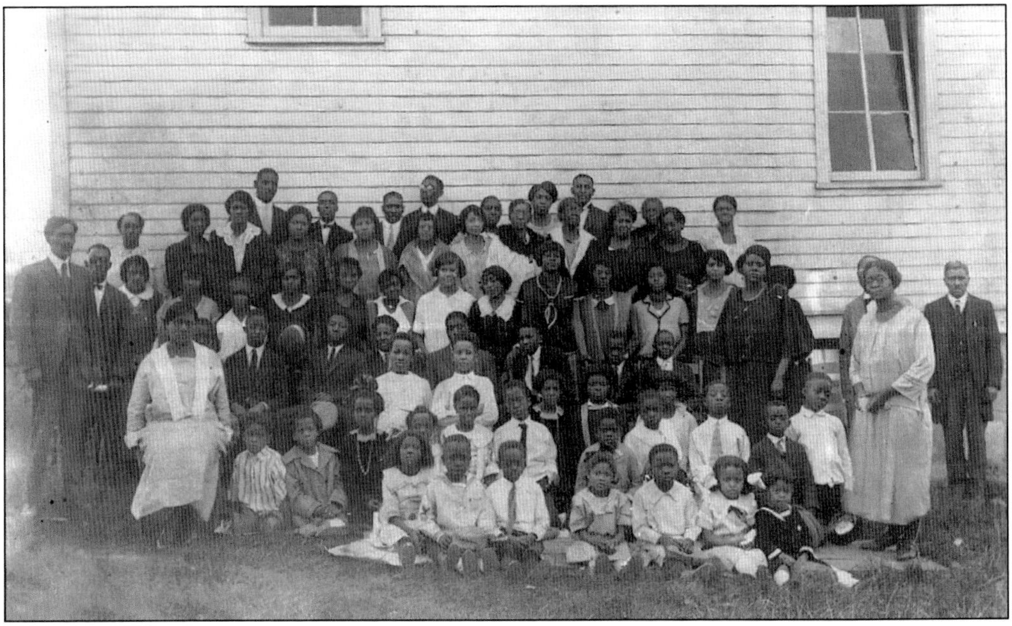

Pictured above is a gathering of worshippers at the Shaffer Chapel A.M.E. Church in 1926. (Hurley C. Goodall.)

Rev. Anthony Jones Oliver, pastor of Shaffer Chapel A.M.E. Church, was instrumental in forming the People's Progress Committee, and worked for expanded employment opportunities for African Americans at local factories, banks, and utility companies. (Hurley C. Goodall.)

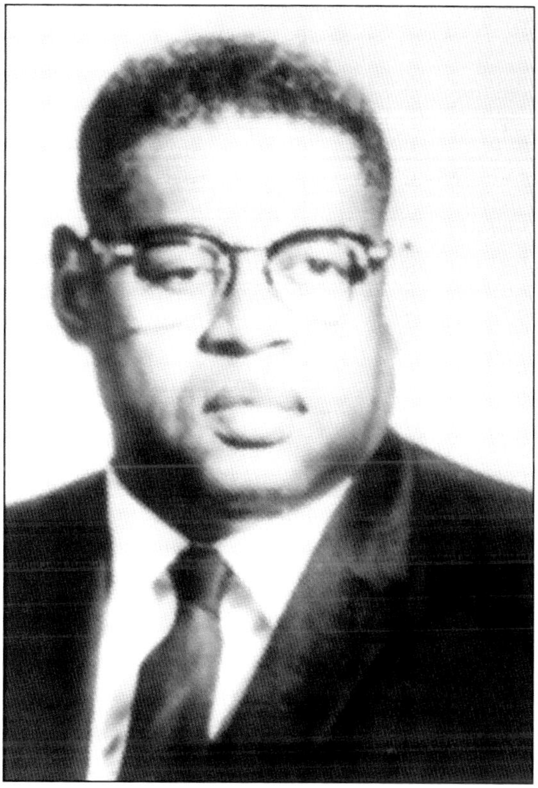

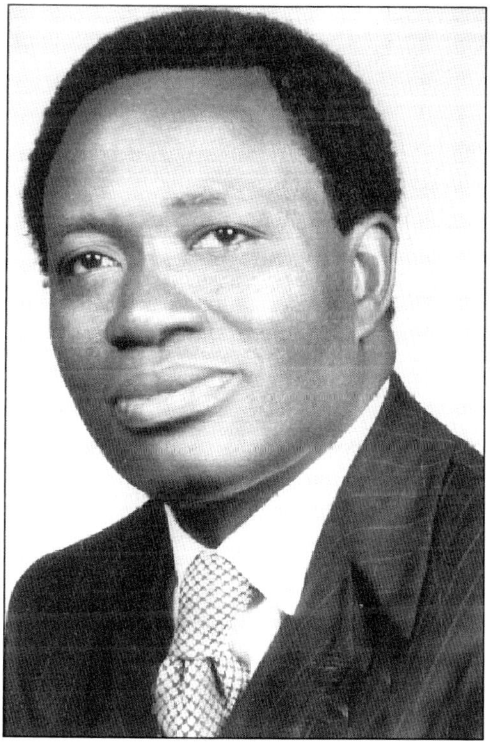

Rev. J.C. Williams, pastor of Trinity United Methodist Church, was an outspoken advocate for civil rights and equal opportunity. (Hurley C. Goodall.)

THE CHURCH AND THE CAMPUS NEIGHBORHOODS

As the neighborhoods adjacent to Ball State grew during the 1920s and 1930s, they became the location for several churches. In the post-World War II period, several of these churches began a ministry to students who were attending Ball State. Two churches, in particular, actively served the spiritual needs of college students. College Avenue United Methodist Church, through its Wesley Foundation ministry, offered programs for college students. Westminster Presbyterian Church became the choice of worship for several leaders of para-church organizations, such as Campus Crusade for Christ, the Navigators, and Inter-Varsity Christian Fellowship. Students who were active in these organizations at Ball State were drawn to Westminster's services.

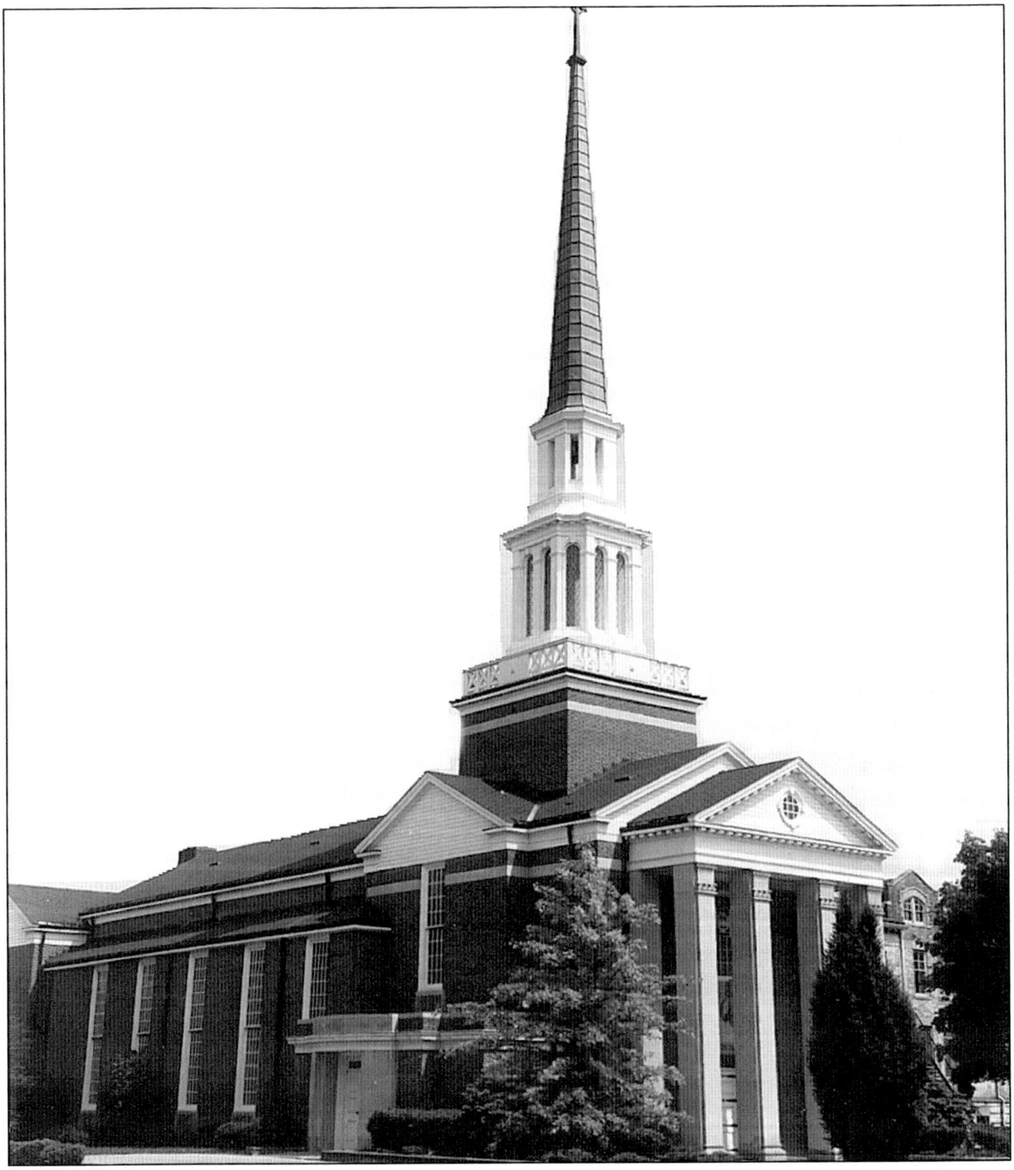

Shown here is College Avenue United Methodist Church, two blocks south of the Ball State campus. The church moved into its present sanctuary in 1959. (BSUA.)

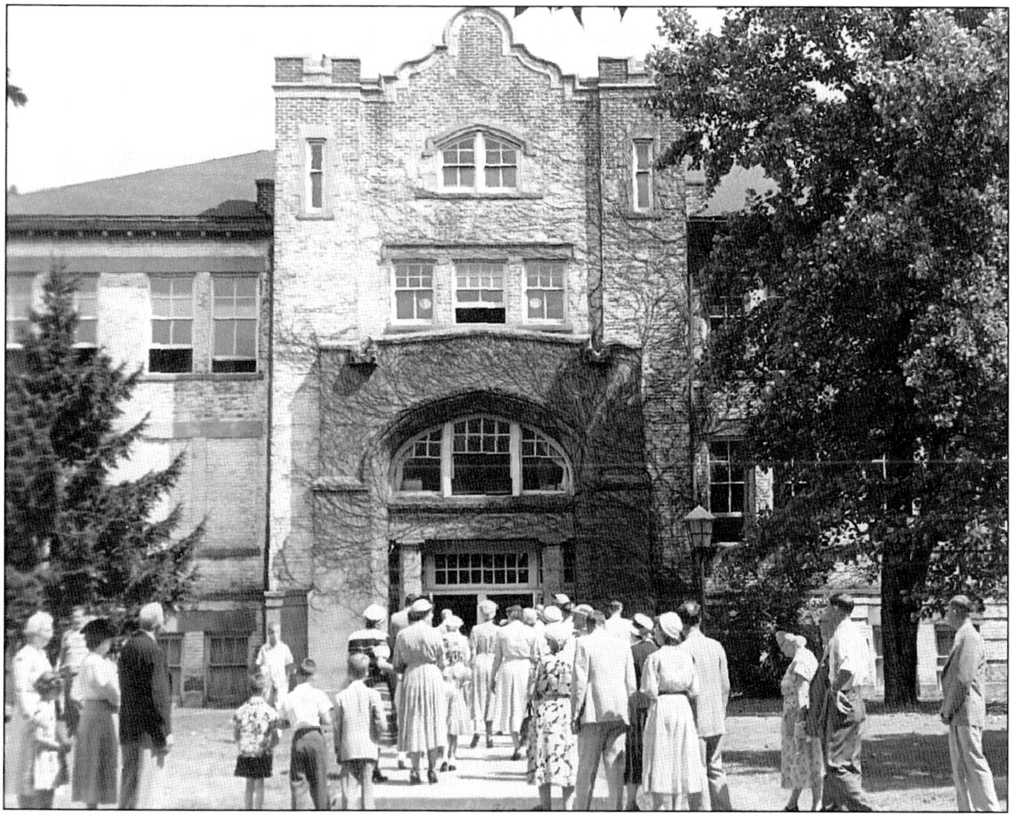

The members of College Avenue Methodist Church worshiped at the Whittier School while awaiting the construction of a permanent sanctuary. This photo shows a group of worshippers preparing to enter the school for Sunday services. (College Avenue United Methodist Church.)

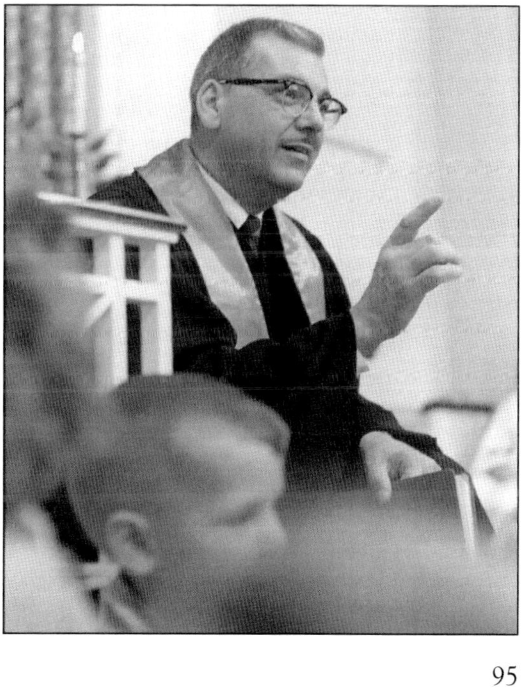

Rev. Donald Barnes held the pastorate at College Avenue Methodist Church from 1952 to 1965, a period of considerable growth for the church. (College Avenue United Methodist Church.)

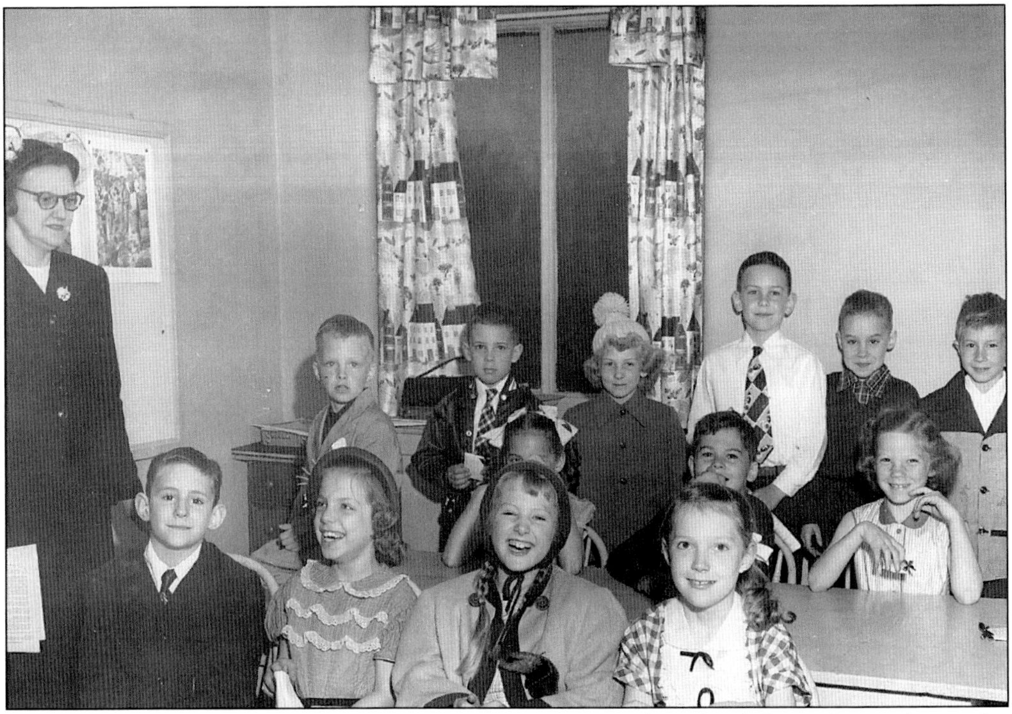

This photo shows a group of young people meeting for a Sunday school class. The teacher at the left is Alice Henman. (College Avenue United Methodist Church.)

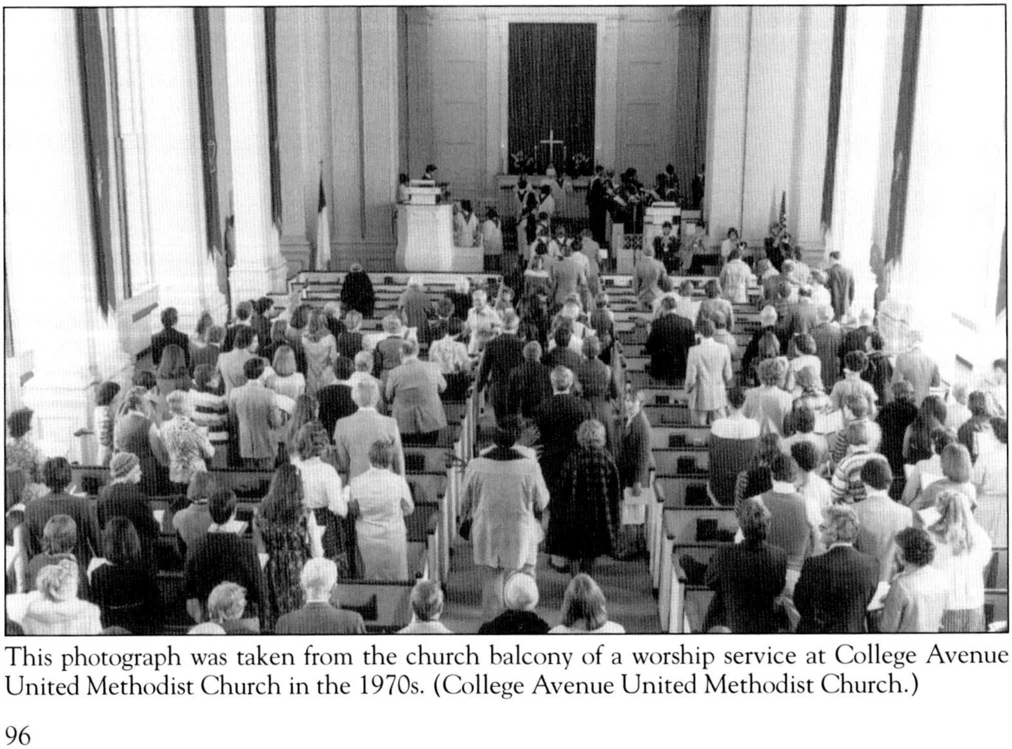

This photograph was taken from the church balcony of a worship service at College Avenue United Methodist Church in the 1970s. (College Avenue United Methodist Church.)

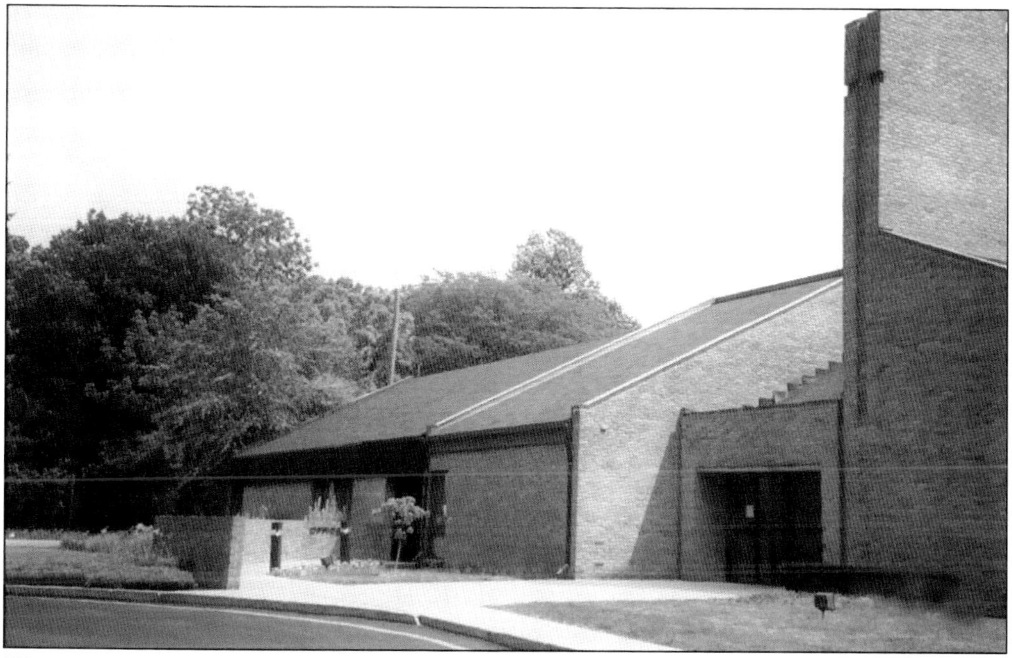

Westminster Presbyterian Church was formed in 1967 when six families purchased the former church building of the Northside Church of God at the corner of Riverside and Tillotson, one block west of the Ball State campus. The church was originally affiliated with the Reformed Presbyterian Church, Evangelical Synod (RPCES). In 1982, the RPCES affiliated with the Presbyterian Church in America (PCA). The church building , pictured above, was completed in 1981. (Deborah L. Geelhoed.)

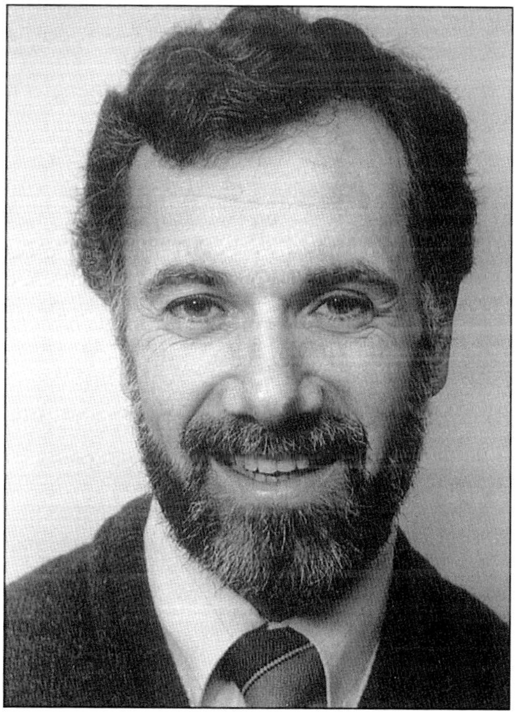

Petros Roukas, a Greek American who received his theological training in both England and the United States, served as the pastor of Westminster Presbyterian Church from 1984 to 1999, a period of rapid growth for the church. (James Garringer.)

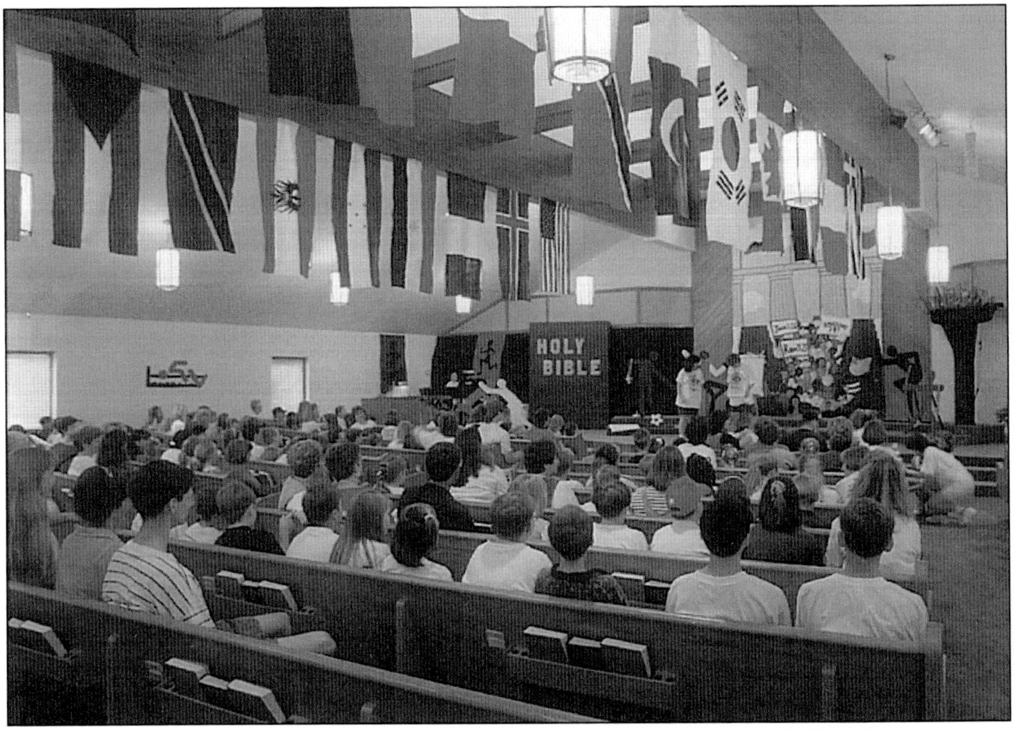

In 1979, Westminster Presbyterian Church began an ambitious summer Bible school program that brought attendance from hundreds of children in the church community and in the nearby neighborhoods. This photo shows a gathering of the children in the summer Bible school. (James Garringer.)

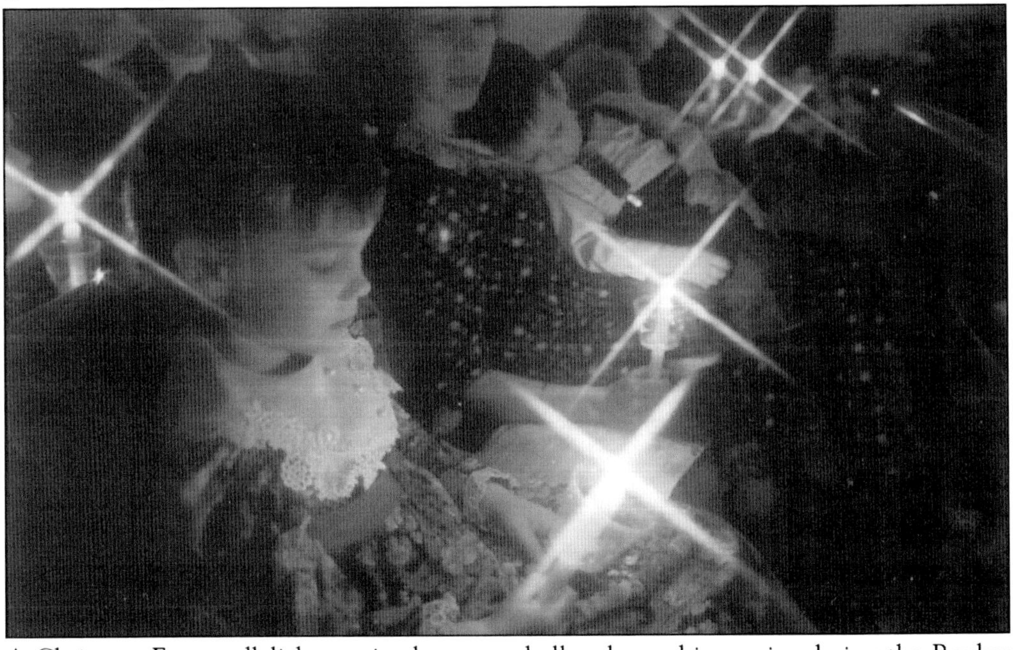

A Christmas Eve candlelight service became a hallmark worship service during the Roukas years at Westminster Presbyterian Church. (James Garringer.)

Five

The Machinery of Government

In *Middletown*, Robert and Helen Lynd paid little attention to Muncie's political system and the manner in which politics and government were exercised in the city. In fact, the Lynds appeared to be somewhat dismissive of the attitude of Munsonians toward their government, especially bemused by the local attitude that politics could be handled in an almost casual, informal fashion. "There is no area in Middletown's life, save religion, where symbol is more admittedly and patently divorced from reality than in government," they wrote in *Middletown in Transition* (p. 322).

In *Middletown in Transition*, the Lynds gave considerably more attention to politics, even going so far as to label a section of the book, "The Machinery of Government" (pp. 319–372). In this section, the Lynds were openly critical of Muncie's political system, which they described as antiquated, sometimes corrupt, and lacking in the ability to make changes for the better in the community. Most shocking of all to the Lynds was the apathy among the citizenry regarding a desire for more effective, progressive government, especially in regard to solving some of the city's most serious problems. Nevertheless, Muncie's city administrations had their share of memorable personalities, as these photographs demonstrate.

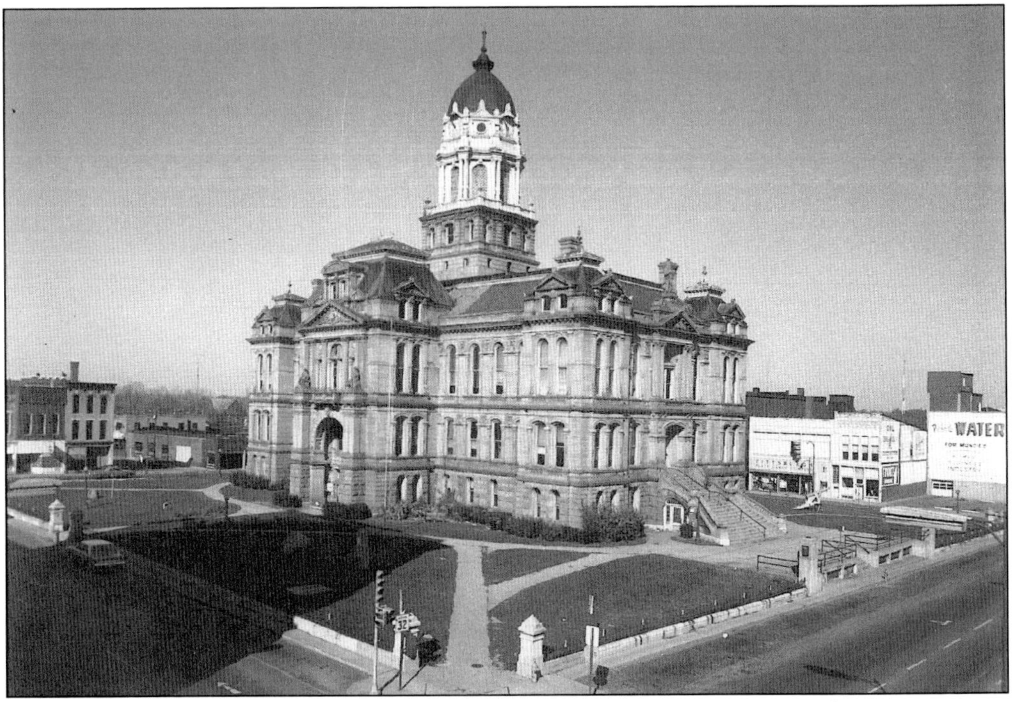

The historic Delaware County Courthouse was razed in 1967 to make way for a new county building. The Delaware County Courthouse was indicative of many stately county courthouses in central Indiana. (BSUA-SG.)

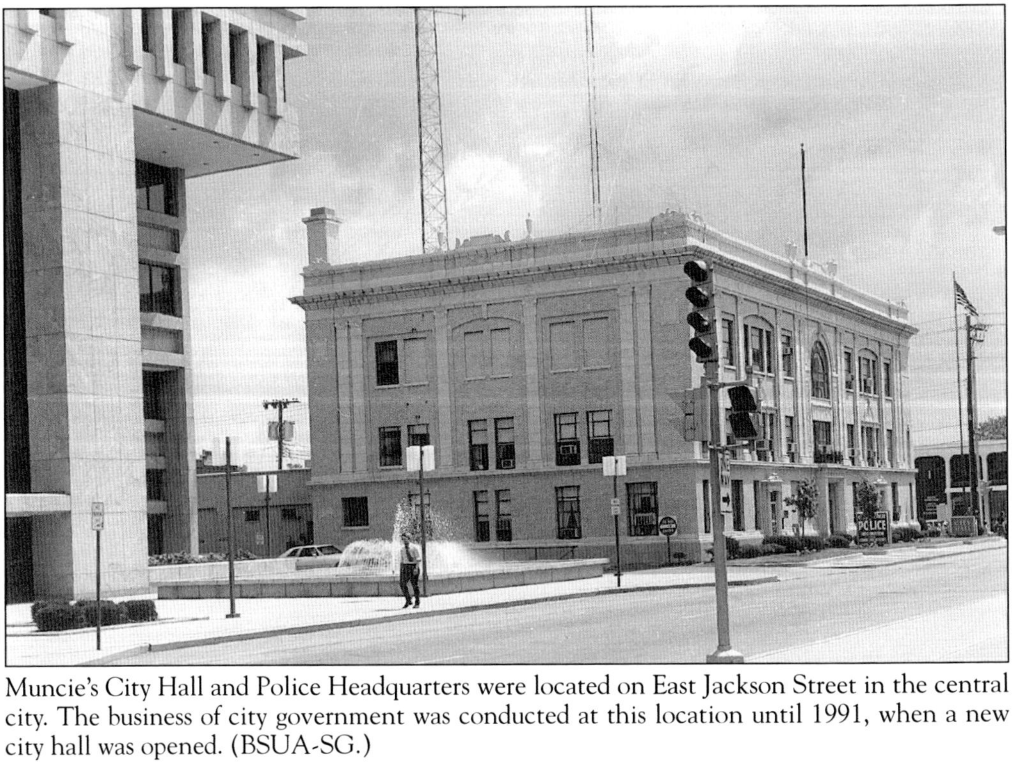

Muncie's City Hall and Police Headquarters were located on East Jackson Street in the central city. The business of city government was conducted at this location until 1991, when a new city hall was opened. (BSUA-SG.)

Pictured is George Dale, mayor of Muncie from 1930 to 1934. The word used most often to describe Dale was "feisty." A crusading editor and publisher by profession, Dale took on the Muncie power structure with reckless abandon, challenging the local business establishment, the newspapers, and the influence of the Ku Klux Klan in Muncie. (BSUA-SG.)

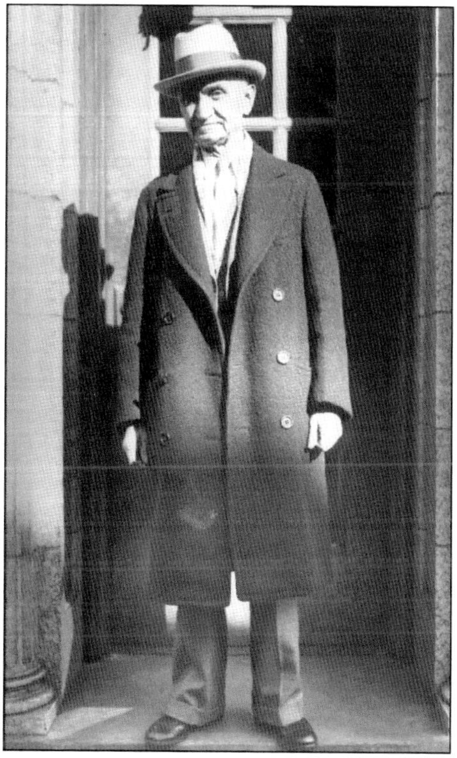

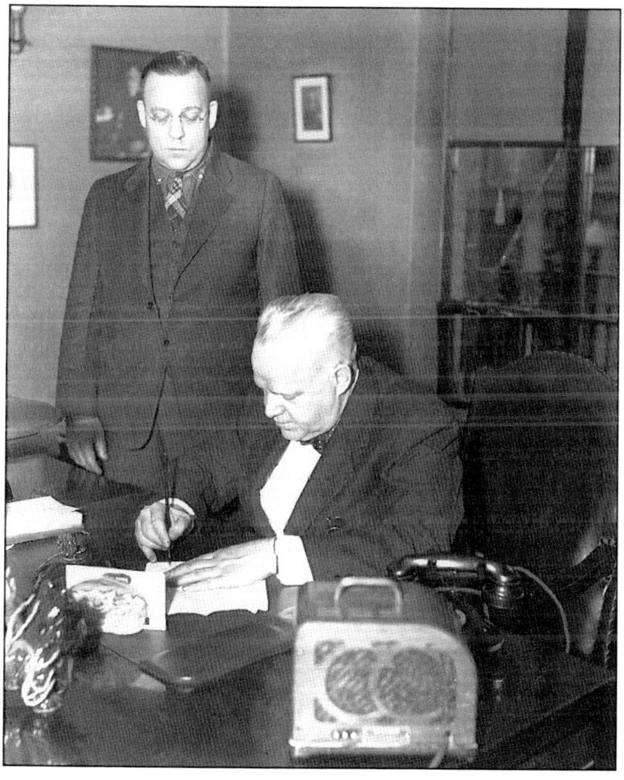

Rollin H. Bunch (seated) was mayor of Muncie from 1914 to 1917, 1918 to 1919, and again from 1935 to 1938. Bunch was known as an urban populist who drew much of his support from working class Munsonians. (BSUA-SG.)

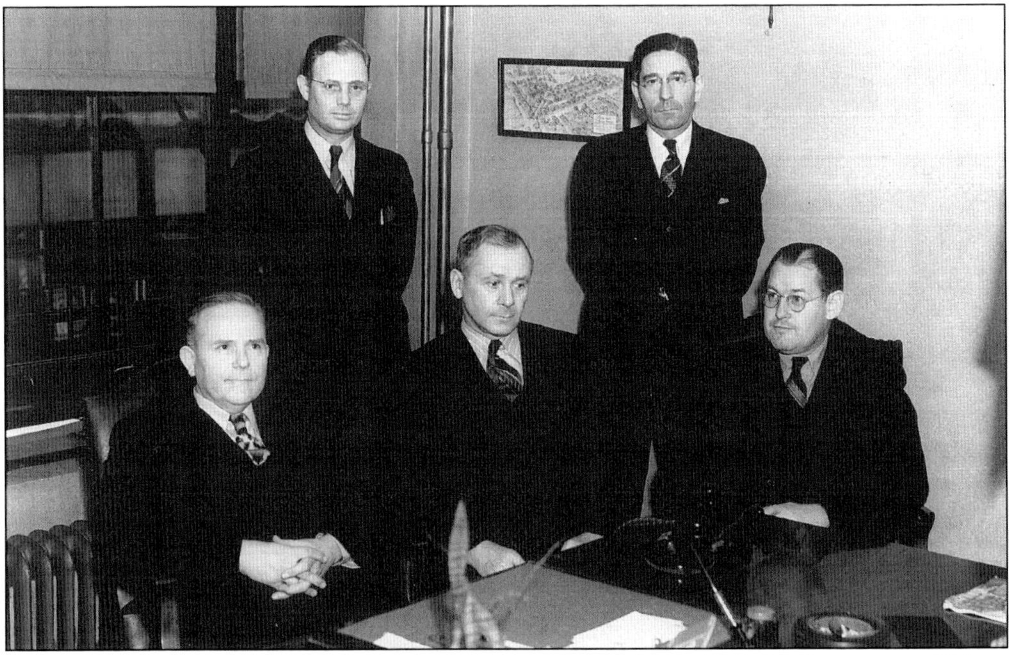

Ira G. Wilson, seated at left, was mayor of Muncie from 1938 to 1942. In this picture, Wilson is shown with several executives from General Motors Corporation. General Motors operated two major factories in Muncie during the Depression—a transmission plant and a Delco battery facility. (BSUA.)

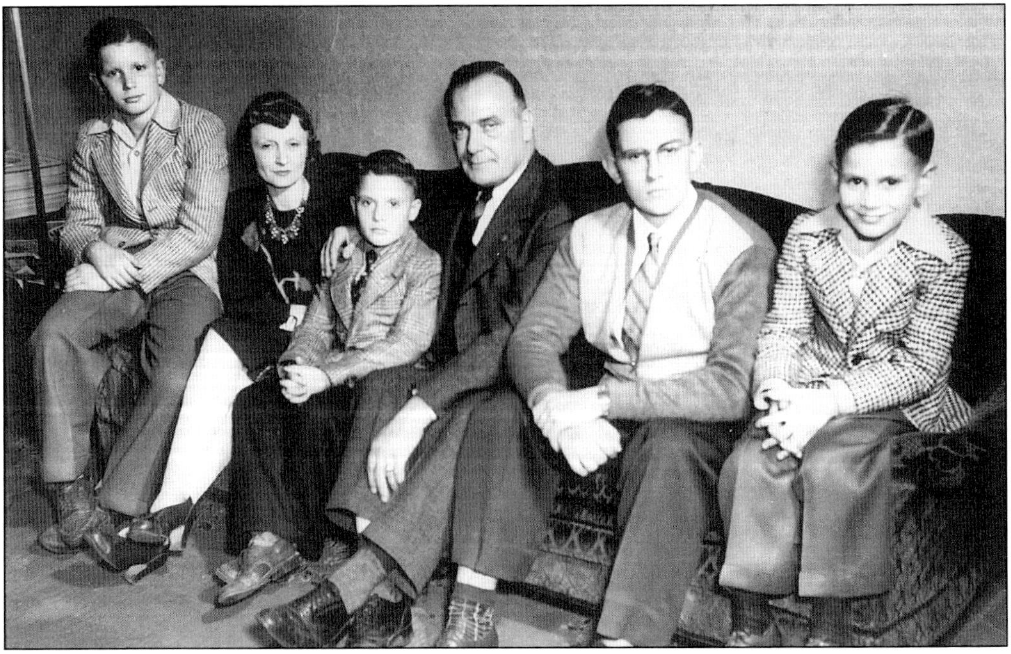

John C. Hampton was mayor of Muncie from 1926 to 1929, and 1943 to 1947. Hampton was a Republican and one of the party's leading vote-gatherers during his career. In this photo, he poses with his family—his wife Reba and sons, from left to right: John, David, Bill Blaney (a stepson), and Philip. (BSUA-SG.)

Campaigns and Campaigners

One of Muncie's unique claims to political recognition concerns the fact that, in every presidential election since 1932, Muncie has voted for the winning candidate, with the exception of 1960 when Richard Nixon's local vote total surpassed that of John F. Kennedy. Few communities across the United States can match Muncie's record in showing a preference for the candidate with the most national appeal. Writers such as Ron Grossman of the *Chicago Tribune* (September 2, 1992) and Ed Field of the *Economist* (November 2, 1996) have pointed out how national trends and candidate preferences have consistently worked their way into Muncie's political consciousness. Field even went so far as to refer to Muncie as the "quintessential home of the swing voter." Regardless, Muncie's political history during the 20th century has seen numerous candidates for national office visit the city during their campaign stops.

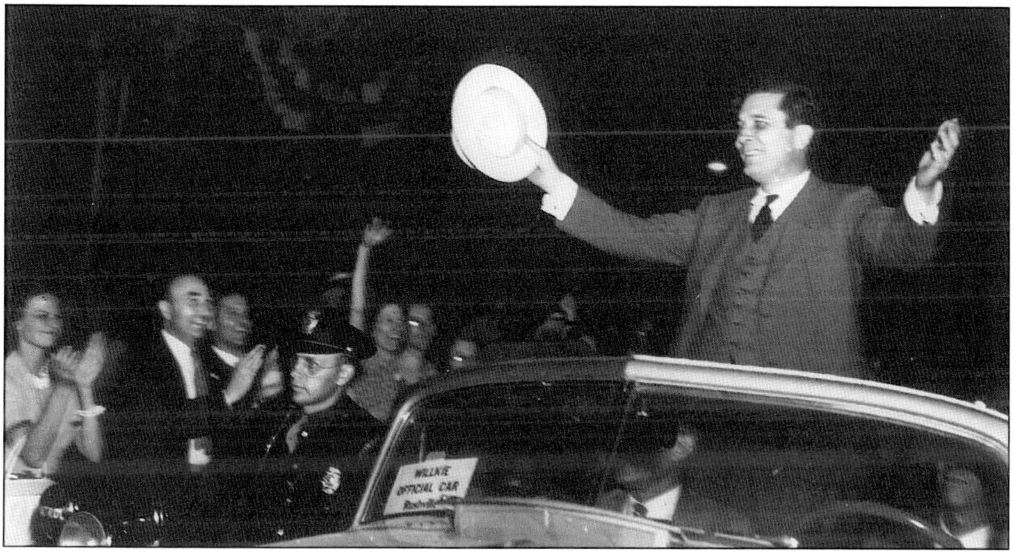

Wendell Willkie, a native Hoosier, won the Republican presidential nomination in 1940. In this photo, Willkie is shown campaigning in Rushville, 50 miles south of Muncie, at a political rally. (BSUA-SG.)

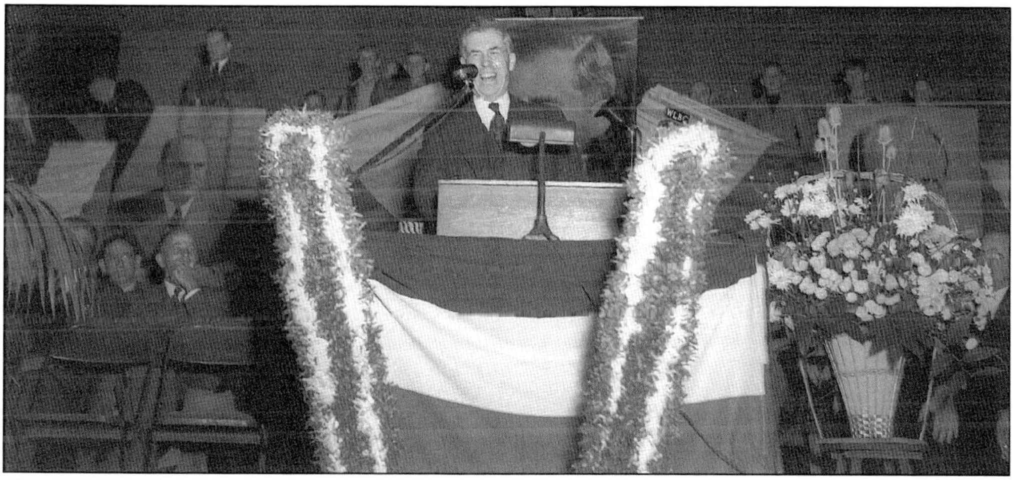

Henry A. Wallace, Democratic candidate for vice president in 1940, campaigned in Muncie at the Fieldhouse in support of President Franklin D. Roosevelt and his drive for a third presidential term. (BSUA-SG.)

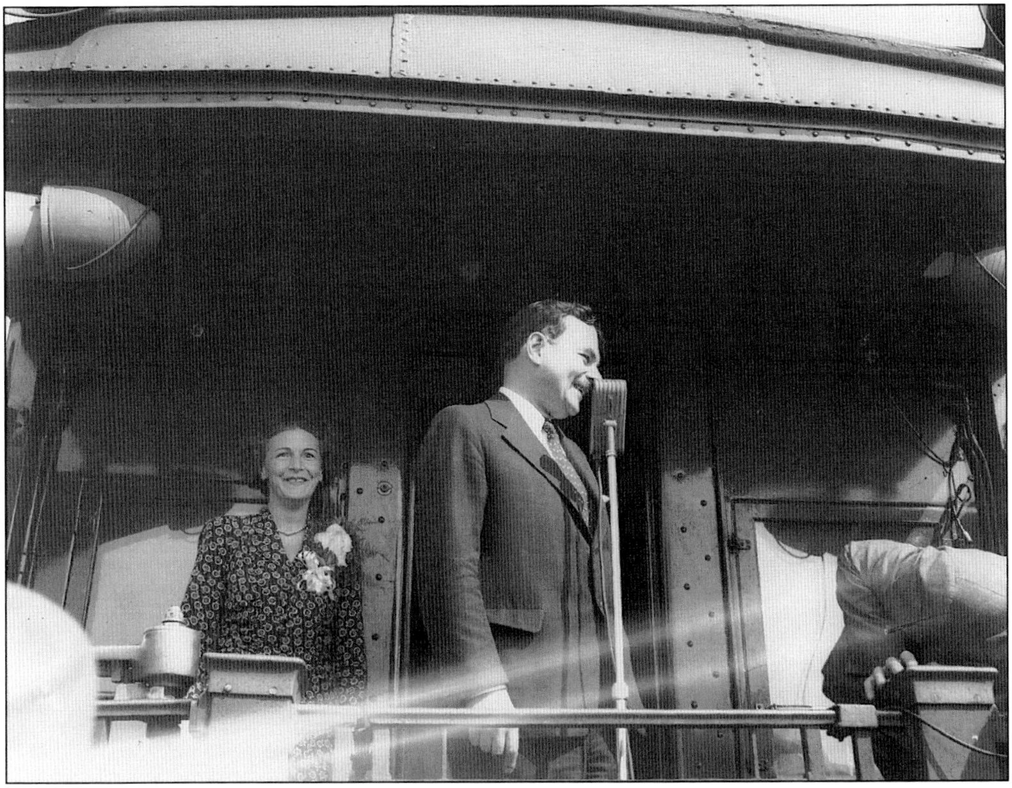

Thomas E. Dewey, Republican presidential candidate in 1944, whistle-stopped through Muncie with his wife, Frances. (BSUA-SG.)

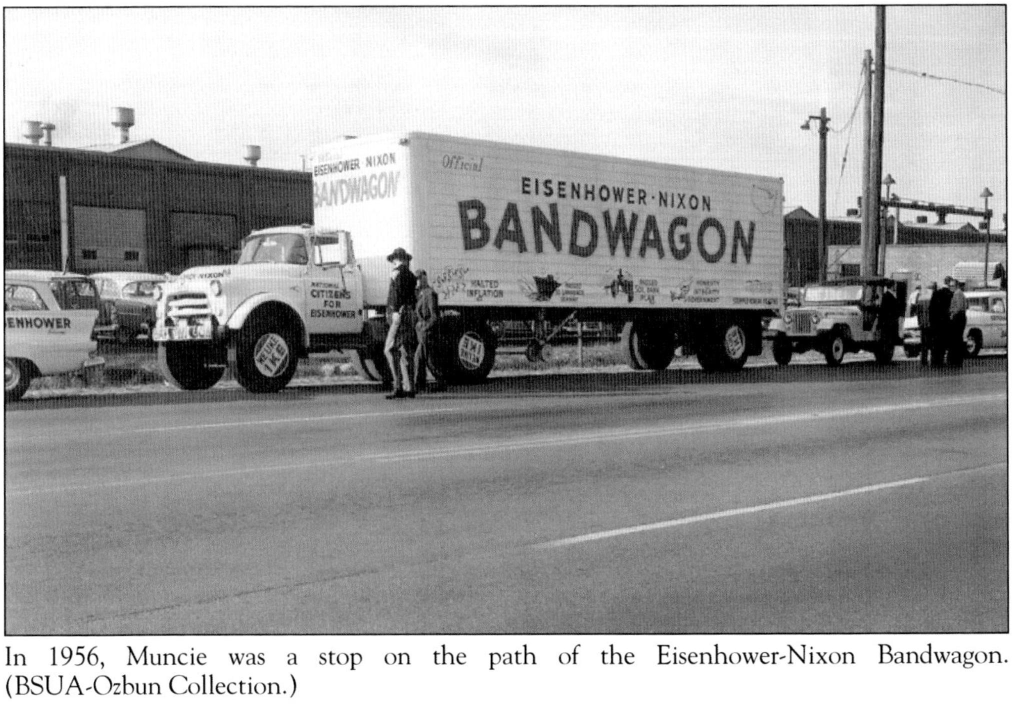

In 1956, Muncie was a stop on the path of the Eisenhower-Nixon Bandwagon. (BSUA-Ozbun Collection.)

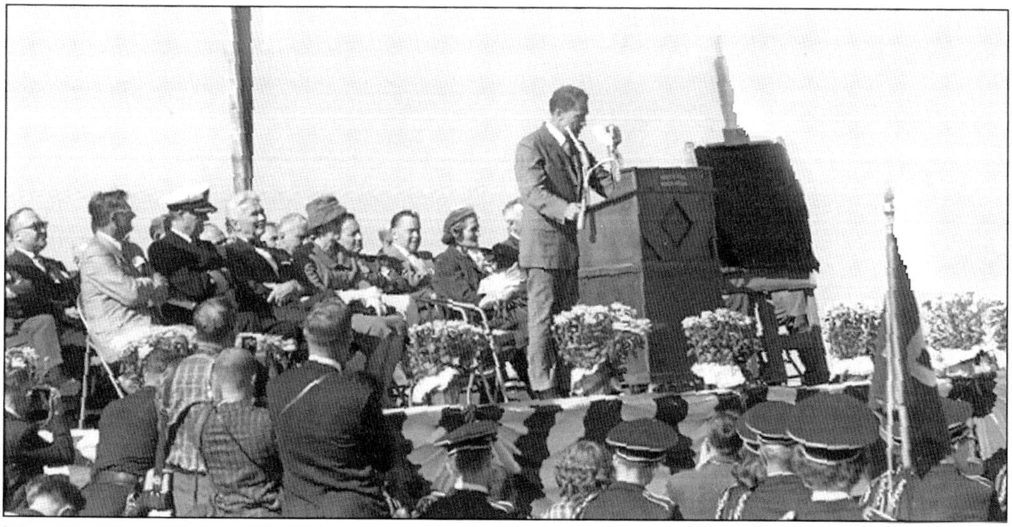

Vice President Richard M. Nixon gave the dedicatory address for the opening of Johnson Field at the Delaware County airport in 1958. (Roger Pelham.)

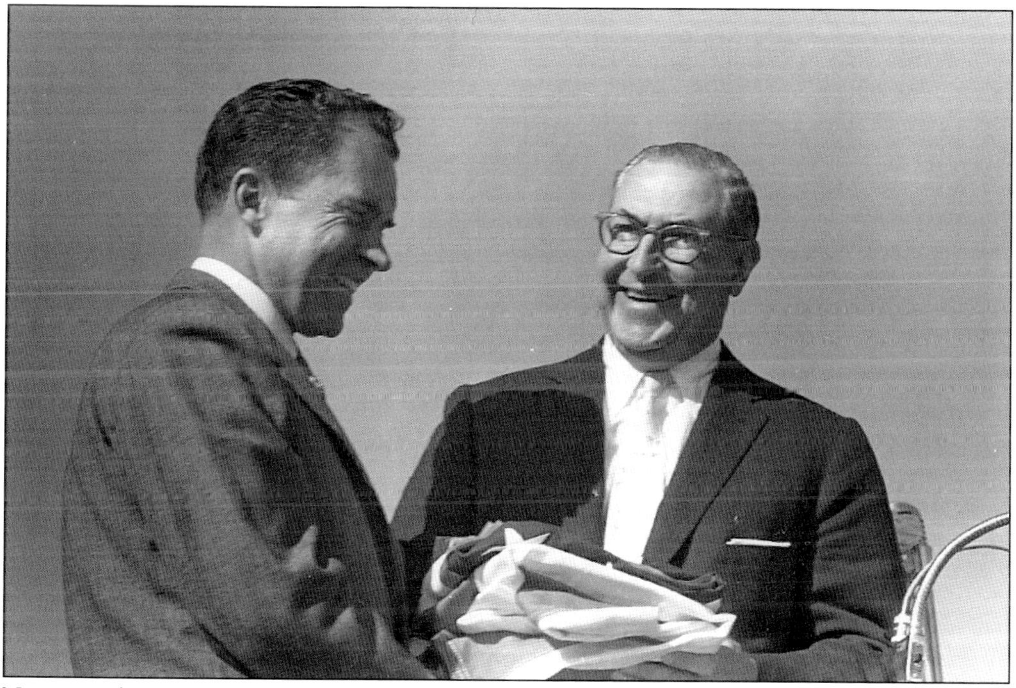

Nixon is shown in this photograph with Abbott Johnson, a Muncie industrialist and civic leader, for whom Johnson Field was named. (Roger Pelham.)

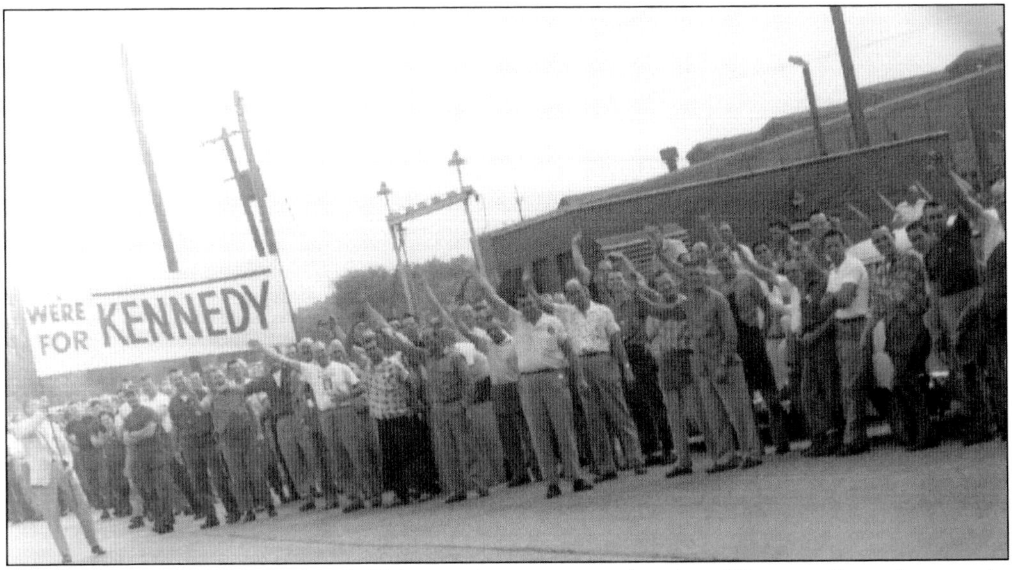

Members of the UAW lined Kilgore Avenue outside the Warner Gear factory in 1960 in anticipation of Senator John F. Kennedy's arrival in Muncie. (BSUA-Everett Ferrill Collection.)

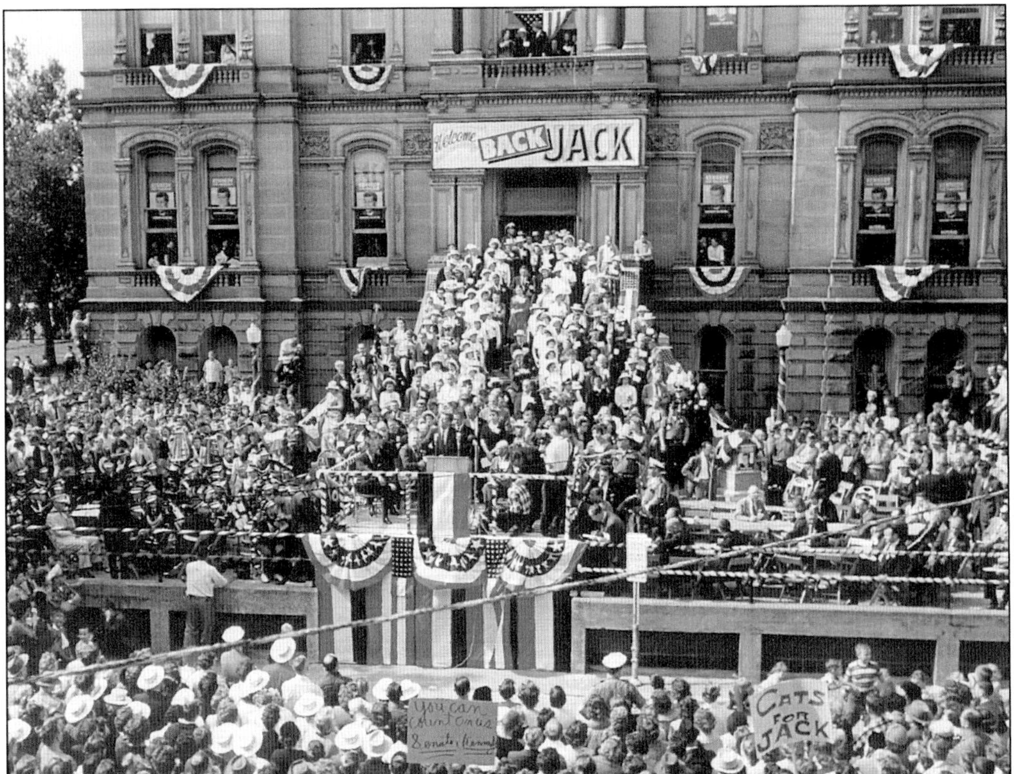

John F. Kennedy addressed a crowd numbering in the thousands at the Delaware County Courthouse during the presidential campaign of 1960. Kennedy's appearance was one of the most memorable political rallies in Muncie's history. (BSUA-Marshall Hanley Collection.)

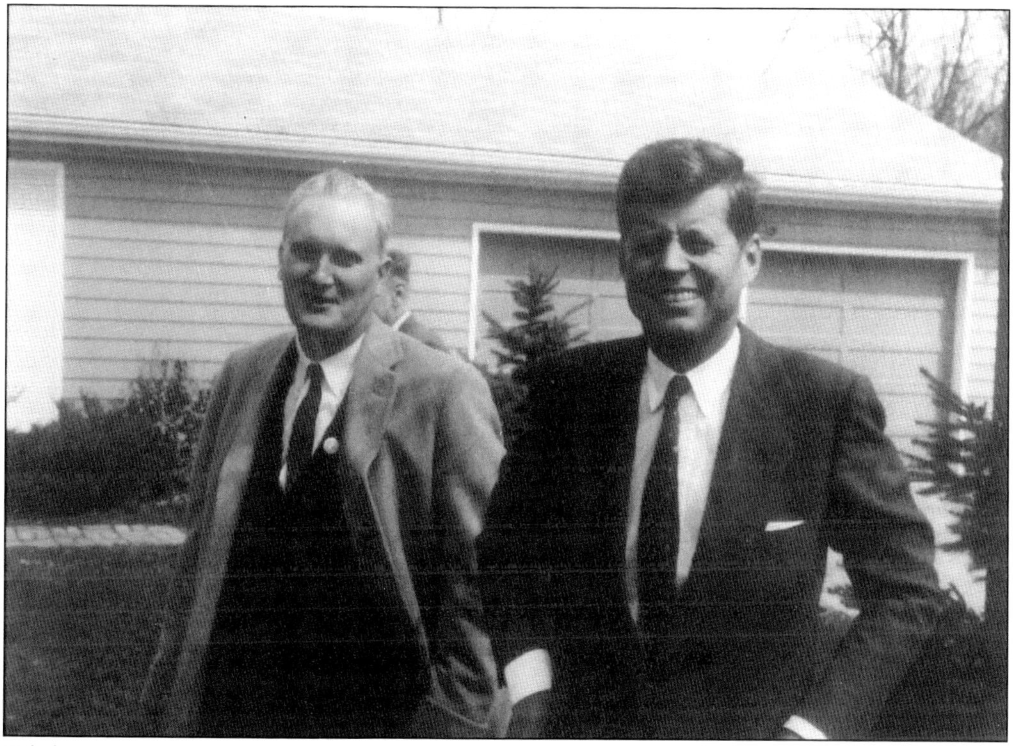

While in Muncie, Kennedy was a guest of local attorney Marshall Hanley, left. (BSUA- Marshall Hanley Collection.)

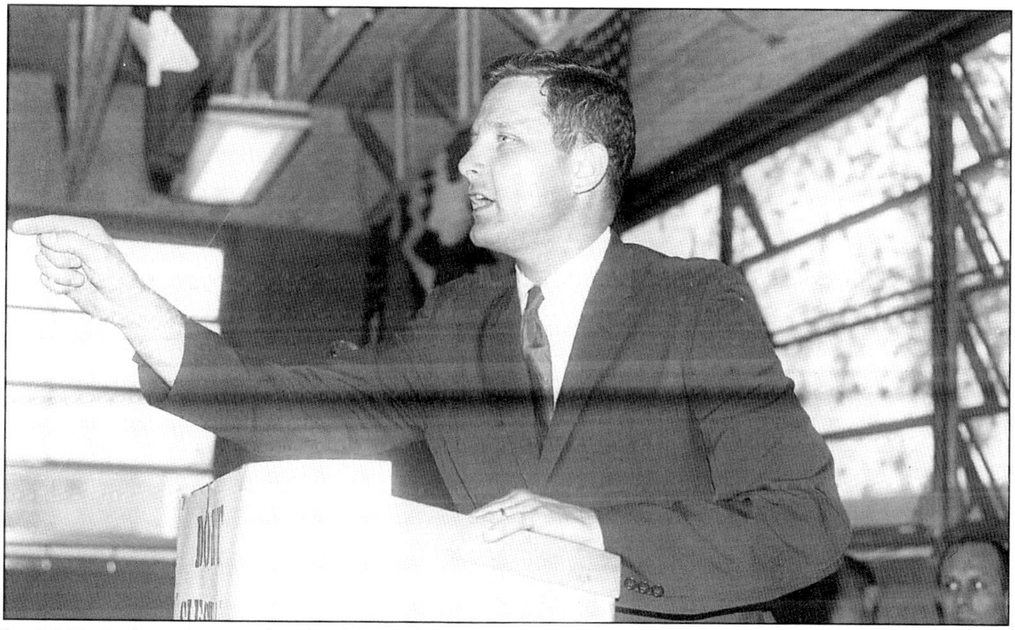

In 1962, Indiana's race for the United States Senate between incumbent Republican Homer Capehart and Democratic challenger Birch Bayh was especially heated. In this photo, Bayh addressed a group of labor supporters at the UAW hall on Madison Street. (BSUA-Everett Ferrill Collection.)

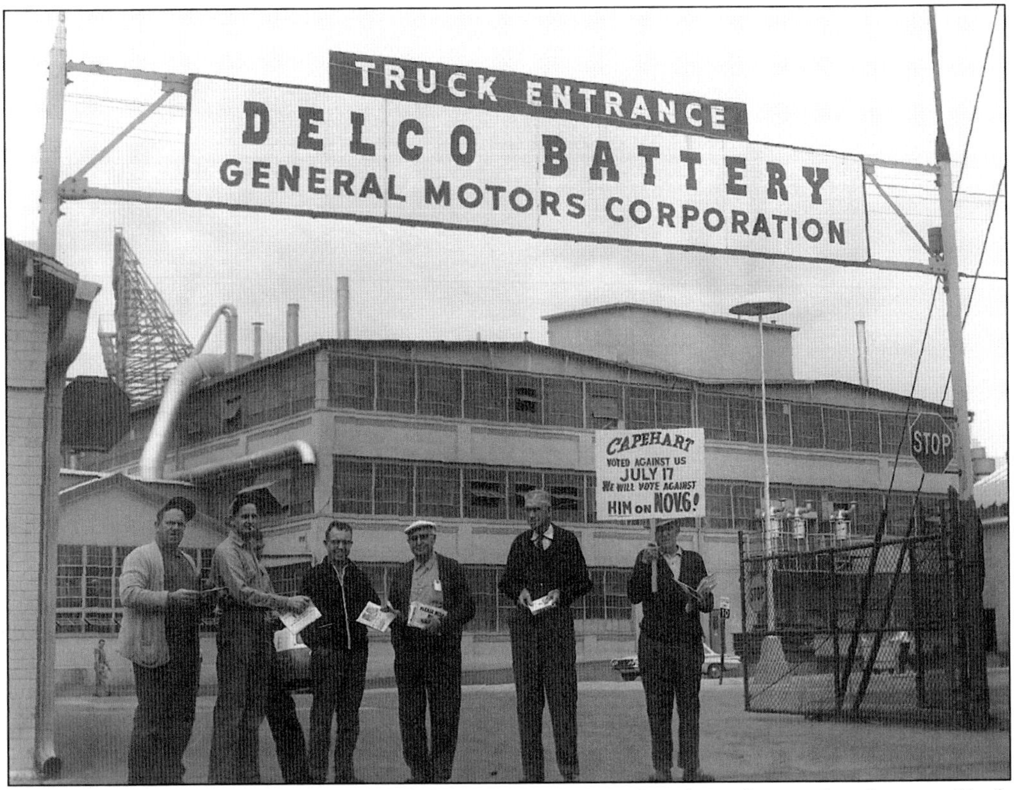

Several members of the UAW showed their opposition to Capehart during the election. Bayh defeated Capehart in the November election. (BSUA-Everett Ferrill Collection.)

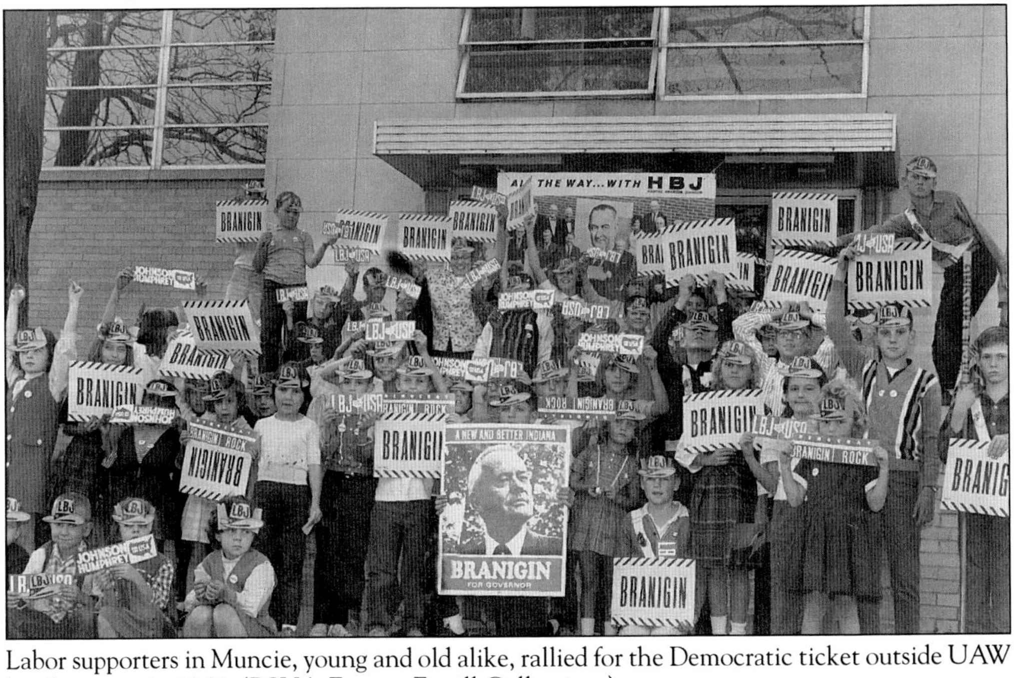

Labor supporters in Muncie, young and old alike, rallied for the Democratic ticket outside UAW headquarters in 1964. (BSUA-Everett Ferrill Collection.)

THE LOCAL SCENE

Politics in Muncie have been competitive between the two political parties, Democratic and Republican, throughout the city's history. During the early part of the 20th century, the Republican Party dominated local government. During mid-century, the Democratic Party rebounded, helped along considerably by the support it received from the ranks of organized labor. In the 1980s and 1990s, the Republicans held the mayoralty more often than the Democrats, but were checked by Democratic control of the City Council. If the Lynds were to visit Muncie once again, they would not be surprised by what they would observe in the local political situation.

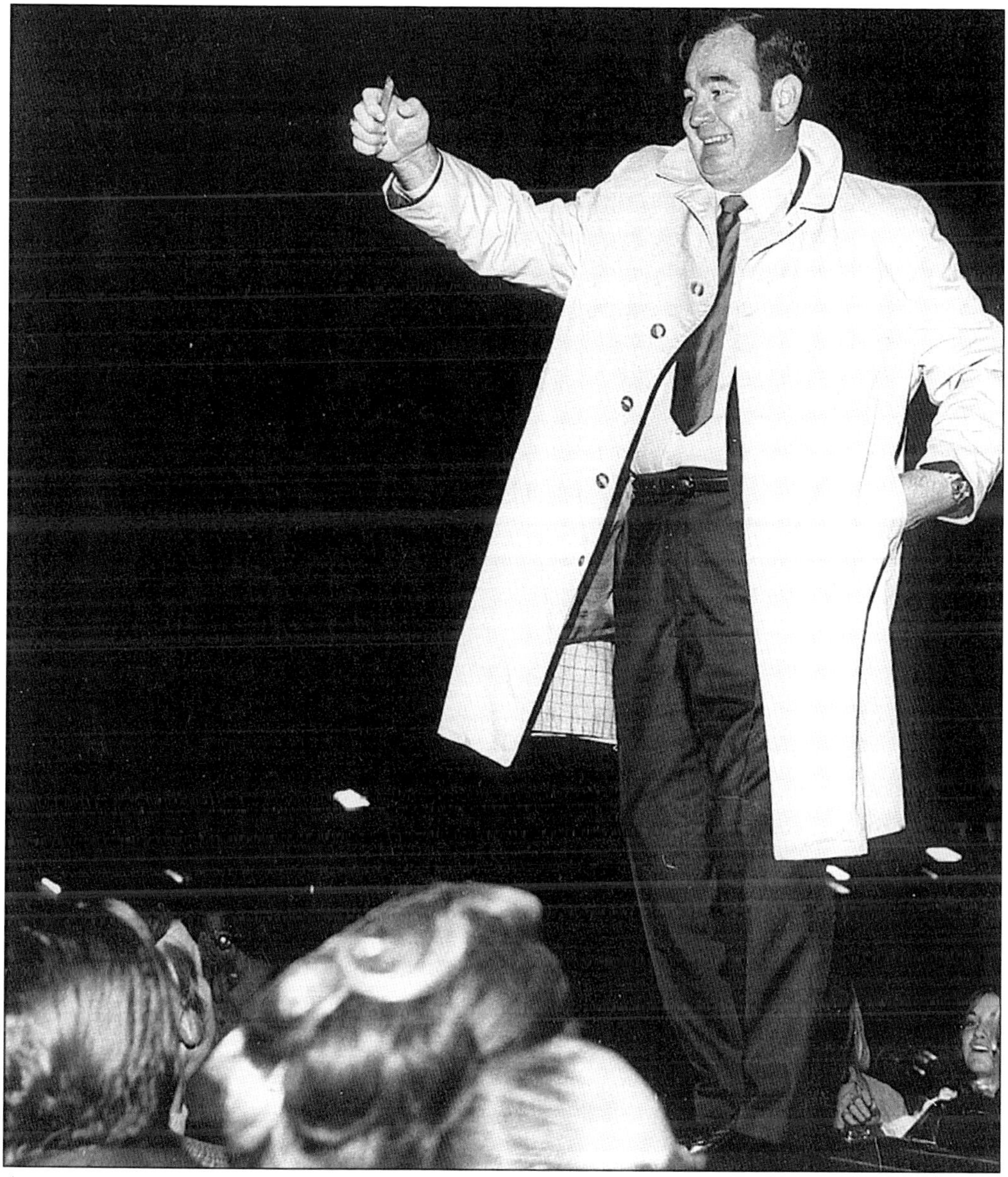

A major political figure in Muncie and Delaware County politics for over a quarter-century was James Patrick Carey. In this photograph, Carey greets his supporters after his victory in the county sheriff's race in 1970. (BSUA-James P. Carey Collection.)

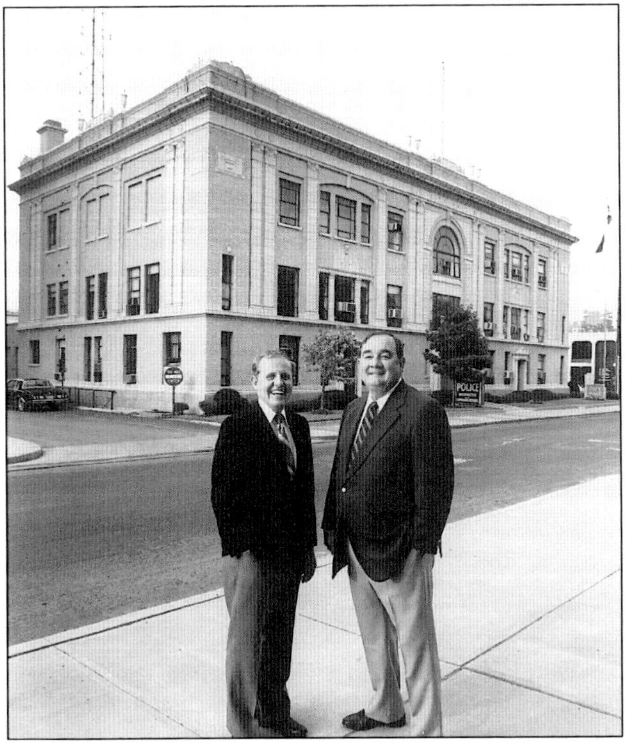

In 1979, Carey ran for mayor of Muncie for the first time. His opponent was Republican attorney Alan Wilson, left. The race between Carey and Wilson became the subject of *The Campaign*, the first film in the six-part documentary, *Middletown*, directed by Peter Davis and produced by the Public Broadcasting Service (PBS). The documentary was shown nationwide in 1981–1983. In 1979, Wilson defeated Carey, a result which most analysts considered an upset. In 1983, however, Carey rolled to a landslide victory over Wilson. (BSUA-James P. Carey Collection.)

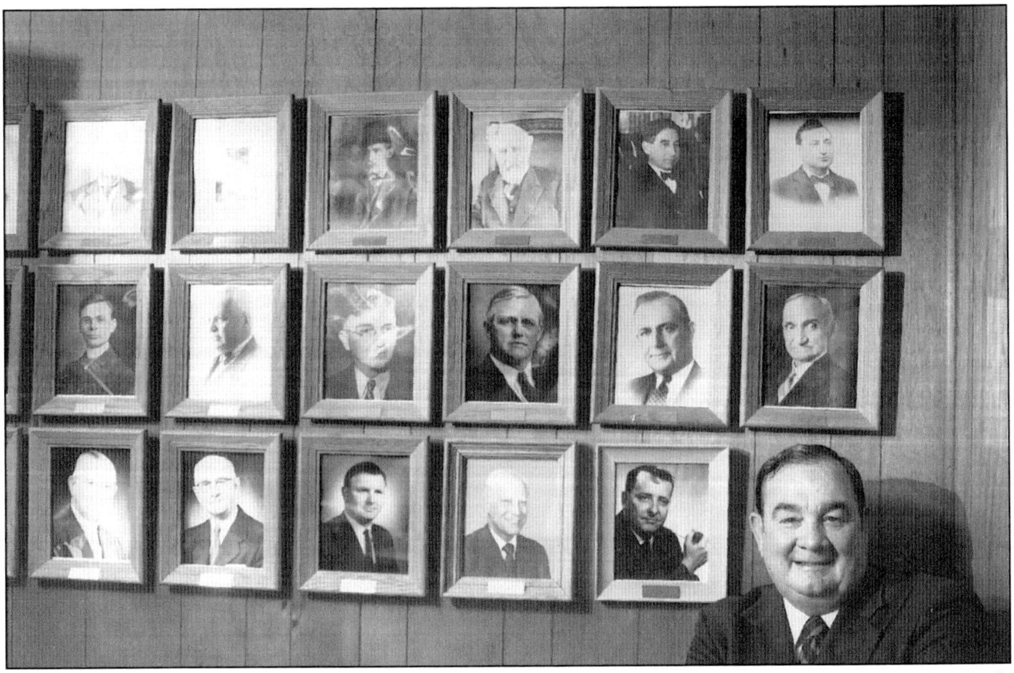

Carey poses in the mayor's office alongside a collection of portraits of his predecessors. An Irish American, Carey once declared that the political leader which he admired most was Richard J. Daley, also an Irish American, who was the mayor of Chicago from the mid-1950s to the mid-1970s. (BSUA-James P. Carey Collection.)

An energetic campaigner, Carey engages in the political art of baby kissing during a St. Patrick's Day event. (BSUA-James P. Carey Collection.)

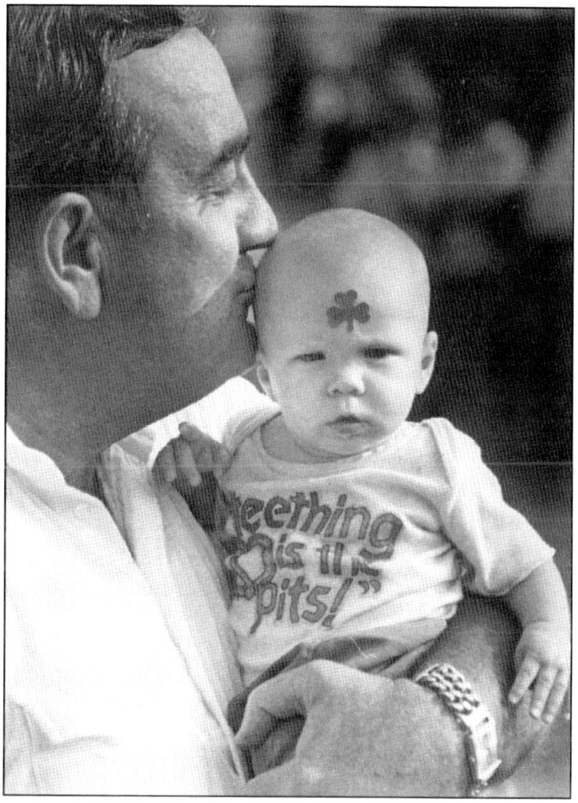

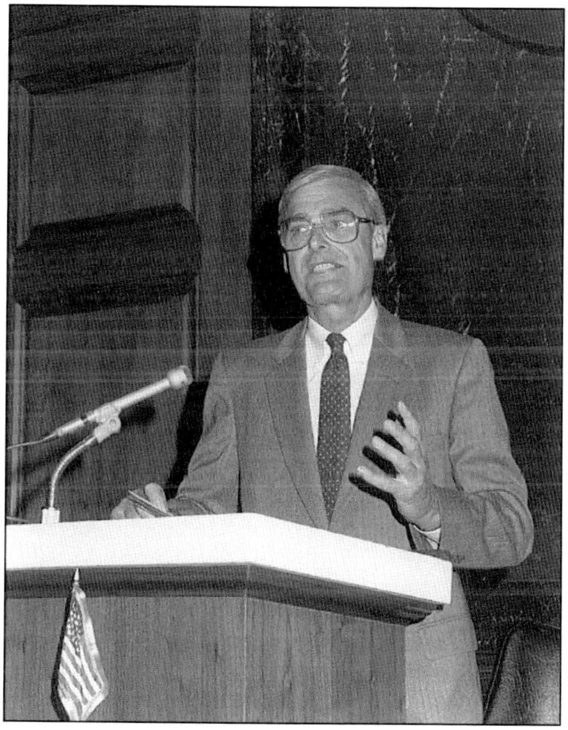

State Representative J. Roberts Dailey, Republican member of the Indiana General Assembly from 1976 to 1986, is pictured at left. From 1980 to 1986, Dailey was the Speaker of the House of Representatives. (BSUA-J. Roberts Dailey Collection.)

Daniel Kelley Jr. was a leader in the Muncie local of the United Steelworkers of America and a member of the Muncie City Council longer than any other African American. (Hurley C. Goodall.)

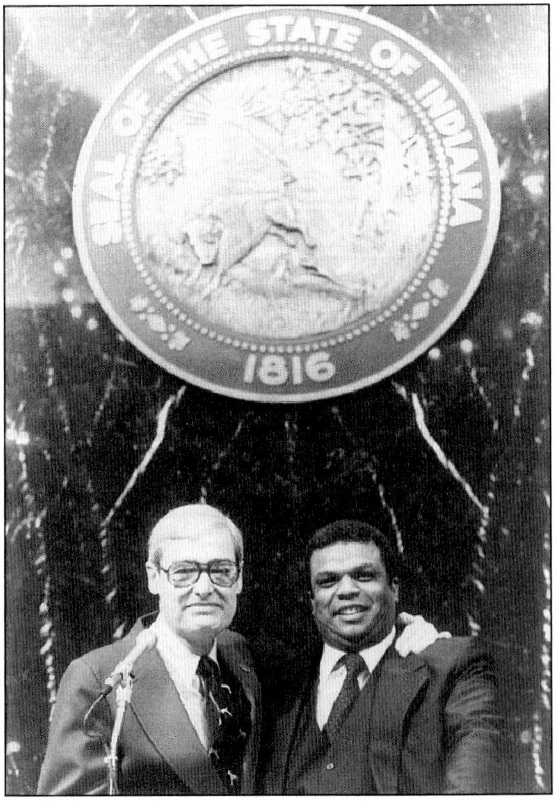

J. Roberts Dailey, Republican, and Hurley C. Goodall, Democrat, represented Muncie and Delaware County in the Indiana House of Representative for much of the 1970s and 1980s. Together they formed an influential duo for advancing the interests of the community. Dailey held the powerful position of Speaker; at the same time, Goodall held a leadership post in the minority and was also a founder of the Indiana Legislative Black Caucus. (BSUA-J. Roberts Dailey Collection.)

CONCLUSION

A Community In Search of a New Identity

Beginning in the mid-1990s, the pace of de-industrialization in Muncie accelerated. In 1996, the Borg Warner Automotive Corporation announced the sale of a major segment of its business to an enterprise in Mexico. In 1998, Ball Corporation announced the impending move of its headquarters from Muncie to Bloomfield, Colorado, a decision which meant that Muncie would no longer be known as the home of the company with which it been synonymous for over a century. While the economic impact upon Muncie of Ball's move to Colorado was only modest, the community was nevertheless forced to deal with the reality that one of its major corporate partners was leaving the city. Then, almost immediately after the Ball announcement in 1998, General Motors Corporation declared that it was closing its Delco battery manufacturing plant in Muncie, a move which also signaled the end of GM's direct involvement with Muncie.

Given these unexpected developments, the community and its civic leaders were forced to make some decisions about the future identity of the city, given that the years of being an industrial center were coming to a close. The community possessed some definite strengths, however. Since the end of World War II, Muncie had become the regional center for health, higher education, retailing, and finance in east central Indiana. It was also making rapid strides toward becoming a center for youth sports, with nationally known programs in soccer, volleyball, and softball. A new initiative in community recreation and cultural activity was underway. Efforts were also being undertaken to lure new manufacturing businesses to the community, businesses that were oriented around high technology. The 21st century promises to be considerably different than the 20th century for this quintessential American community.

THE PHILANTHROPIC IMPULSE

Muncie's transition from its industrial past began in the mid-1980s when members of the Ball family and other civic leaders initiated several new programs in art, culture, and local history. Aided by philanthropic support from the Ball Brothers Foundation and the George and Frances Ball Foundation, two of Indiana's largest private foundations, the community embarked upon a new era of cultural awareness. In addition, several community leaders actively promoted the establishment and growth of the Community Foundation of Muncie and Delaware County, an organization which provided support to educational institutions, social service organizations, and other non-profit groups.

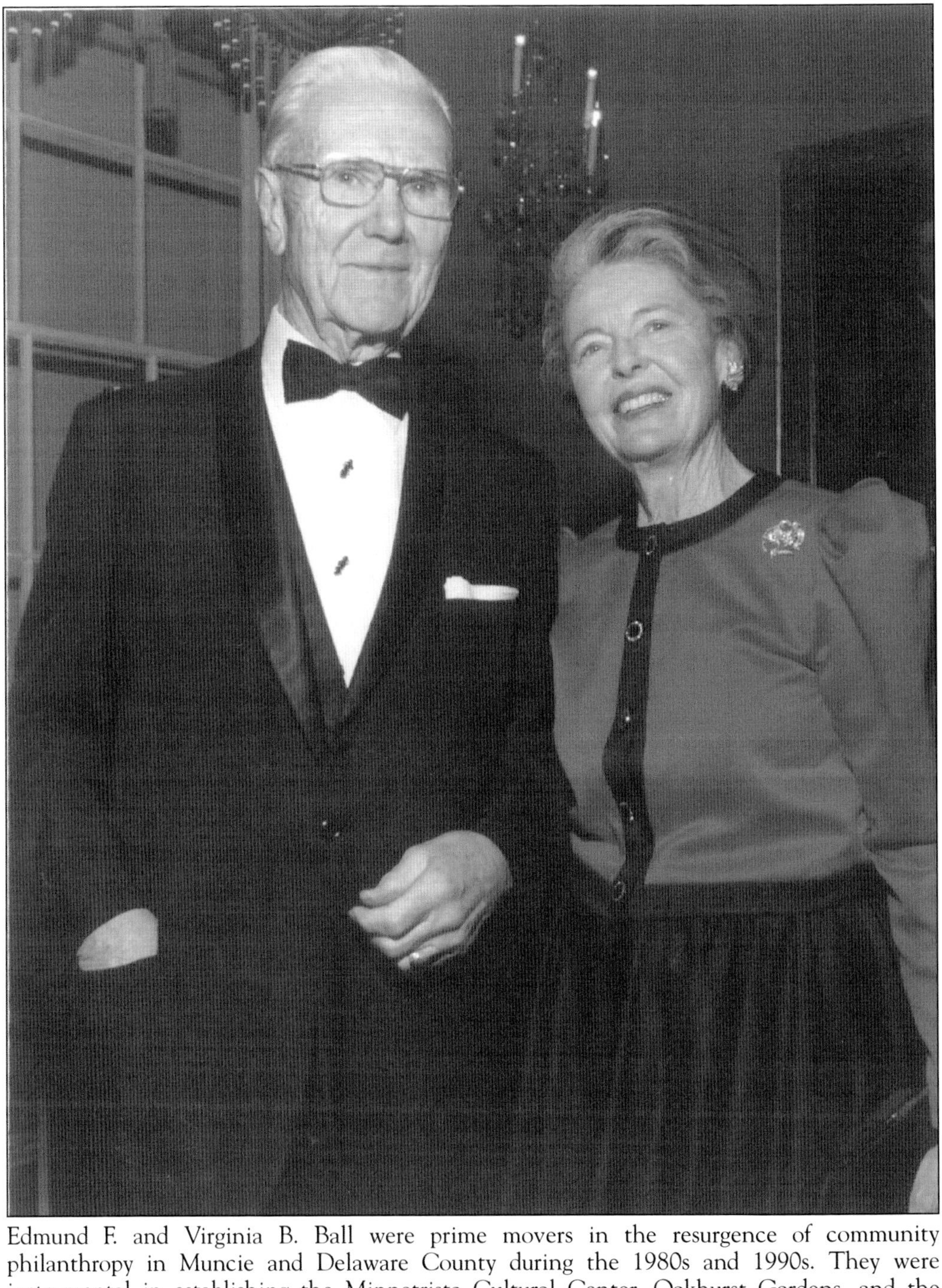

Edmund F. and Virginia B. Ball were prime movers in the resurgence of community philanthropy in Muncie and Delaware County during the 1980s and 1990s. They were instrumental in establishing the Minnetrista Cultural Center, Oakhurst Gardens, and the Community Foundation of Muncie and Delaware County. In addition, they remained major benefactors of Ball State University through an endowment for a distinguished professorship in telecommunications, as well as the establishment of the Virginia B. Ball Center for Creative Inquiry. (Ball Associates.)

John W. and Janice Fisher have been major benefactors of Ball State University—specifically of programs in wellness, exercise physiology, and athletic training. John Fisher built a 42-year career as an officer of Ball Corporation, retiring in 1986 as chairman and chief executive officer. During his leadership of the business from 1970 to 1986, Ball Corporation made the transition from a privately-held business with annual sales approaching $200 million, to a publicly traded corporation with annual sales exceeding $1 billion. He also served one term as the head of the National Association of Manufacturers in 1979–1980. (Ball Associates.)

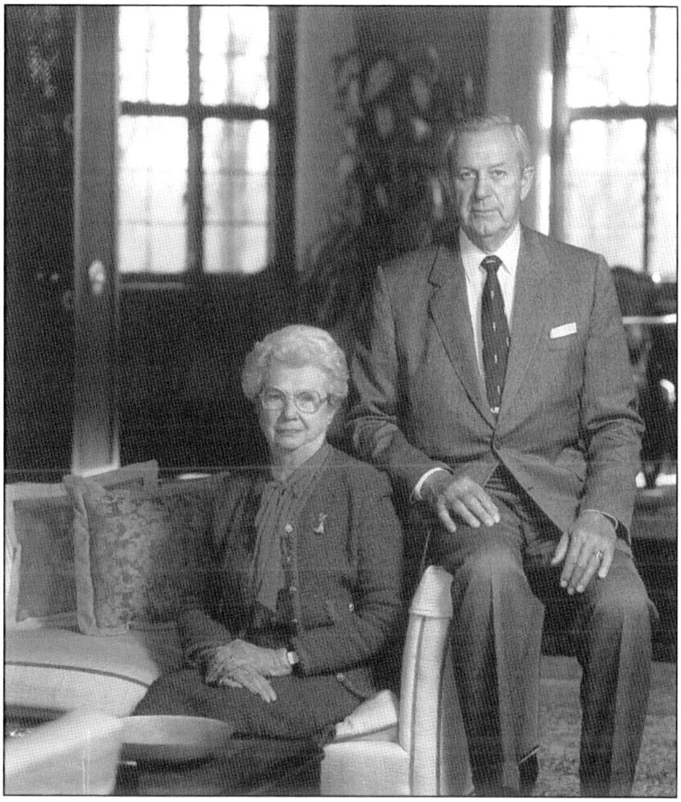

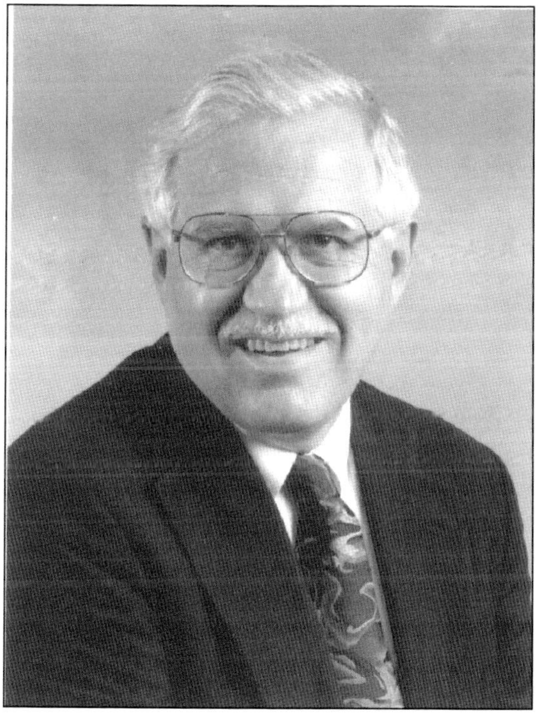

Douglas A. Bakken became the executive director of the Ball Brothers Foundation in 1983. An active participant in the non-profit community throughout Indiana, Bakken has also been a persuasive advocate for many programs of civic improvement in Muncie and Delaware County. (Ball Associates.)

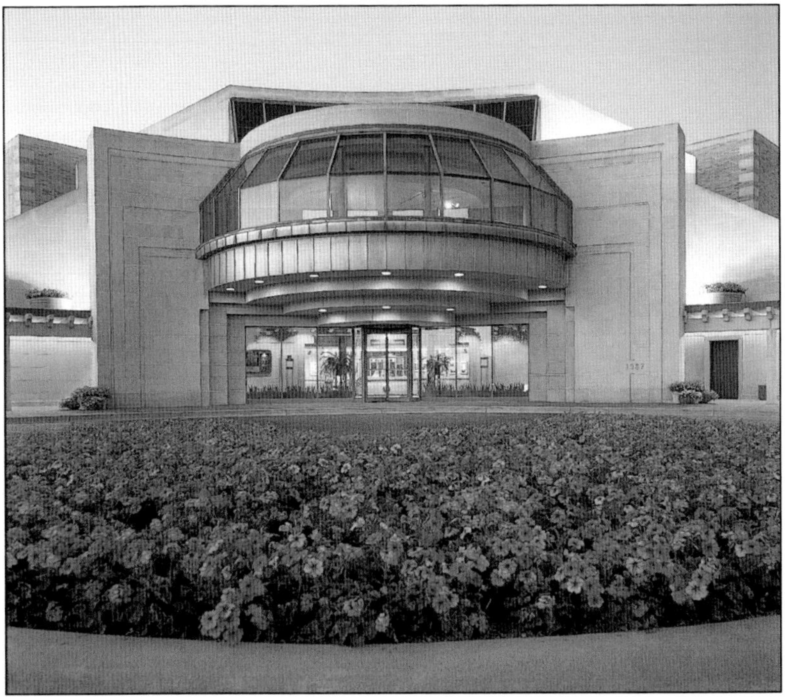

The Minnetrista Cultural Center opened in 1988 and was the symbol of the new approach to cultural and local history that took root in Muncie during the 1980s. The Minnetrista Cultural Center was a project supported by the Ball Brothers Foundation and the George and Frances Ball Foundation. (Minnetrista Cultural Center.)

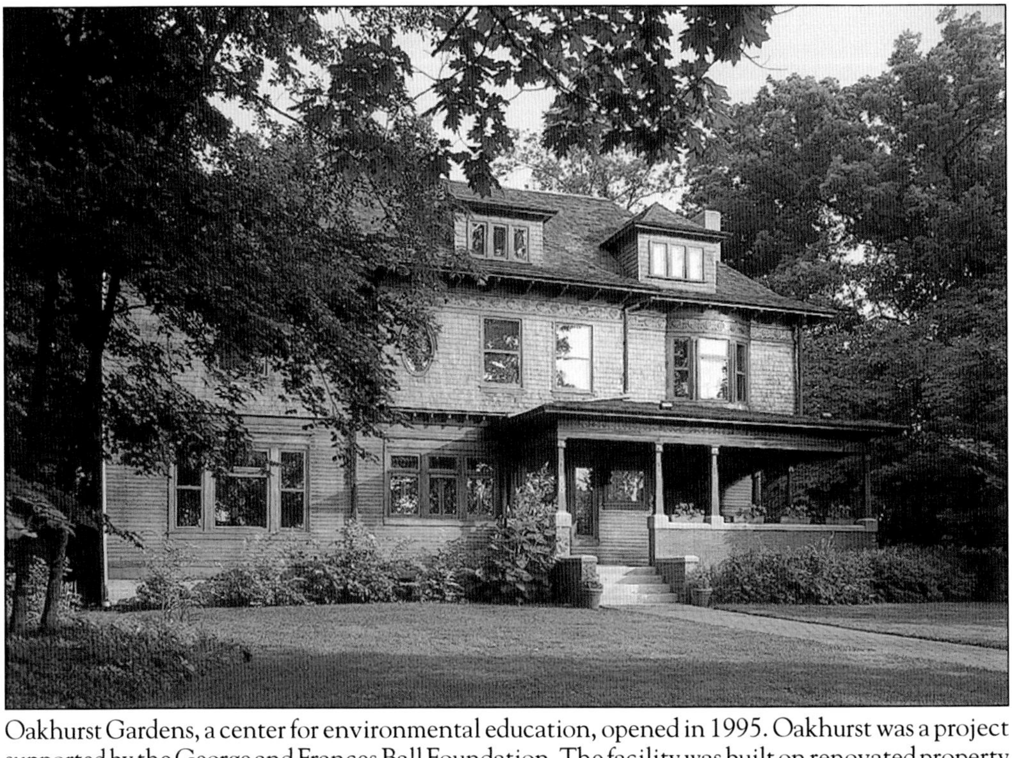

Oakhurst Gardens, a center for environmental education, opened in 1995. Oakhurst was a project supported by the George and Frances Ball Foundation. The facility was built on renovated property that was originally the home of George and Frances Ball. (Minnetrista Cultural Center.)

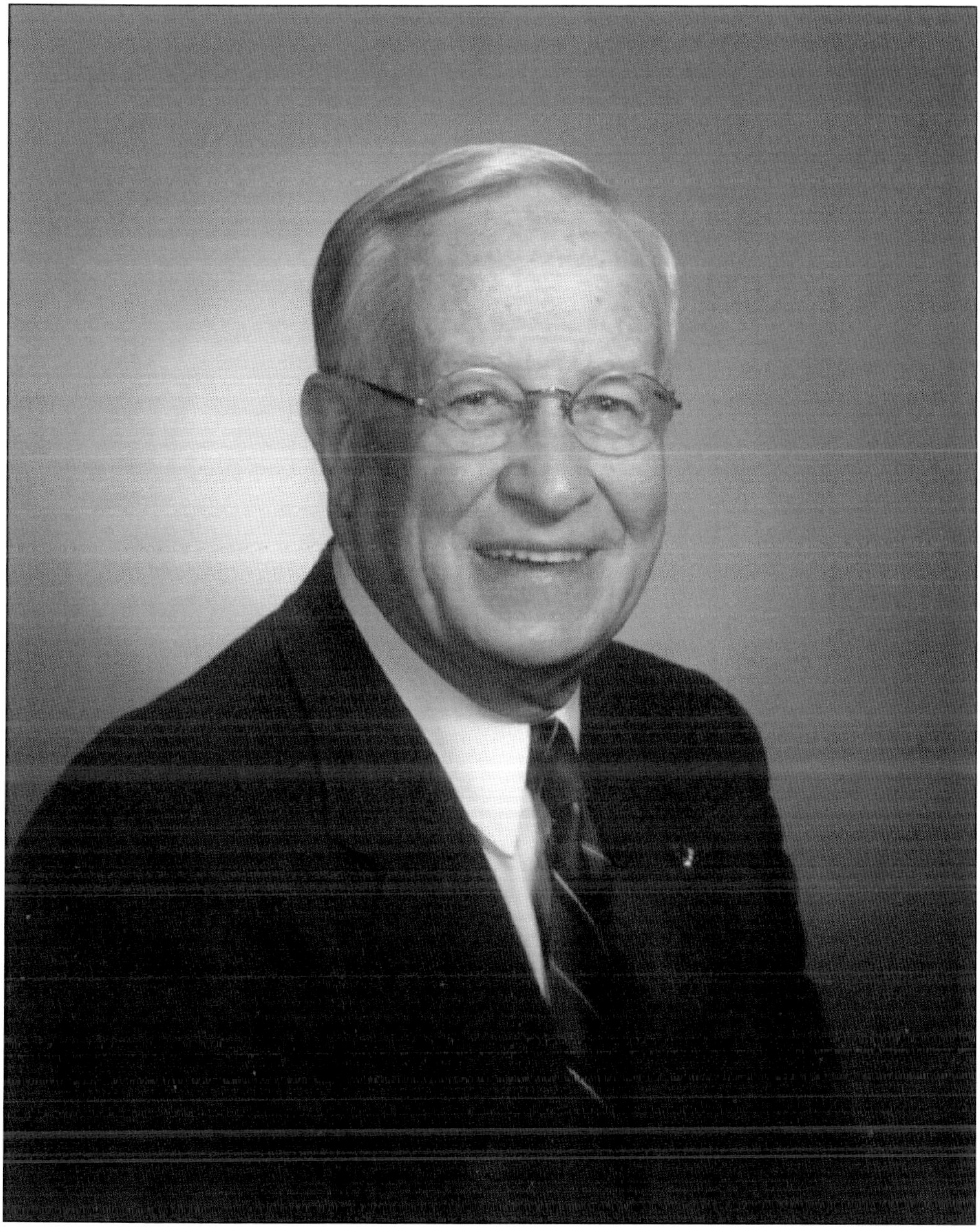

AN ENTREPRENEURIAL COMMUNITY

During the 1970s and 1980s, Van P. Smith was an articulate national and international spokesman for entrepreneurialism and the importance of the small business sector of the economy. The chief executive officer of Muncie's Ontario Corporation during that period, Smith was chairman of the United States Chamber of Commerce in 1984–1985 and literally traveled the world giving speeches in support of entrepreneurialism and free enterprise. (Ontario Corporation.)

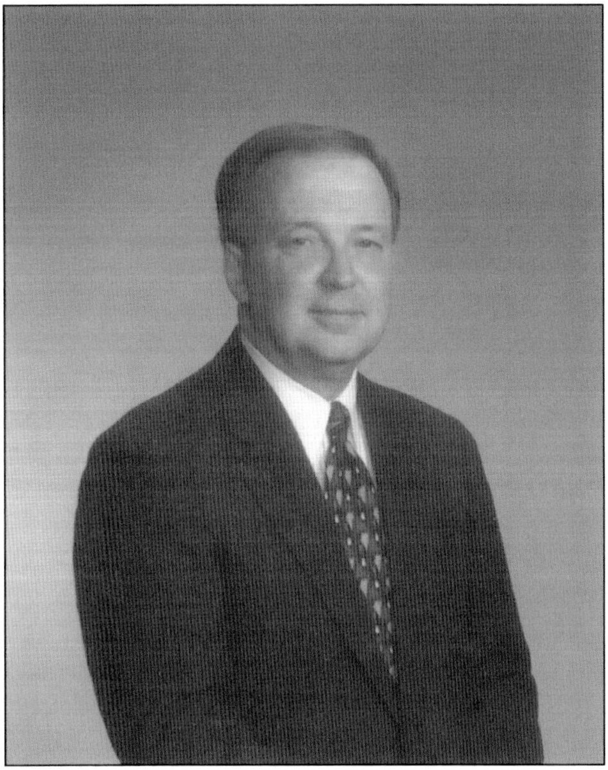

Kelly N. Stanley, the current president of Ontario Corporation, was elected chairman of the United States Chamber of Commerce for 2000–2001. Ontario Corporation was one of the few American companies ever to have two of its presidents serve as chairman of the United States Chamber of Commerce. (Ontario Corporation.)

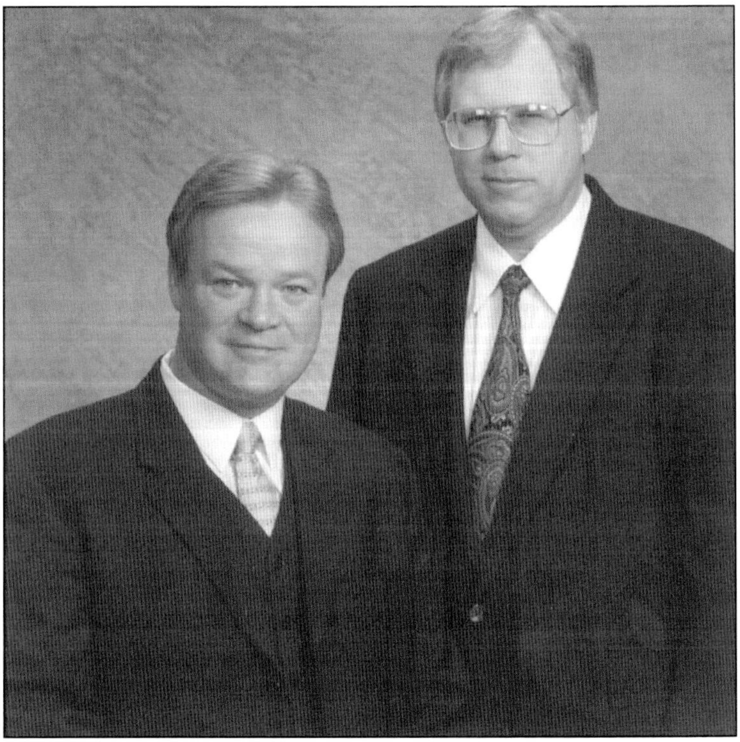

Wil Davis, left, and Ron Fauquher, right, teamed up in the 1970s to form a computer service business called Compusoft. As the business grew, it attracted the attention of Ontario Corporation which purchased the company in 1985 and renamed it Ontario Systems Corporation. Operating as a subsidiary of Ontario Corporation, Ontario Systems Corporation employs over 250 people and does business around the world. (Ontario Corporation.)

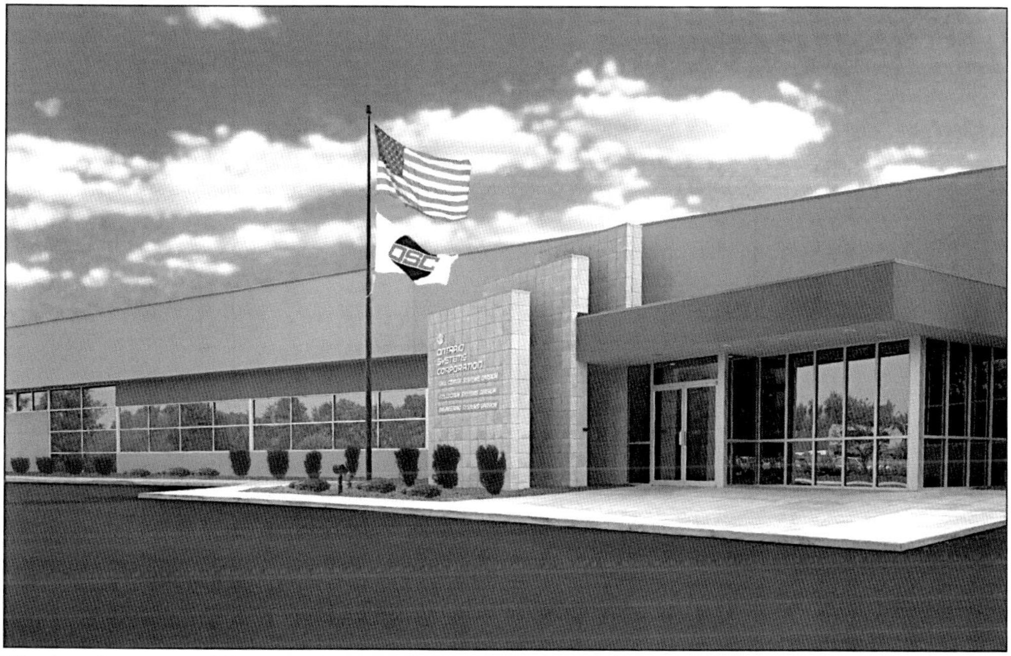

The headquarters of Ontario Systems Corporation, one of Muncie's fastest growing companies, is pictured above. (Ontario Corporation.)

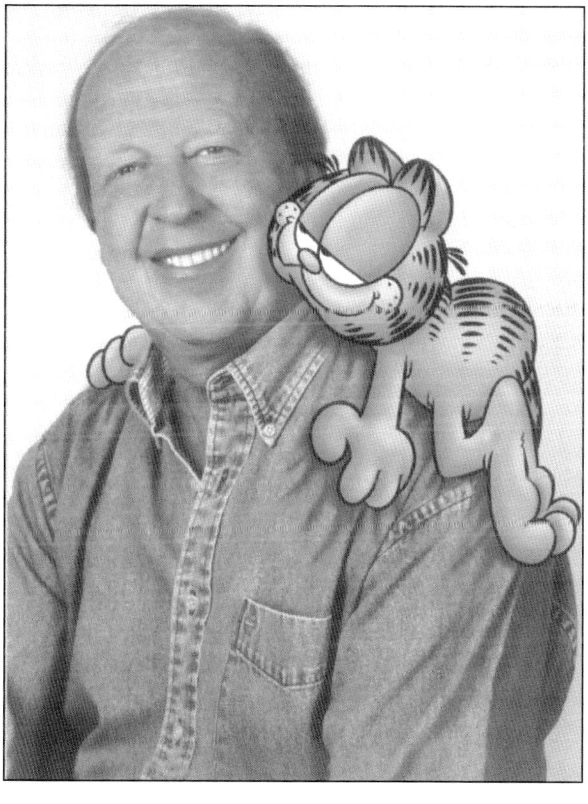

Jim Davis, creator of Garfield and other characters in the Garfield comic strip, works from the headquarters of his business, Paws Incorporated, in northeast Delaware County. (Paws Incorporated.)

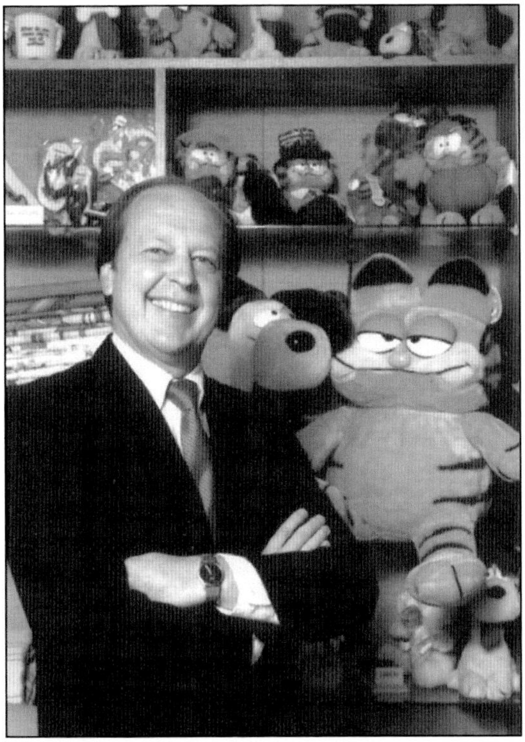

In this photograph, Davis is surrounded by a multitude of products that have been licensed by Paws. The Garfield strip appears in more than 2,600 newspapers, and Garfield products are sold worldwide. Davis has a simple message to his employees regarding the success of the company: "Take care of the cat and the cat will take care of you." (Paws Incorporated.)

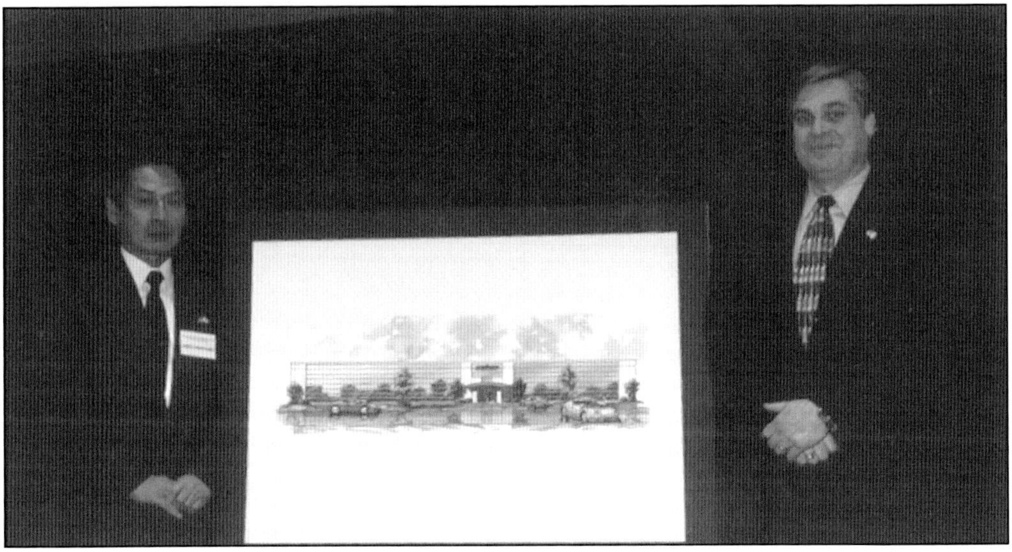

A major new development in Muncie's industrial profile occurred in 1998, when Keihin Aircon North America, a division of Keihin Corporation, announced its decision to build a manufacturing facility in Muncie. The company specializes in the manufacture of parts for air conditioners used in vehicles made in the United States and Canada by the Honda Motor Company. Shown in this photograph of the announcement ceremony are Hideo Nishigama, president of Keihin Aircon North America, and Dan Canan, mayor of Muncie. They flank an artist's conception of the Keihin Aircon facility. (Keihin Aircon North America, Incorporated.)

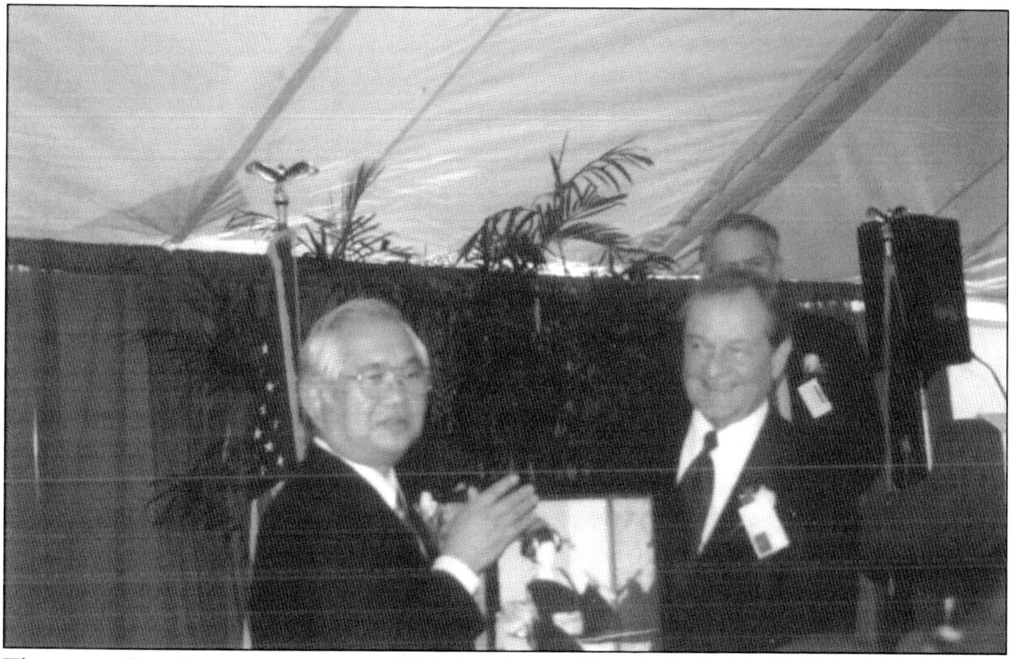

The groundbreaking ceremony in 1999 for the Keihin Aircon manufacturing facility was attended by Indiana Governor Frank O'Bannon, right, and Mideo Otsuka, past president of Keihin Corporation. (Keihin Aircon North America, Incorporated.)

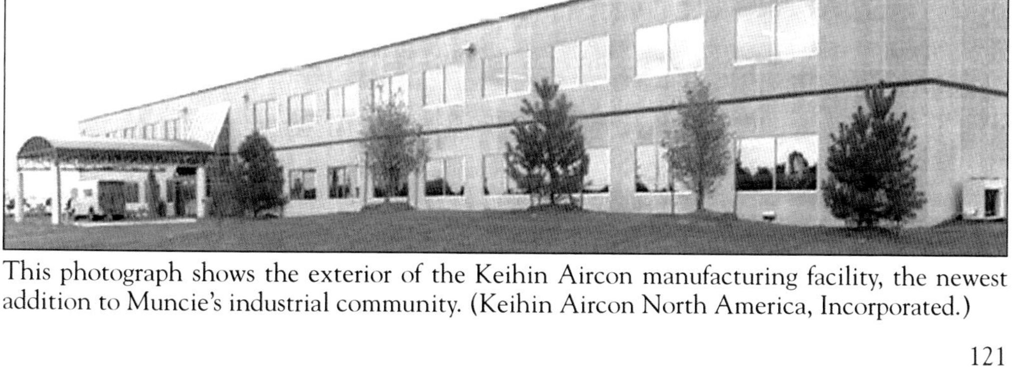

This photograph shows the exterior of the Keihin Aircon manufacturing facility, the newest addition to Muncie's industrial community. (Keihin Aircon North America, Incorporated.)

Ball State University: The New Mainstay of the Community

By the 1980s, Ball State University had emerged as the dominant economic and educational enterprise in Muncie. The employer of over 3,500 people, including faculty, administration, and support personnel, the university's economic impact on the community exceeded $400 million annually. As an educational institution, Ball State had also made some noticeable strides since it obtained university status in 1965. It boasted an internationally respected program in exercise physiology and adult fitness, one of the largest undergraduate colleges of business in the United States, and Indiana's only public college of architecture. In 1973, Ball State joined the Mid-American Conference (MAC), an athletic affiliation which placed the university within a respected group of regional, public universities in the Midwest. During the 1980s and 1990s, Ball State began the development of several academic programs that considerably broadened its curriculum. These included an expansion of its telecommunications offerings, programs in computer science and athletic training, and offerings in the field of industry and technology.

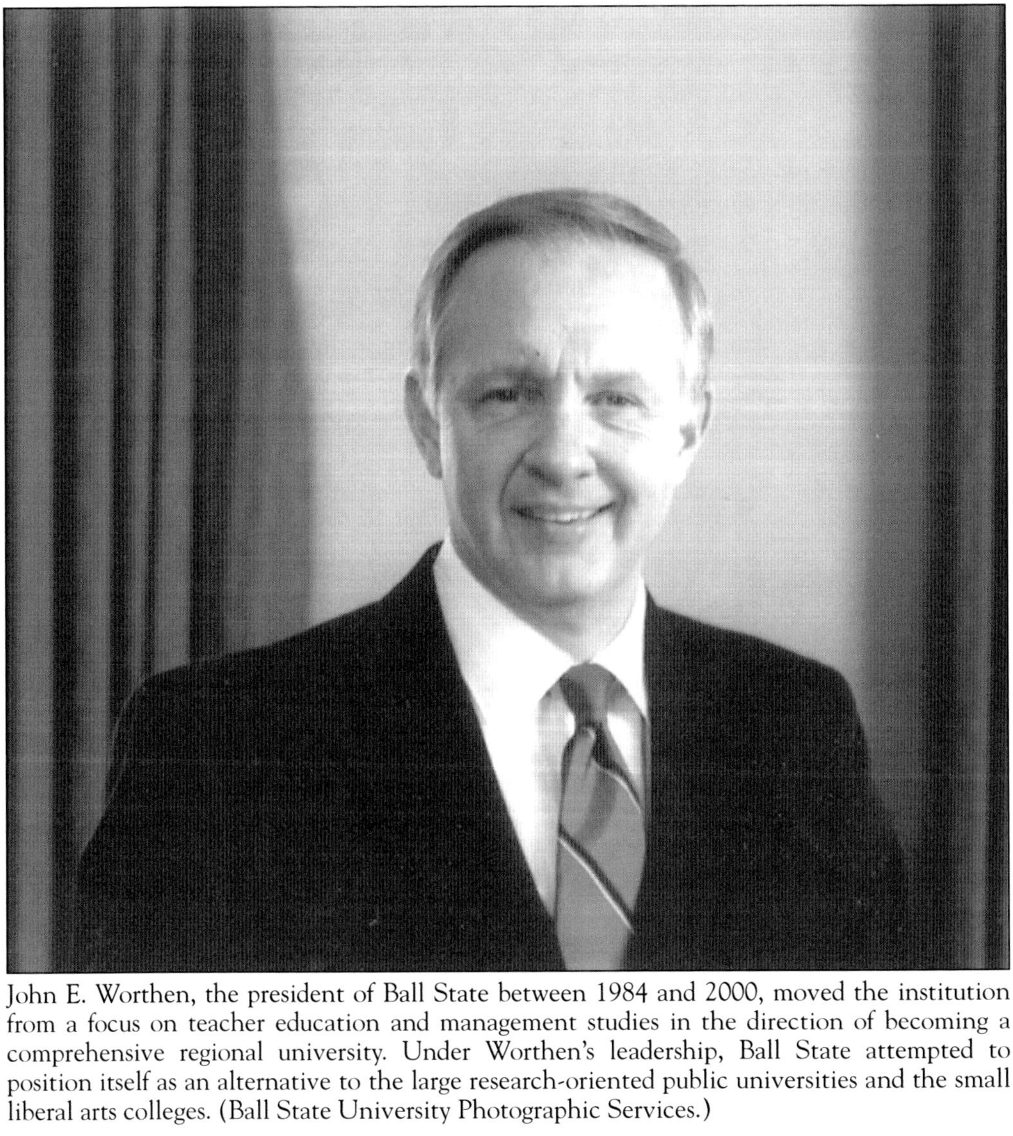

John E. Worthen, the president of Ball State between 1984 and 2000, moved the institution from a focus on teacher education and management studies in the direction of becoming a comprehensive regional university. Under Worthen's leadership, Ball State attempted to position itself as an alternative to the large research-oriented public universities and the small liberal arts colleges. (Ball State University Photographic Services.)

David L. Costill was the founding director of the Human Performance Laboratory at Ball State. Costill conducted extensive research for agencies of the federal government, the United States Olympic Committee, and several corporations who were active in the business of athletic training. The results of his research, especially for distance runners and swimmers, were used by athletes and coaches around the world. (BSU Photographic Services.)

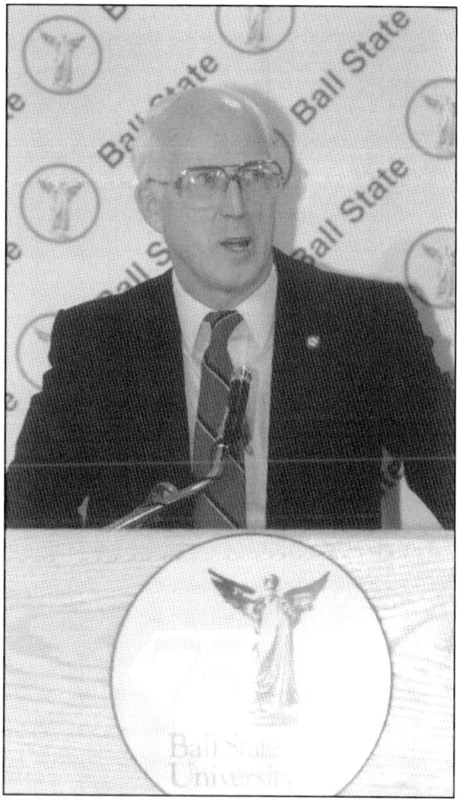

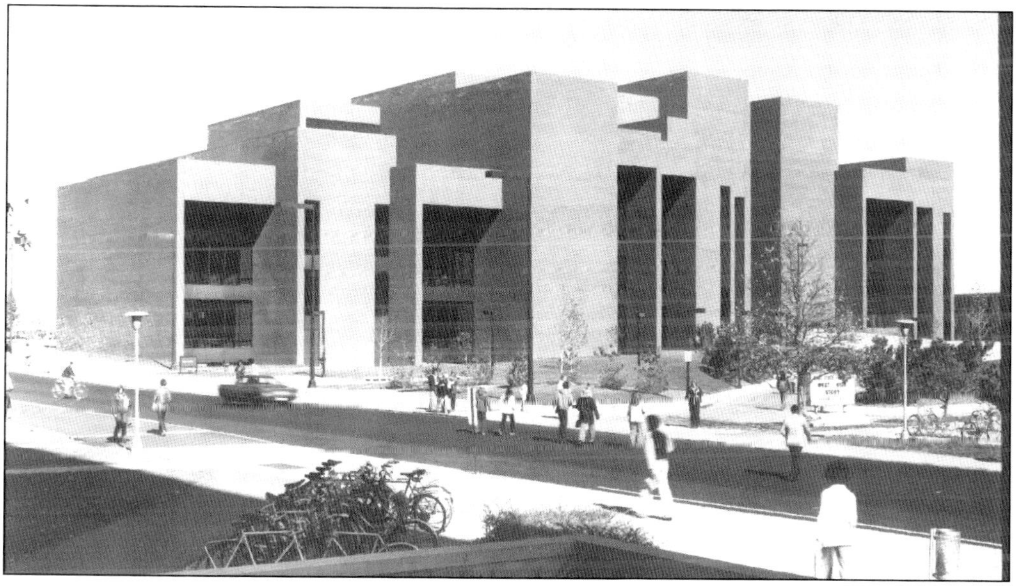

Bracken Library, named in honor of Alexander M. Bracken, the president of the Ball State Board of Trustees from 1956 to 1979, was completed in 1975. The library became the central academic building on campus and the hub of many of the new developments in teaching technology which were introduced in the 1980s and 1990s. (Ball State University Photographic Services.)

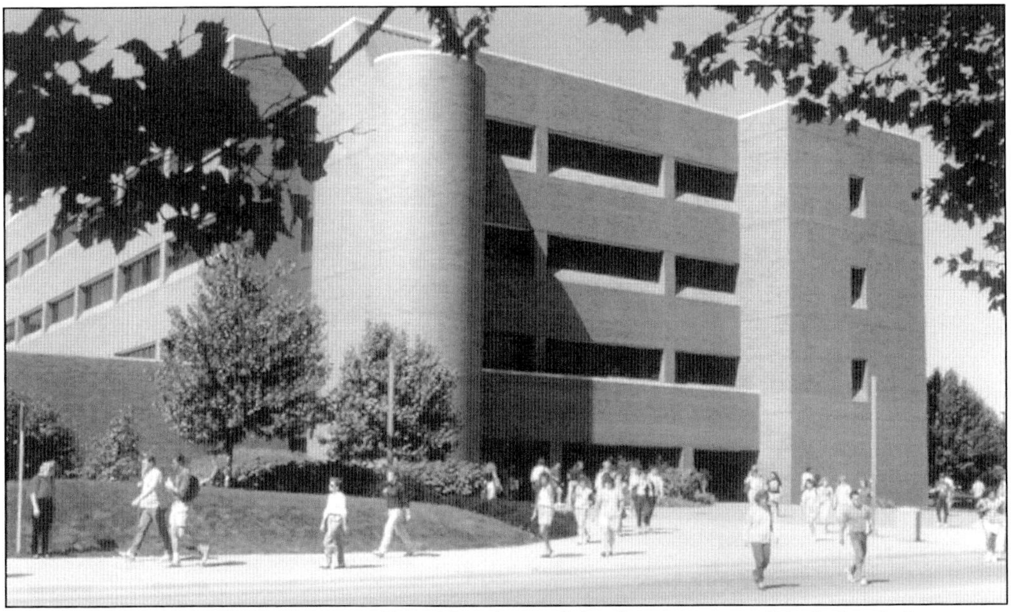

Completed in 1985, the Robert P. Bell Building housed the departments of English, Mathematics, and Computer Science, as well as the university's Computer Center. Named in honor of Robert P. Bell, president of Ball State from 1981 to 1984, the building underscored Ball State's emphasis on computer literacy for students and faculty. (Ball State University Photographic Services.)

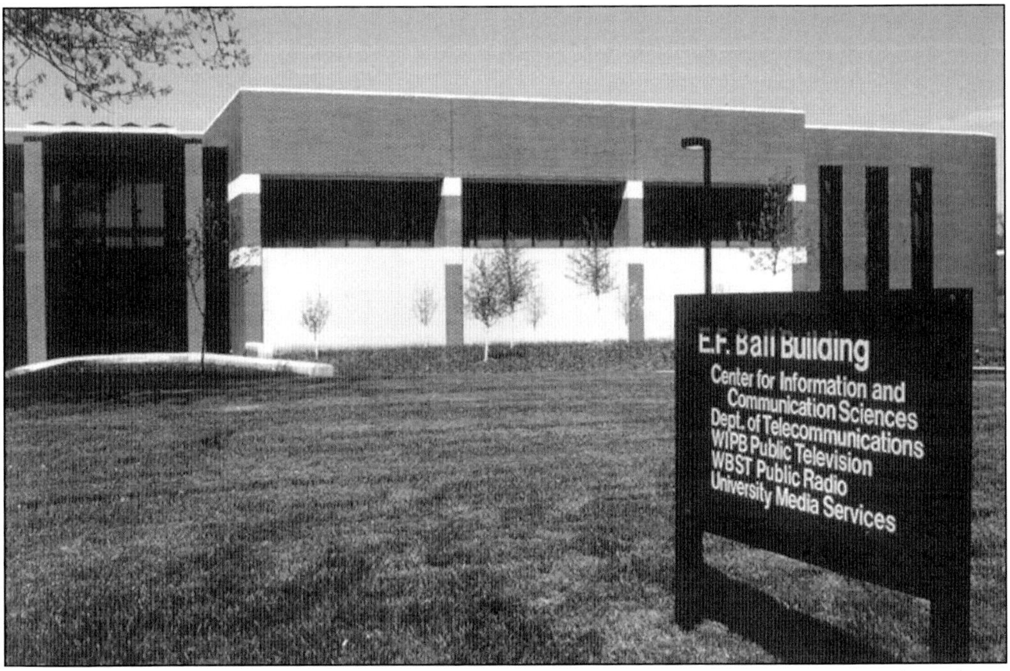

Completed in 1988, the Edmund F. Ball Building housed the undergraduate and graduate programs in the information sciences. The Ball Building became the central campus site for Ball State's commitment to using advanced technology to improve the teaching and learning process. (Ball State University Photographic Services.)

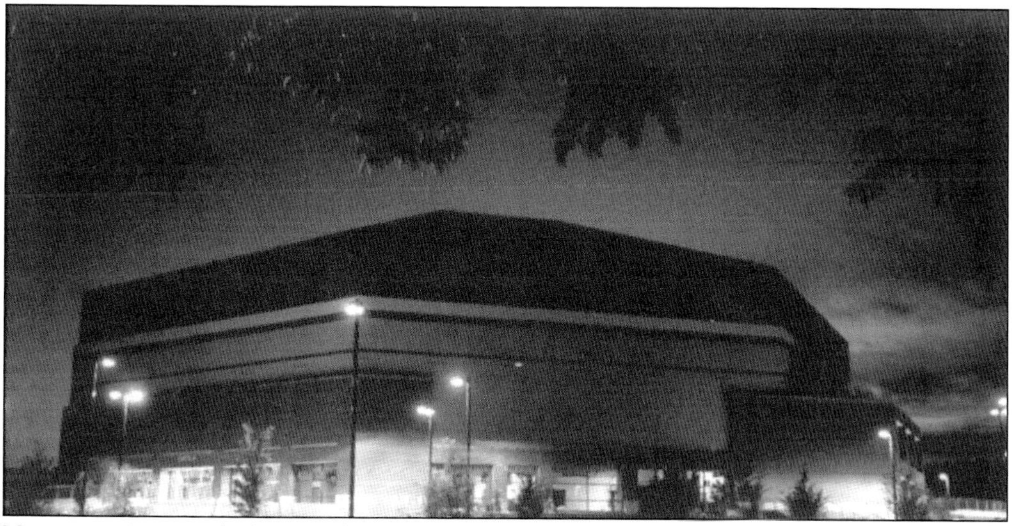

University Arena, which opened in 1994, was the site of athletic contests in men's and women's basketball, and men's and women's volleyball. During the 1990s, Ball State developed the most successful athletic program in the Mid-American Conference, winning the conference all-sports trophy more than any other conference member. Following the retirement of President John E. Worthen in 2000, the University Arena was renamed in his honor. (Ball State University Photographic Services.)

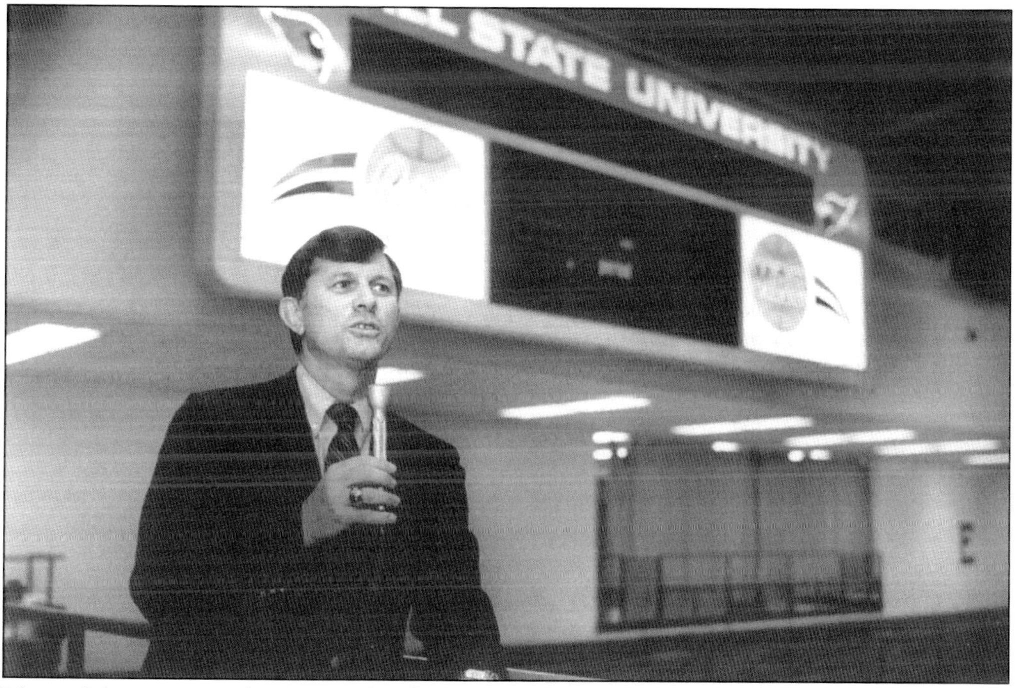

Morrie Mannies was the voice of Ball State athletics as well as local high school sports for over 40 years. A graduate of Ball State, Mannies began broadcasting the high school basketball games of Muncie Central High School in the 1950s. He is currently the broadcaster with the longest-running affiliation with any university athletic program in the United States. (Ball State University Sports Information.)

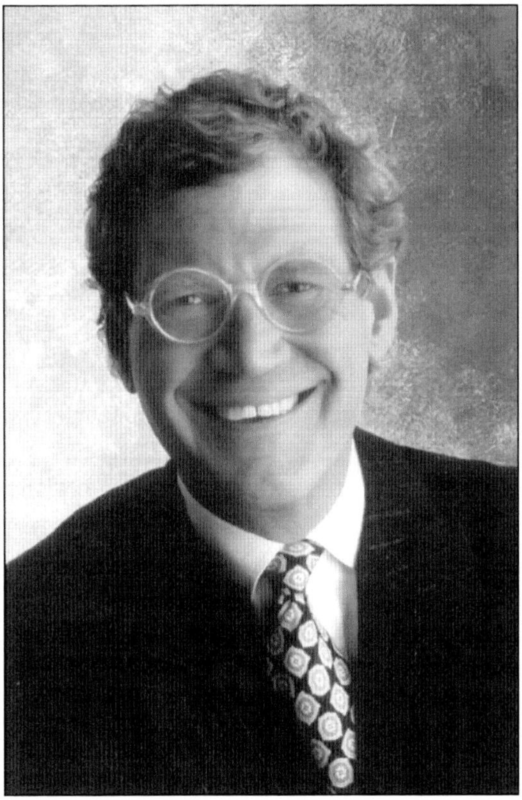

Television personality David Letterman graduated from Ball State in 1970. He became a national figure during the 1980s and 1990s, famous for his "Top Ten" lists. (Ball State University Photographic Services.)

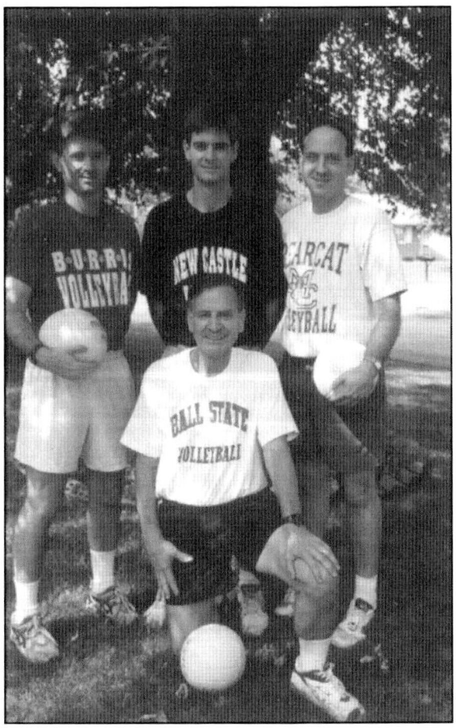

Ball State University, the Burris High School, and east central Indiana became a hotbed of scholastic and intercollegiate volleyball during the 1980s and 1990s. Credit for this development belongs to the Shondell family, and specifically Don Shondell (pictured here kneeling), men's volleyball coach at Ball State for almost 40 years, and one of the winningest collegiate volleyball coaches in the United States. Also pictured are, from left to right: Steve Shondell, coach of the girls' volleyball team at Burris High School (and winner of 11 state championships in the sport), John Shondell, coach of the girls' volleyball team at New Castle High School (20 miles south of Muncie), and David Shondell, coach of the girls' volleyball team at Muncie Central High School (winner of three state championships). (Don Shondell.)

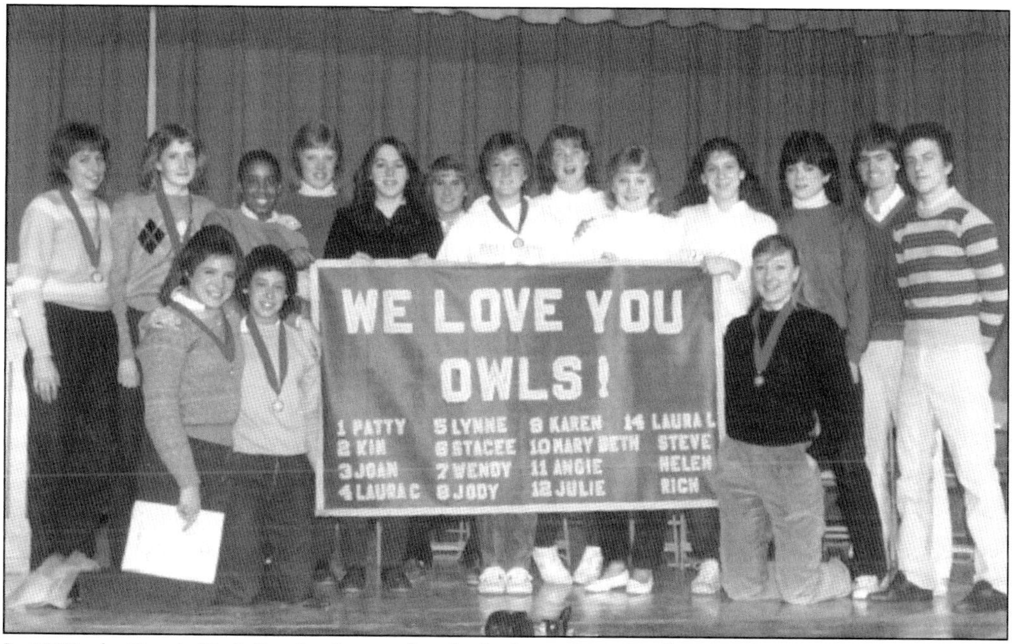

In 1983, the Burris Owls finished second in the Indiana State High School Volleyball Tournament. This achievement marked the beginning of an era when Burris dominated high school volleyball in Indiana and became a respected national competitor in the sport. (Don Shondell.)

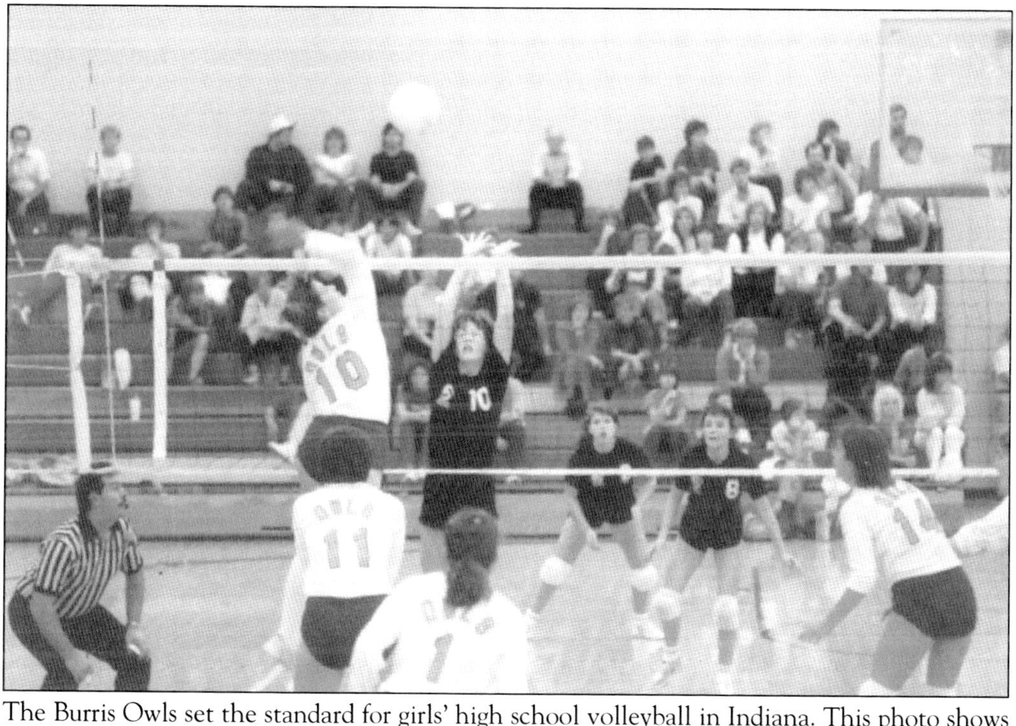

The Burris Owls set the standard for girls' high school volleyball in Indiana. This photo shows the Burris players in action against Daleville in 1985. Going into the match, the Burris team was ranked number one in the state, the Daleville team number two. (Don Shondell.)

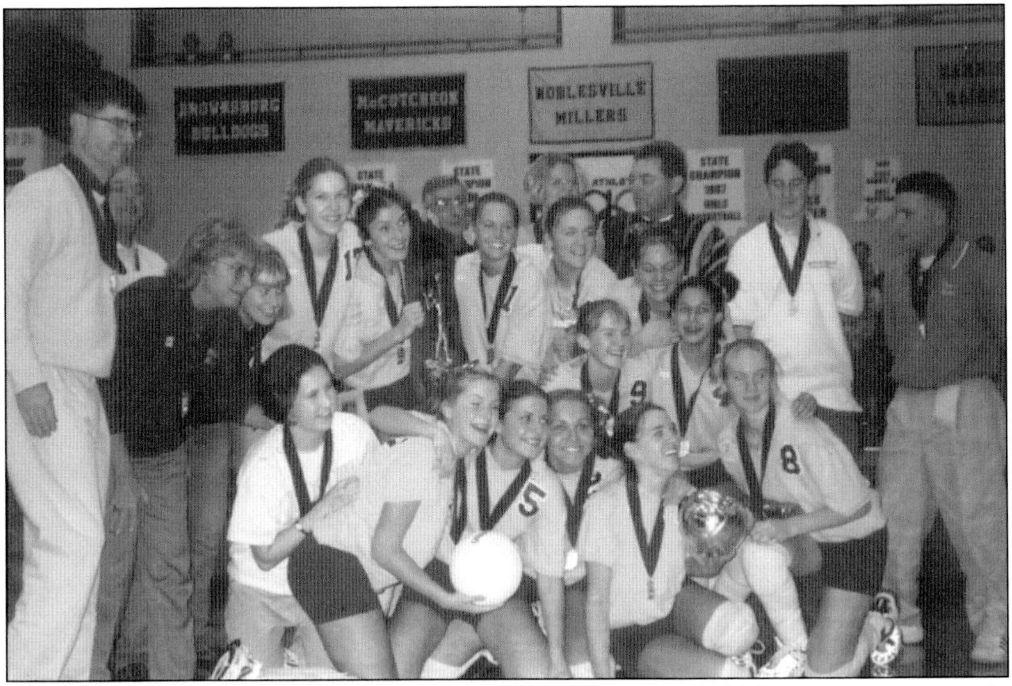

In 1999, the Burris Owls girls' volleyball team won the school's 11th state tournament. In this photo, the team members gather for a celebratory picture after the conclusion of the tournament. (Don Shondell.)

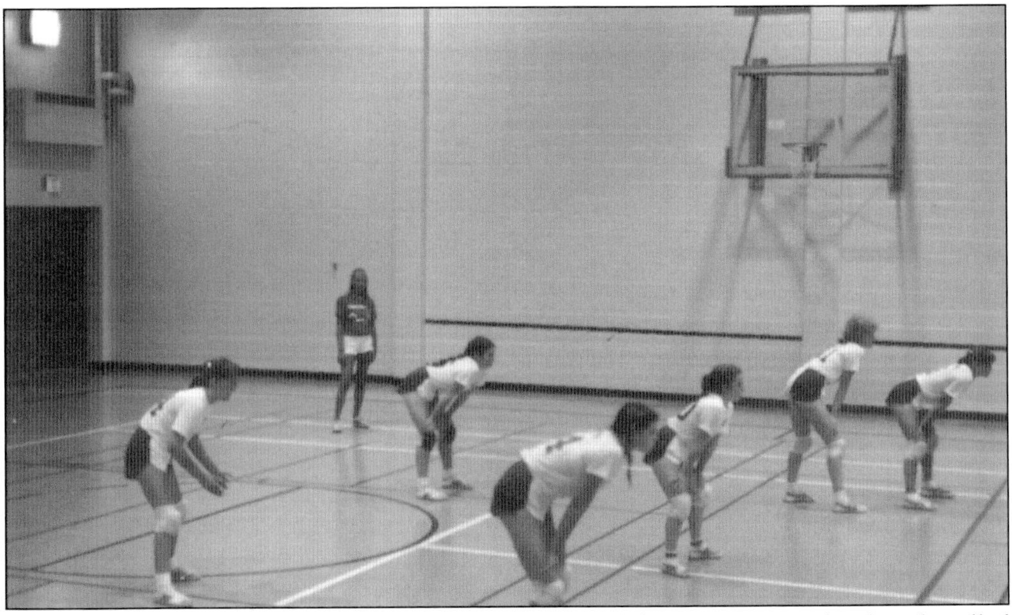

Under the direction of the Shondells, an age-group club program was developed, called Munciana. Teams enrolled in the Munciana program played in tournaments across the country during their off-seasons from high school competition. This photo shows the Munciana 14-under team in action at the Junior Olympic National Tournament in Omaha, Nebraska, in 1983. (Don Shondell.)